The Fortune Hunters

Also by Charlotte Hays

Being Dead Is No Excuse:
The Southern Ladies' Guide
to Hosting the Perfect Funeral
(with Gayden Metcalfe)

Somebody Is Going to Die If
Lilly Beth Doesn't Catch That Bouquet:
The Official Southern Ladies' Guide
to Hosting the Perfect Wedding
(with Gayden Metcalfe)

The *Fortune Hunters*

Dazzling Women and the Men They Married

Charlotte Hays

ST. MARTIN'S PRESS ≋ NEW YORK

www.stmartins.com

Library of Congress Cataloging-in-Publication Data

Hays, Charlotte.
    The fortune hunters : dazzling women and the men they married / Charlotte Hays. — 1st ed.
      p. cm.
    ISBN-13: 978-0-312-24646-4
    ISBN-10: 0-312-24646-3
  1. Women—Psychology.   2. Marriage.   3. Rich people. I. Title.

HQ1206.H383 2007
306.872'308621091821—dc22

2007019665

First Edition: August 2007

10 9 8 7 6 5 4 3 2 1

For

Julia Morgan Hall Hays

Julia Lipscomb Goodrich

Gayden Metcalfe

Josie Pattison Winn

Contents

Author's Note

Great fortune hunters embody a set of characteristics visible to the observant eye. No woman in this book embodies all these qualities. Nor do I purport to get into the minds of these inscrutable souls. Their motives and inner beings are known only to themselves.

Acknowledgments

The nicest acknowledgment I can give many who helped me with this book is a silent acknowledgment. I thank you heartily for helping me find people and phone numbers and for your insights and tips.

Exceptions to the rule of silence are Deborah Grosvenor, who conceived of the project; Reagan Arthur, who originally bought the book; and Charles Spicer of St. Martin's, an editor with a wonderful touch, who lived with me through its long parturition. My gratitude overflows.

The risk of naming names is that one will leave out somebody who deserves thanks. But I shall take that risk to thank those who have been friends and supporters while I labored on this book: my old friend and wonderfully forbearing colleague Gayden Metcalfe, Harley Metcalfe, Ireys and Charles Nelson, Gretchen and Houston Winbiggler, Ginny Hardy, Bruce Eggler, James Glassman, Michelle Bernard, Grace and Phillip Terzian, Anita Blair, Karlyn and James Bowman, Christine and Jeff Rosen, Gwyn Guess, Luci Goldberg, Jayne Ikard, Joan Mower, Charlotte McGee, Hebe Smyth, Hugh and Mary Dayle McCormick, Yaniv Soha, Tom and Donna Bethell, Lisa De Paulo, Eugene Ham, Bland Currie, Mary Glassman, Ed Goodrich, Judy Bachrach, Sandra McElwaine, Clinton Bagley, Heath Thompson, the entire Robertshaw family, Jon Newlin, Mayree

Smyth, Amelie Cagle, and Emily and Harry Griffith. I have an awful, awful feeling that I am leaving out people who are dear to me, but I've been the beneficiary of so many kindnesses along the way that this is almost certain to happen.

Preface

WHY I WROTE THIS BOOK

Somehow early on, in those halcyon days when I toiled for an alternative newspaper in New Orleans, it became clear that I was destined to chronicle the lives of society ladies—it happened during Carnival season. I wrote a piece about the ins and outs of being one of the city's debutantes who were presented at Mardi Gras balls. Next came my exposé of the Junior League of New Orleans and then my revelations about the local art ladies. The die was cast.

Although this book is the logical consequence of the kind of reporting I started doing all those years ago in New Orleans, it does have roots closer to the surface. I had been living in New York and working as a gossip columnist, first for the *New York Observer* and then for the *New York Daily News,* but was, as they say, betwixt and between when I received a call from a well-known author and man about town. Would I be interested, he wondered, in working with Carroll Petrie, a South Carolina model who had been close to the Duchess of Windsor, on her autobiography? I knew almost nothing about her other than that she was the recent widow of Milton Petrie, a noted philanthropist.

When I first went to see Mrs. Petrie, who received me in her Fifth Avenue apartment, it was clear she was ambivalent about wanting to tell her story—which included being married to a titled playboy, a marriage that literally went up in flames when he died in a racing accident, and three subsequent marriages—but it was just as plain that she did *not* want to tell it. I suppose it might have been a mistake on my part to harp on the theme of candor in our first meeting. Even after it became obvious to me that she had no intention of doing an autobiography, I couldn't stop thinking about it. For somebody who'd written society pieces most of her adult life, this saga, from South Carolina to Paris to Fifth Avenue, with a friendship with Eva Perón thrown in for good measure, was catnip, the *pièce de résistance,* but unfortunately Mrs. Petrie was resisting.

About the same time as I visited Mrs. Petrie, I wrote an article on forces of nature for the *New York Observer*—it featured such forces as Arianna Huffington, whose career I had followed avidly since she emerged as the girlfriend of a highbrow London journalist who set her on her march to fame and fortune; Lynn Wyatt, the Texas socialite; and Pat Buckley, then the doyenne of New York society. I followed the forces-of-nature article with "Ladies in Waiting," also published by the *Observer,* which dealt with "baby Pats," or the rising generation of social dominatrixes who would run New York's black-tie circuit in the twenty-first century. Carolyn Bessette Kennedy was one of them.

Ladies, ladies, ladies: You'd think I'd had enough, but women who aspire to—and obtain—power and money through marriage or other sorts of liaisons with men are endlessly fascinating, from Madame de Pompadour, Louis XV's mistress, to the modern fortune hunter. For much of history, marriage or being a powerful man's mistress was how women made it, so to speak. I was intrigued by these women, and I had to figure out why some succeed brilliantly while others, perhaps even more beautiful, fall by the wayside. In retrospect, it was inevitable that the literary agent Deborah Grosvenor and I would hit upon the idea of a book on women who married super rich. Of course, it might also seem odd that an unmarried, penny-pinching journalist would undertake such a book, and I'll admit it—several times I was at my wit's end trying to get to the bottom of what makes these women, a breed unto themselves, tick.

In writing the book, I trod in the sacred footsteps of Sheilah Graham, another gossip columnist, who did not marry money but wrote about how to do it. Graham is best remembered today for having been F. Scott Fitzgerald's mistress in his down-and-out days in Hollywood, but she was also a prominent Hollywood columnist who in 1974 wrote *How to Marry*

Super Rich: or Love, Money, and the Morning After. Even now, *How to Marry Super Rich* is a delicious read, but I felt the time had come to reexamine the subject. If nothing else, the cast of characters has changed, though it must be noted with some degree of awe that the redoubtable Marylou Whitney, nearing or past eighty (depending upon the speaker) and married to a gallant four decades her junior, has the distinction of having made it into both books.

Quite a bit has changed since Marylou began her marital career in the 1940s—the job of the fortune hunter is evolving. Cornelius Vanderbilt Whitney fell for Marylou Hosford in the 1950s in part because she was a great cook. It's hard to imagine, say, John F. Kennedy Jr. marrying somebody because she could whip up a cheese soufflé. The trophy wife of today is more likely to be her mate's intellectual peer (if not his superior, as in the case of Arianna Huffington and the dim but rich Michael Huffington—they reversed the *Pygmalion* roles, with Arianna playing Henry Higgins to Michael's Eliza Doolittle during their brief but, for Arianna, lucrative marriage).

The social milieu has also changed. The older women in this book started out in a world still dominated by the aristocracy, but the younger ones thrived in a more glitzy, money-obsessed world of fast deals and a churning economy that picked people up and threw them down before they had time to learn what a strawberry fork is. But the fortune hunter does not look back to the elegance of the past. Pamela Harriman, whose father and brother sat in the House of Lords, was the consummate fortune hunter in that she always looked forward. She used her heritage when it might impress people—the stationery and place cards at her Georgetown house bore the ostrich feathers of her family coat of arms, which no doubt made the Democratic Party stalwarts who gathered there feel that they'd truly arrived—but she never waxed nostalgic for a lost world or the good old days. A fortune hunter is interested in only two periods of history: the present and the future. A fortune hunter may have *a* past, but she doesn't dwell on *the* past.

Although the world around her has changed, the fortune hunter, a hardy perennial, has not. Some of the same qualities that made Madame de Pompadour one of the richest and most powerful women in France make Mercedes Bass one of the richest and most powerful women in Texas. Both women were ineffably cheerful when their men were around, great as nest builders, and adept at making a man comfortable. The word that comes to mind is *courtesan,* though de Pompadour was officially a courtesan and Mrs. Bass practices her arts as a wife.

In researching this book, I learned that the fortune hunter is a woman utterly without peripheral vision. She has total focus. This is reflected in all sorts of ways, her brave decision to move to a big town where the money is if she's from a small town and her ability to pay complete attention to whomever she is pursuing, or whoever might simply prove useful. You will notice that all the women in this book are known for being able to fix a look of rapt attention on a man. The Look is something all fortune hunters intuitively know about; indeed, it is their most lethal weapon. The Look is as sexy as lingerie, and if you can't stare with near religious awe while Mr. Rich goes on and on about something that would put the non–fortune hunter in a coma, you're probably not cut out for marrying super rich.

As Sheilah Graham did, I asked myself if I wished I had married a millionaire while there was still time (you can't start fortune hunting later in life). Graham, who claimed to have turned down a marquis to nurse Fitzgerald through his pitiful decline, said no—she valued her independence too much. She did sound a bit wistful at the prospect of finding some nice older millionaire. In my case, as the anti-belle growing up in the Mississippi Delta, surrounded by real belles destined to marry cotton planters, I knew early on that I was fated never to be a belle (but to write about them). I could do all the Atkins and Botox in the world and I still wouldn't be fortune-hunter material. I could never get the Look just right—even if I were looking at billions. But for these special women I must confess a certain admiration.

If I had a tiara, I'd doff it in their honor.

The
Fortune Hunters

1

PROSPECTING FOR GOLD:
What Kind of Woman Does It Take?

After the feminist shenanigans of recent decades, it is not politically correct to speak of great fortune hunters unless you're referring to those who dive into the ocean to hunt for sunken treasure. Yet many of the most dynamic women of our day launched themselves the old-fashioned way, through a dazzling marriage. Even Hillary Rodham Clinton, the standard-bearer of feminist values, began her march to fame and fortune with a trek to the altar and went on to solidify her stature by standing by her man, a character-building duty the fortune hunter is not infrequently called upon to perform.

Fortune hunting, like diving for treasure, is a real job. Some women strive to be CEOs; others prefer to wed them. Is one endeavor really morally superior to the other? I once knew the daughter of a prominent feminist, a nice woman, struggling to make it in an intellectual profession. I always felt she'd have been happier as, say, a real-estate agent who spent her time off shopping and accessorizing. Why are some jobs more "authentic" than others? Fortune hunters are not dopes who sit by the pool all day reading Harlequin romances. They are talented women who make a conscious decision to pursue a particular career path. Of course, it is not always possible to know a woman's inner thoughts and real motivations, though her life story allows for reasoned speculation. Indeed, the best way to assess the job requirements is to look at the lives of women who've succeeded. Though the ladies in this book are all different, you will pick up certain common themes that run through their lives.

Fortune hunting has been a valid occupation for women throughout the ages. It probably started when the first Neanderthal fortune hunter made goo-goo eyes at the fellow with the largest collection of pelts. The roster of worthies includes the Byzantine striptease artist, famed for the lewdness of her dancing, who became the Empress Theodora, helpmeet to Justinian; Jacqueline Kennedy Onassis, who wasn't endowed with the wealth to support the grand life to which she was accustomed; and plus-size model Anna Nicole Smith, who zeroed in on her Adonis when he had one foot in the grave and then battled his children in court over the estate. The issue of how to marry super rich is something we don't talk about in polite company. Still, mothers from time immemorial have told their daughters that it's just as easy to love a rich man as a poor one. As a single former gossip columnist, I might seem an odd cicerone for travel in these realms of gold. But I have devoted much of my professional life to observing the rich and what it takes to succeed in this highly competitive arena. The requirements may not be what you expect at all.

Beauty is the first thing that leaps to mind as a requirement. Beauty helps, no doubt about it. But it is not a *sine qua non* for fortune hunting. Several women in this book are drop-dead gorgeous; others work hard to make themselves attractive. All take pains to maximize nature's gifts, whether extravagant or modest, with diet, exercise, and designer couture. If necessary, there is also the magic of a good plastic surgeon. The aspirant who happens to be blessed with natural beauty recognizes the value of her asset. But she knows that she cannot afford to be passive with it. She is well aware that even great beauty can be squandered. We've all heard about ravishing women who've ended their days in trailer parks. What makes one stunning woman waste her advantage on a poor man while a less beautiful one comes within a constitutional crisis of becoming queen of England?

Marrying super rich is more a matter of talent and enterprise than beauty. "You'll never make it on your face, so you'd better be interesting," New York socialite Nan Kempner recalled her father, the millionaire California Ford dealer Albert Schlesinger, admonishing her. Instead of sulking because she wasn't a natural knockout, Kempner made sure she was fascinating. She cultivated a self-deprecating wit (she was amusingly frank about her plastic surgery and love of shopping), joie de vivre, love of couture—and a svelte figure that was often compared to a celery stalk. Intelligence, she showed, always counts more than awe-inspiring looks. None of the women in this book are bimbos (though some do a good imitation). Smart and versatile, they are a special breed distinguished by a specific set of qualities. All, to some degree, embody these traits. Just what are they?

A fortune hunter is a woman who doesn't wait for her ship to come in—she swims out to meet it. More than anything, she is an activist who believes that she is in control of her destiny. Cinderella she is not. (Left to her own devices, Cinderella would have been stuck in a dead-end housekeeping job.) Nor is the fortune hunter a Sleeping Beauty. Nobody is more wide-awake than the fortune hunter. She may dream of a bright future, but she doesn't simply build castles in the air. She must be tough enough to withstand rough patches and bad publicity because the rich—and the would-be rich—are prone to messy scandals. (This is particularly true if Mr. Rich happens to be married to another woman at the outset of their courtship.) Her resilience is such that some have called into question the depth of her feelings. She is not somebody who, as the Victorian author of doggerel put it, "looks before and after, and pines for what is not." One woman in this book was so unstoppable that she managed to marry a richer man so quickly after a nasty divorce—as in the next day—that the discarded mate publicly accused her of bigamy. Did she die of shame? Did she cower in her room? She sailed along serenely, head held high, on the arm of her new billionaire.

A fortune hunter is a chameleon who is able to pick up the hues of her surroundings. Her vivid imagination enables her to reinvent herself as circumstances unfold. When one door closes, she opens another. A Chicago-bred Pan Am attendant in this book transformed herself into a New York sophisticate who claimed to have grown up in a thatched cottage in England. Some have enough diversity on their résumés for a dozen ordinary women. Arianna Huffington is a virtuosa of variety whose curriculum vitae includes brainy Oxford undergraduate, highbrow critic's ingenue, bestselling author, cult aficionado, gal about town, multimillionaire's wife, divorcée, right-wing hostess, and left-wing pundit. Acting, closely allied to reinvention, is another basic skill. A fortune hunter is always a consummate actress, though smart enough never to up-stage her mate. Princess Diana forgot this rule, and Prince Charles was not pleased by the realization that the crowds had not come to see him. Acting can be designing a whole new persona or telling little white lies. When Georgette Paulsin wanted to meet Robert Muir, the Los Angeles real-estate baron who became her first husband, she pretended to be a reporter from *Time* magazine. In contrast, there is also the woman who is so lovely that she seems to have simply slipped into a Midas marriage without premeditation—New York's reigning socialite, the designer Tory Burch, did this. Twice.

When on the prowl, all women try to be in the right place. The quin-tessential fortune hunter takes this to the next level and is *always* in the right place at the right time. She familiarizes herself with the terrain. Her research is often as simple as asking a friend about a man or checking the obituary pages to keep abreast of what rich widowers have recently come on the market, a tactic employed by small-town hunters reading the *Town Tatler* as well as big-game hunters studying the *New York Times* obits. Every serious fortune hunter must confront the question of venue. She must ask: Where shall I ply my trade? Sheilah Graham addresses this question in her classic *How to Marry Super Rich: or Love, Money, and the Morning After*. "What," Graham asks, "does a woman—or a man—have that others do not, to close the deal? You can sleep with a man for twenty years and you are lucky to get bus fare. If you dig in a coal mine, you are likely to come up with coal. If you go to Coney Island, you get a Nathan's hot dog. You have to go where the rich are."

Outside of certain places the fortune hunter would never dream of setting foot—Appalachia comes to mind—millionaires are widely dis-persed. You can find them even in Arkansas and Mississippi. However many eligible men there may be in many parts of the country, they tend to congregate in certain centers of wealth. New York—in Graham's day and ours—is a particularly happy hunting ground. Not only do the rich-est of the rich live there, New York is not a closed society. You can be a chorus girl one minute and Mrs. Donald Trump the next (and an ex–Mrs. Trump the next). Texas, of course, is a superlative breeding ground of multimillionaires, as is Palm Beach (if your taste runs to the more mature rich). The important thing, whether you are on the Riviera or in a small town in Arkansas, is to get out and see and be seen—by rich men. Melania Knauss was—unusually for a supermodel—given to spending quiet evenings at home. If she hadn't been talked into attending a party at New York's Kit Kat Club (where Donald Trump was another guest), she might still be the singular Miss Knauss rather than the third Mrs. Trump. It is not without significance that in a *New York* magazine piece on how to be an "It" girl, Nan Kempner advised aspirants to entertain "constantly." "I've always liked being noticed, and I work hard at it," Kempner admitted.

A fortune hunter can turn the wrong place into the right place. New Orleans, even before Katrina, was not a town known for its profusion of the very rich. Yet one woman in this book got her start while working as a maître d' in a New Orleans restaurant, proof that character triumphs over an inauspicious beginning. Still, it should be pointed out that most of the women in this book courageously left the provinces for greater opportunity. Wherever she settles, the fortune hunter wisely minimizes contact with the non-rich. There's the story (told by Graham) of the boy whose grandfather asked if he'd like to marry a rich girl. "I guess so, Grandpa" he said. "Here's how to do it," his grandfather offered. "Don't date poor girls."

Cultural attainments are highly desirable. Believe it or not, a good art history course can do you as much as regular Botox injections. Though a deep academic background would be a waste, if not downright annoying, a familiarity with antiques and other finer things of life comes in handy. A rich man doesn't want a nitwit who might embarrass him. Jacqueline Kennedy Onassis is the best possible role model. Though not an intellectual, she was clever and sophisticated and she created a White House that wowed Nobel laureates, novelists, and nabobs. Jackie's mentor, New York socialite and art collector Jayne Wrightsman, learned the hard way. She had not had Jackie's advantages. Her husband, Charles, employed tutors and curators to make up the deficiency. He was "brutally demanding." "If she didn't do everything perfectly," a Wrightsman friend told writer Francesca Stanfill for a *Vanity Fair* profile, "he made it clear that there would be consequences."

A patina of culture has always been advisable, but now more may be required. "The trophy wife doesn't exist anymore," John Fairchild, who made *W* magazine the authoritative handbook for social climbers, wrote in 1995. "Now a wife has to be more than beautiful. She has to have brains." Older fortune hunters were more inclined to skip college and work as models (still a popular career choice). Younger ones frequently are professionals. Carolyn Bessette, though beautiful enough to be a model, was a fashion publicist instead. Marie-Josée Kravis, a respected economist, displaced dress designer Carolyne Roehm as the wife of eighties leveraged buyout king Henry Kravis. A self-made man is particularly susceptible to the allure of a cultivated woman. A socialite who preferred to remain anonymous recalled a proposal of marriage from such a man. On the night they met, "I got myself out of the gutter and into good clothes," this romantic stated, "and now I need to marry somebody like you to take me to the next level." She declined, but you get the idea: You may have to settle for somebody less gracious than Lord Fauntleroy.

The fortune hunter, said a woman who knows, must be willing to live in a world that is "full of self-made men who got where they are with total ambition and still have raw elbows. It's sometimes not a place of kindness, thank-you notes, and flowers." The fortune hunter may have to take a page from the gossip columnist's book. I once had a call from a snooty public relations man who, pompously informing me that his clientele was made up of members of *real* society, chided me for writing about new-money types. He asked me to a fund-raising event that supported some patrician-approved charity. There I met some lovely people, received several kind invitations to Tuxedo Park, a blue-blood stronghold in New York state, and had an absolutely scintillating chat about the art of portraiture. Not to belabor the point, I felt as if I'd been in an exotic aviary. The next day I called the publicist. "Goody for you to be able to prey on old money," I said. "But as a gossip columnist, I am forced to prey on new money." The simple fact is that most money is new money, and even the most brilliant fortune hunter may not become Mrs. Astor right off the bat. A 1998 survey by the U.S. Trust Corporation, which manages money for the very rich, shows that only a minuscule 4 percent of those surveyed said that they had been born rich. Slightly more than a fourth (26 percent) said they hailed from the upper middle class. Still, take heart, because as you'll see, one of the least pleasant husbands in this book was the possessor of a grand name redolent of American wealth.

For the most part, it is the rich who make fortune hunting such a challenging profession. Fortune hunting is demanding because the rich are demanding. That certainly is what F. Scott Fitzgerald had in mind when he remarked that they are different from you and me. Whether spoiled by inheriting lots of easy money or growing ruthless in the pursuit of lucre, they expect—no, they require—deference. When Princess Diana became angry with Prince Charles, he simply didn't know how to react. She was supposed to defer to him.

Living with the super rich without running afoul of them and being cut out of the will requires the utmost in self-control. You can't throw a tantrum when things aren't going your way. The golden rule: He who has the gold gets to make the rules. The aforementioned Jayne Wrightsman was a paragon of self-control. When Wrightsman died, he left everything to Jayne. One of their grandchildren famously remarked that nobody could begrudge her the money—she had earned it. Of course, the rich aren't always ogres. Some are as nice as you and me.

And then there's sex. When a major stockholder meeting was taking place, Sid Bass didn't show up. A friend staying in the same hotel was asked to get him to the meeting. She said it might not be easy. "They're moving furniture up there from morning 'til night," she reported. You can know every painting in the Louvre, but if you can't play the courtesan, forget it. A fortune hunter is a woman who can never have a headache. It may not be true that one of the best fortune hunters of our day perfected her skills under the tutelage of the renowned Madame Claude, doyenne of an exclusive brothel. True or not, the undying canard says something about the job. The fortune hunter lives with the certain knowledge that there are all too many women eager to replace her. Along with time's winged chariot, she fears younger women. *Fortune* magazine noted, in the story that coined the term *trophy wife,* that having a sexy, young wife "dispels the notion that men peak sexually at eighteen."

The bedroom is important, but it is not the only room in which the courtesan plies her trade. The geisha role is twofold—sex and pampering. Rich men like their women to hover around them. They have needy egos and want to be told they are great, just like the rest of mankind. Learning to cook is a very good idea, even if you know you'll eventually have a large staff. Until the end, Ambassador Francis Kellogg spoke dreamily of the meals his ex-wife, Mercedes, prepared before she hooked a Bass. The wife of a rich man must make his comfort the main purpose of her life. She must make sure that he doesn't get bored. Mercedes Bass goes so far as to ask hostesses in advance who Sid's dinner partners will be, though, truth to tell, nobody is quite sure whether she's trying to ensure that he *does* or *doesn't* enjoy the woman seated next to him. Mercedes knows well what perils lie in wait at a dinner party. She and Bass began their flirtation at a black–tie dinner.

A fortune hunter must be an incomparable wife, but she is all too often no great shakes as a mother. The single-minded focus on Mr. Filthy Rich is the reason. Children often are left at home and go to boarding school before they are out of short pants. Successful fortune hunters would rack up millions of frequent-flyer miles per annum—that is, if they took commercial flights—making sure that their husbands don't spend too much time alone. (One New York woman is so intent on keeping a watchful eye on her portfolio that she refuses to let bad knees prevent her from sharing his morning jog—she bicycles by his side.)

But, of course, sometimes Mr. Rich jogs off the straight and narrow and into the arms of another woman. Few things call upon the fortune hunter's sangfroid more than this challenge. She must refuse to panic—and she must refuse to bolt unless she knows that bolting will make her richer than Mr. Rich. Nan Kempner faced this challenge when husband Thomas Kempner, chairman of Loeb Partners, the investment banking firm founded by his grandfather, set up housekeeping with his longtime mistress in the mid-1990s. Nan did not hang her head in shame. She did not abandon the couple's lavish Park Avenue apartment to another woman. She did what had to be done. "Nan Kempner threatened to take him to the cleaners," Fox News gossip columnist Roger Friedman reported, "so Tom returned." Nan died in July 2005, still married to Tom.

Still, a fortune hunter should walk down the aisle knowing that a marriage lived in the spotlight will die in the spotlight if it fails. Even golden girl Blaine Trump, the well-bred Mrs. Trump—she was married to Robert Trump, Donald's brother—was forced to learn this lesson in 2005. She had been married to Robert for twenty years. "Blaine was alerted to the relationship by anonymous phone calls, *WWD* reported yesterday," the *New York Daily News* reported. "Blaine is extremely popular, but in New York, the friends tend to follow whoever gets the money," the article went on to note (attributing the quote to "a realist"). But Blaine herself is a realist: I'll never forget the day she was kind enough to phone me on her car phone and out of the blue. I was a gossip columnist at the *Daily News*—her call was my first sign that media-savvy Blaine's pet, William Norwich, engaged in hush-hush negotiations with his employer, had left his perch at the *New York Post* only a few hours before our most pleasant chat. Don't count Blaine out—a woman who prepares for the translation of her Boswell may well survive the loss of a husband.

Perhaps we're dwelling too much on the demands and not enough on the rewards. Mr. Rich may require constant pampering. But I've put up with some pretty awful bosses in my time, and not a single one has ever whisked me off to St. Moritz on his private jet, turned me loose at the diamond counter in Tiffany's, or bought me an apartment on Fifth Avenue. These are the sorts of gifts regularly bestowed on fortune hunters. In return for playing second fiddle, she lives in a world of addictive comforts (imagine never standing in line at a ticket counter). She can go anywhere, see anything. Museums name wings after her. And, if she is patient, she will most likely inherit. A successful fortune hunter might even flip the roles and end up with a charming boy toy of her own late in life. We must all get our daily bread, and who's to say that making money is more virtuous—or more fun—than marrying it?

There is one weighty issue that remains to be addressed. What's love got to do with it? When I began this book, I didn't expect to discover much in the way of love. I had assumed that the women who famously married big money had gone about it coldly, methodically, and with calculation, just as you would any high-stakes business deal. Romance be damned. "This is not a book about love stories," I repeatedly told friends. You will find, as you meet these women, that I was not entirely right. As Mother said, it *is* just as easy to love a rich man—sometimes.

2

The Power of Beauty
and
the Philandering Marquis

*B*eauty has always been women's passport to wealth and power. From the beginning of recorded history, beautiful women have used their looks to gain fortunes and elevate their social status.

A woman's beauty can change the course of history. Remember Helen of Troy? She had the face that "launched a thousand ships"—it also launched the Trojan War. Madame de Pompadour, one of the most powerful behind-the-scenes players in the history of the French court, was once Mademoiselle Poisson—Miss Fish. She became Louis XV's "declared mistress," a quasi-official role. When Miss Fish demanded that Louis ennoble her, she became Madame de Pompadour.

Madame de Pompadour did not found a noble line, but numerous aristocratic families were established on a woman's beauty. England's dukes of St. Albans, for instance, are descended from Nell Gwynne, an actress and orange seller in London's Covent Garden who became King Charles II's favorite mistress. When Nell called her son by the king a bastard, Charles was shocked. "For what else should I call him?" canny Nell asked. Charles legitimized the boy and made him a duke.

This is the story of a woman who—like Madame de Pompadour—used her radiant good looks to become a marquise. She did not become a political power. But she had a life full of adventure and, despite several false starts and a tragedy that filled the gossip sheets, ended up enormously rich. She is not as well known as her great friend the Duchess of Windsor, but her tale has a happier ending. She lives on Fifth Avenue, is still, in her eighties, possessed of a willowy beauty, is a contributor to good causes and the toast of New York society, though a few, it must be said, remember certain youthful indiscretions.

Beauty wasn't her only gift. She was also ambitious and determined. She started as a belle of the American South, and so it is appropriate that her daughter nicknamed her Scarlett, after Scarlett O'Hara, the determined—and ruthless—Southern belle.

GREENVILLE, SOUTH CAROLINA, 1920S–1940

She has always portrayed herself as a flower of the Old South, well born, a lady to her fingertips. New Yorkers who don't understand the South often insist that Carroll McDaniel Portago Carey-Hughes Pistell Petrie—to give her the full drumroll of her married names—puts on airs. "She claimed to come from landed aristocracy," sneered a critic. These are people who don't know about a distinctively Southern caste: the land-rich, cash-poor gentry. Or perhaps they expect Southern ladies to be more like Melanie, the good girl in *Gone With the Wind,* than Scarlett.

A pretty girl with perfect skin, lustrous hair (which started out darker but became very blond), and smoky blue eyes—the McDaniels say the blue comes from their Huguenot ancestors—Carroll McDaniel grew up knowing that beauty mattered. The South is a region that particularly prizes female comeliness. Carroll, a girl in the 1930s, absorbed the sense of her cousin Ben McDaniel's oft-repeated adage: "You can marry more money in five minutes than you can make in a lifetime." It is the wisdom of the Old (and New) South, a line the McDaniel men still quote to their daughters.

Carroll had advantages and disadvantages, the daughter of a peculiarly Southern, intergenerational family ruled by a severe Baptist matriarch. The family lived on McDaniel Avenue—named for them, originally known as "the road to Mrs. McDaniel's farm"—in Greenville, South Carolina. Greenville, not moss-draped like Charleston, had large trees, historic houses, and was, especially by Southern standards, a large town. If you included the metropolitan area, Greenville numbered more than sixty thousand souls in Carroll's youth. The first McDaniel, a quartermaster in the War of 1812—rumored to have been a slave trader in Charleston—came to Greenville in the 1840s. The family quickly became prominent in local affairs. There were three long-serving Sheriff McDaniels in the latter half of the nineteenth century. Land was the most cherished form of wealth in the Old South, and the McDaniels had a great deal of it. An 1890s real-estate circular described Carroll's neighborhood as "a nice place to raise children and chickens." The street, paved in 1924, had big, old houses, graceful, overhanging giant oaks providing shade, and a profusion of dog-woods and azaleas blooming in the spring. McDaniel Avenue was the best address in Greenville.

Southern belles often have a thing about Daddy. Carroll was named for her father—Carroll had been a man's name in the McDaniel family—but he died when she was seven. The "poor man," as she referred to him, had Lou Gehrig's disease. Carroll; her sister, Camille, older by four years; and their mother, Helen, moved in with the formidable Nora McDaniel, owner of the house on McDaniel Avenue. Many in Greenville felt sorry for Miss Helen, a gracious woman from an old Georgia family, for having to live with her domineering mother-in-law.

Nora McDaniel ruled the McDaniel Avenue roost. She wore high-topped shoes and long black dresses with high necklines. "She looked like Whistler's mother," a neighbor remembered. Nora McDaniel was a famil-iar sight in town, as her chauffeur, Will—also the handyman—drove her to the country to buy fresh eggs and ham. Even after Carroll moved to New York, she sometimes appealed to Nora McDaniel for money. "I re-member Carroll sitting on the porch, begging Miss Nora to give her the money to fly back to New York," said the neighbor. Nora was unmoved. "You came on the train," she said, "and you'll go back on the train."

The McDaniel girls attended Greenville High School, where the city's "nice" children went, a WPA building still in pristine condition, with pic-tures of George Washington and Robert E. Lee hanging in the corridor. The actress Joanne Woodward attended the school several years after Car-roll, who graduated in 1940. Although well-liked, Carroll was never as popular as the more outgoing Camille. Still, Carroll dated a lot, had a twinkle in her blue eyes, belonged to the French and Art Clubs, and worked on the business staff of the *Nautilus,* the school yearbook. "Tell me and I'll tell a million," read the legend under her senior yearbook picture. In the picture, she is a saucy-looking teenager with juicy red lips. There is already a coquettish gleam in her eyes—this is clearly a girl who knows that she is very, very pretty.

Whatever else Mother and Grandmother, whom she remembers as "righteous Baptist ladies," did, they endowed Carroll with an unshakable sense of her place in the world. "The things that were important to us were the land and the [Civil] war," she recalled, "and all of that my grandmother had in her head and passed down to me. I was never allowed to forget who I was. I had a very strong image of what my family was. They were landowners." Still, Carroll yearned to leave Greenville. As a little girl, she dug holes in the front yard, saying she was trying to get to China. "I knew from an early age that I wanted to leave," she said. She wanted to go to New York, but first there was college.

She enrolled in Converse College, in Spartanburg, South Carolina, a school established in 1892 by a rich cotton mill owner named Dexter Edgar Converse to educate his daughter. Converse was known for turning out well-bred young ladies. A year was enough for Carroll. "She was determined to go to New York and make it big," said a contemporary. Carroll was willing to take a financial gamble to get there. "Carroll went to [her mother] and said she wanted her inheritance now," a relative said. According to Greenville lore, Carroll received $8,000, which she planned to use on a modeling course. While her peers were still at college, places like Hollins or Sweet Briar, Carroll McDaniel, at the age of eighteen, boarded a packed wartime train for New York, beginning a life of glamour, tragedy, and triumph.

Greenville from now on would only read about her adventures—marrying a nobleman, making the best-dressed list, decorating yet another apartment. It's instructive to contrast the careers of the two pretty McDaniel sisters. Camille, the more popular, married the state's premier banker and became beloved by the community, a lady who enjoyed a cocktail and being slightly shocking. When she died in 1999, Carroll returned for the standing-room-only funeral at Christ Church (Episcopal). Dressed in what looked to some like a silver ski jacket, Carroll took her small dog inside the church. She was in a hurry to get to the airport. "The poor limo driver hit a tombstone in the churchyard because Carroll was yelling at him," said a relative.

NEW YORK, 1940S

My Sister Eileen, a play that later became the Broadway musical *Wonderful Town,* captures the quintessential New York experience of young women of Carroll's vintage. It's about the adventures of two struggling but ebullient sisters from Ohio who take a moldy basement apartment in Greenwich Village. Occasionally they ask themselves (in the musical version): Why, oh why, oh why did I ever leave Ohio? Carroll's experience was different. She bought a fur coat, almost the moment she got off the train, and took a room at the Hotel Barbizon, "New York's Most Exclusive Hotel Residence for Young Women," on the stylish East Side, at Sixty-third Street and Lexington. It was where "everybody" stayed. Sylvia Plath immortalized it as the Amazon. Carroll did not ask herself why, oh why, she'd left South Carolina. "It was a wonderful time to be here," she recalled wistfully. "It was a glorious time."

With her classic good looks, coquette's smile, and a touch of the ethereal, Carroll had no trouble getting into the John Robert Powers modeling school. Powers was more than a modeling course. The "Powers Girls" were special—there was a song and a movie about them. Along with developing runway skills, Powers Girls learned how to select the right clothes, the ins and outs of proper etiquette. They learned not only how to eat correctly, they learned how to eat nutritiously. Former First Lady Betty Ford and actresses Lauren Bacall, Ava Gardner, and Paulette Goddard were Powers Girls. Through her Powers training, Carroll landed a job as a model at Bergdorf Goodman, one of the world's leading department stores, famous for its splashy window displays on Fifth Avenue. As college girls from Greenville began coming for adventure in New York, they noticed that Carroll was meeting "a lot of influential people." She soon lost track of her old friends from home, at least the female ones.

"She was the kind of girl who set the Thames on fire," said a socialite who knew her then. "Guys don't forget a girl like that. No two ways about it, she was a knockout." The Depression had ended, releasing pent-up energy and making New York the most exciting place imaginable. "When I came to New York, it was the Stork Club and El Morocco," Carroll said, "but the Stork Club didn't last. From my point of view, the El Morocco was the most glamorous club in the world. It had an atmosphere that was magic and which you couldn't get any other place."

Carroll was a regular at the El Morocco—Elmo's to initiates—on

Fifty-fourth Street, just off Fifth Avenue. Inside, beyond the velvet rope, were the club's plastic palm trees and signature blue zebra-striped banquettes, the backdrop of numerous newspaper photos of that glamorous era. El Morocco opened only in the evening for dinner and dancing. It had evolved from a speakeasy in the 1930s, and until it fell on hard times in the early 1970s (there was later a failed attempt at reviving the sacred club), it was home to Europeans with titles, American debutantes, and plutocrats. El Morocco drew, author Neal Gabler has noted, the remnants of Old Guard society and the more established Hollywood stars to its "elegant din." Humphrey Bogart was banned after a particularly nasty drunk. ("You don't get to be the Boris Karloff of the supper club scene overnight," Gabler said.) The maître d'hôtel, always attired in white tie and tails, perfected the art of power seating. "In those days, it was jewelry, furs, and feathers," recalled Dorothy Strelsin, a New York socialite and former entertainer. "You were dressed up, you were noticed, you were glamorous. If the maître d' didn't know the woman, he'd say there were no reservations. If you weren't glamorous, he'd seat you on the wrong side."

Carroll McDaniel never sat on the wrong side. She had a huge smile and syrupy Southern accent that some could barely understand. She was a lot of fun, so much so that she sometimes joined New York society debutantes Cobina Wright Jr. and Brenda Frazier as Bob Hope's "girlfriends" on his Tuesday radio show. Hope gently teased the girls, and they had to keep up a polite banter. Though Carroll never smoked or drank—it's bad for the skin—she was "a little sexier" than most Powers Girls, said a women who knew her in those days. "She was a completely social creature," said this woman who never liked her, "and it was blatantly clear what she was trying to do—marry money." "She was always on the go with somebody or other. A lot of zillionaires gave her gifts," said another. "Carroll," said Venezuelan-born socialite Reinaldo Herrera, who is married to fashion designer Carolina Herrera, "is one of those women who have continuously been beauties. That is the source of her charm and self-assurance."

"When the war started," Carroll recalled, "all the South Americans came to New York, which made it exciting." Carroll loved Latin dances—and Latins. Her relationship with one Latin in particular says something about her willingness to risk censure to get something she wanted. He was Alberto Dodero, an Argentine shipping magnate and mentor to Aristotle Onassis. It was rumored that Dodero had helped Nazis escape Germany after the war. He was friendly with Argentine dictator Juan Perón. Eva Perón—who would become Carroll's friend—adored him. He bought Eva fabulous jewels from Van Cleef & Arpels. Estranged from his wife, an American chorus girl, Dodero offered Carroll a trip around the world. It was not the sort of invitation Southern belles of that day customarily accepted. Carroll did. The *New York Daily Mirror*, a popular source of gossip, reported that Dodero had "lavishly" entertained "Miss McDaniel," taking her to Buenos Aires, Spain, Italy, and Paris. According to the *Daily Mirror*, Dodero gave Miss McDaniel jewelry valued at $250,000. The headline: QUEEN OF HEARTS LIKES DIAMONDS TOO. The relationship was most likely platonic—Dodero "loved being surrounded by beautiful women, but he couldn't *do* anything," according to a woman who knew everybody. The trip turned out to have been a good gamble: "She met an old Argentine man who brought her to Paris, where she met the Marquis de Portago," said a titled contemporary.

PARIS, NEW YORK, 1949–1950S

The Marquis de Portago spotted her having lunch with two friends (men, of course) at Maxim's in Paris. He sauntered over to their table, ready for another challenge, another conquest. A professional race car driver in his early twenties, Portago looked more like the precursor of James Dean in *Rebel Without a Cause* than a Spanish nobleman. A cigarette (unlit—he was a health nut who also had an aversion to baths and dentists) invariably dangling from his lower lip, the slim, wavy-haired marquis with the grimy leather jacket was undeniably one of the most glamorous men in Europe. A *Life* magazine portrait would hail him as a "noble daredevil" who had been "born 400 years too late." "I like the feeling of fear," he was quoted as saying. "After a while you become an addict and have to have it." He was shown in a picture as a baby being held by his godfather and namesake, King Alfonso XIII of Spain. People spoke of him as the next Porfirio Rubirosa or Aly Khan, famous playboys. Carroll's companions shooed him off, making it abundantly clear that Don Alfonso Cabeza de Vaca y Leighton, seventeenth Marquis de Portago, thirteenth conde de la Mejorada, *grandee* of Spain—known as Fon—was not welcome at their table.

Although Portago loved picking fights in nightclubs, he left without provoking a scene this time. The next night he saw her again, at an embassy reception, without her centurions. "He walked straight towards me," Carroll recalled. They chatted briefly, and then the young nobleman asked Carroll to marry him. Even for a woman used to having men fall at her feet, this was unexpected. "That's a very funny thing to say," Carroll told him. Fon explained that he expected to die young and wanted a wife and family before it happened. He added that he preferred an American wife. "I'm a woman and we usually marry in terms of family," Carroll demurred. Carroll required a bit of pursuing, but she must have known that if she played too hard to get for too long, Fon's mother, Olga, the tiny and witty Marquesa de Portago, would put a stop to it.

Olga wasn't shy about telling people that the American woman was out to "capture" her darling Fon. Olga complained of Carroll's age—she was seven years older than Fon. "I'm not sure my grandmother would have wanted my father to marry anybody," said Andrea Portago. Some felt that the real reason Olga didn't like Carroll was that they were too much alike. Olga had, in her day, captured both a fortune and a title. A former Irish nurse, she married an American multimillionaire, Frank J. Mackey, the polo-playing founder of Household Finance. Olga inherited the bulk of Mackey's $5 million estate when he committed suicide in the spring of 1927. By the end of that year, she was the Marquesa de Portago. Don Antonio, Fon's father, was a playboy, heroic soldier, gambler, and sportsman— but not rich. Olga's money and Don Antonio's title fell in love. It was ironic, a reporter once noted, that the noble Portago family was supported by the interest middle-class Americans paid on loans to buy their Philcos. When Fon was short of cash, he'd swoop down on Biarritz, the Côte Basque town where Olga, who controlled the family finances, lived in a magnificent villa, and charm his mother. Olga was unable to persuade Fon to give up the American woman.

After making a not very serious feint at being uninterested in marriage, Carroll accepted Fon's proposal. They were married in 1949, the same year the *Daily Mirror* reported on her travels with Dodero. The wedding took place in Biarritz. The couple went first to the town hall for a civil wedding, as required by French law, and then to a Catholic church, St. Charles, not far from the imperial chapel Napoléon III and the Empress Eugénie built for their summers in Biarritz, for a religious ceremony. Carroll had become a Catholic, which can be a difficult decision for a Southern Baptist. A picture shows a dazzlingly handsome couple emerging from the church: Carroll in a long white dress and Fon in striped pants. "Fon Portago had lots of girlfriends," said a friend of Carroll's, "but he married Carroll—over his mother's dead body—because she was sexy and beautiful." "He was a love of a man, always ready to help and very correct," a friend reminisced in a documentary. Some had a different view: "If he hadn't been a marquis," said a New York socialite, "he would have been a truck driver."

Carroll and Fon lived at 40 avenue Foch, known as the millionaire's row of Paris. Baron Georges Haussmann, architect to Napoléon III, created avenue Foch to give the rich easy access to the Bois de Boulogne, the fashionable park, modeled on London's Hyde and Regent's Parks. It is the widest street in Paris, with large, shady sidewalks that are ideal for the neighborhood's many children and their nurses. The Arc de Triomphe—avenue Foch is one of the streets that radiates from this monument—is at one end, a sight as emblematic of Paris as the Plaza Hotel is of New York. It was a long way from McDaniel Avenue. Olga lived next door when not in Biarritz.

Although Olga never accepted her daughter-in-law, Carroll quickly became absorbed into her new life. "She was very good-looking, and they became part of the social life of Paris," said the late socialite John Galliher. She was so beautiful that the couturier Dior encouraged her to wear his clothes, which he gave her without charge. Even Olga's carping about the American daughter-in-law, the woman with a past who had stolen her adorable son, couldn't put a damper on Carroll's zest for her new role. Everybody knew that Carroll simply loved being a marquise.

Carroll was proud of Fon. She took him to Greenville for the Christmas season of 1950. Their visit rated a feature in the local newspaper, with a photograph of a radiant, stylish couple fresh from shopping and taking in plays in New York, accompanied by their two dogs, Spooky, a Maltese terrier, and Duchesse, a miniature poodle. Carroll took courses in antiques and art. She was beginning to know more about furniture and china than did the European aristocrats in her circle. The avenue Foch apartment was spacious and furnished with fine antiques. There was a den where Fon kept his trophies and records of the Latin music he loved.

Through Olga, oddly enough, Carroll became friendly with the most famous American woman living in Paris, the Duchess of Windsor. The duke and duchess, who had lived in exile since his abdication in 1936, were sometimes Olga's houseguests at Biarritz, and Olga and the duchess played bridge together. Carroll and the duchess found that they enjoyed the very same pastimes: shopping and going to spas. "We got on because we were both Southerners," Carroll said of the Baltimore-born Wallis Simpson. Carroll was a guest when the Windsors hosted their first weekend house party at the Mill, their French country house. "The Duchess of Windsor taught Carroll how to run a house," said a friend. (A household tip from the duchess: Always have your servants iron the sheets after your nap.)

The friendship with the Duchess of Windsor became an important part of Carroll's legend. It's almost impossible to find an article of any length about Carroll that doesn't highlight her famous friendship. One of the things that people inevitably remember about her dinner parties was that the Duke and Duchess of Windsor were frequent guests. When Carroll married a third time, the couple who had broken all the rules to marry conferred a kind of cachet by attending.

Carroll loved her Dior clothes, her title, and her life in Paris, but the marriage was not a happy one. Fon continued to hang out at the Eléphant Blanc, the famous nightclub, with his Sancho Panza, Edmund Gurner Nelson. Nelson was Fon's codriver and a former elevator operator at the Plaza Hotel in New York, where the Portago family stayed. Nelson had also been a pugilist. He scouted attractive women for Fon, and the two often started bar brawls. Fon was always sober—he drank only milk.

As Carroll and Fon began to lead separate lives, he became involved with another American model, the stunning Dorian Leigh. Leigh was one of the most sought-after models of the late 1940s and '50s, the signature face of Revlon's Fire and Ice lipstick and the sister of Suzy Parker, another famous model. Leigh accompanied Fon when he went on the road to racing events. Dorian was a free spirit who claimed, with some justification, to be the inspiration for her friend Truman Capote's joyfully promiscuous Holly Golightly in *Breakfast at Tiffany's*. If Fon gave Dorian a signal in the Eléphant Blanc, she left him to pursue whatever girl had caught his fancy that night. Carroll did not make much effort to cultivate her mother-in-law. Dorian went all out to woo Olga, who, according to reports, may have paid for her Paris apartment. Dorian wrote in her autobiography that Carroll was "several years older [than Fon]—not only in years but in experience with men. Fon said defensively, after hearing some gossip about Carol's [sic] premarital adventures, 'when I married her, she became a lady.'"

Carroll is a careful woman, always concerned about doing the right thing, presenting the right image. During "the crazy years at St. Moritz" (as the documentary about Fon describes the time), a New York socialite saw Carroll's facade crack. Fon was training the Spanish bobsled team he founded in St. Moritz. "Portago got these guys together—they were just a bunch of maniacs," said the New Yorker. "One day we were all sort of sleeping in a hotel room at the Palace [Hotel], and there's this banging on the door, and it's Carroll. 'Fon! *Fon!* Are you in there?' He'd disappeared, obviously, with somebody. She's usually under very careful control, but she was crazy at that moment. Boy, when she lost her temper, she was really quite something."

Andrea recalled that her mother was "often in tears" during the Paris years. Dorian was the most serious of Fon's affairs, and they had a son together. Fon's only legitimate son with Carroll, Antonio—Anthony— was born on March 24, 1954. Dorian's son with Fon, Kim, who looked so much like his father, was born a year and a half later, on September 21, 1955. Carroll "hated the humiliation" and fought to prevent her children from learning of Kim's existence. This was complicated when Kim went to live with his father's family in Biarritz. Olga adored him.

"Fon loved Carroll," insisted his sister, Sol, the Marquesa de Moratalla. "She was his first great love, but he loved Dorian, too. He liked clever women. Fon and Dorian would do crossword puzzles for hours. The other women were flattering for him." Whenever women pressured Portago to divorce Carroll, he flippantly replied, "I'd love to, but I'm Catholic." Even so, Carroll moved back to New York and into an apartment at 1030 Fifth Avenue. Andrea Portago believes that her father was "devastated" by Carroll's return to New York, but he did begin the process of obtaining a divorce (which Olga opposed—she didn't care for Carroll, but she didn't want a divorce in the family, either). He began a very public fling with the actress Linda Christian, who was divorced from matinee idol Tyrone Power.

Hailed by the writer Taki as "the femme fatale to end all femme fatales," Christian had had an affair with Errol Flynn while still in her teens. She would go on to have headline-grabbing romances with Baby Pignatari, the celebrated Brazilian playboy, and producer Mike Todd, who later married Elizabeth Taylor. Fon's sidekick Nelson spotted her deplaning at Paris's Orly Airport. Nelson assured Fon that she was bound to turn up at the Eléphant Blanc—she sounded American, and all the Americans went there. Christian did go to the famous nightclub. She left her seat and returned to find Fon sitting in it. She asked him to leave. "What? Are you seriously turning down a Marquis of Spain, who was held in the arms of a king?" Fon teased. "When he had left our table, my friends competed for the privilege of recounting his biography: he never allowed himself to remain serious about anyone; his last girl friend had three times attempted suicide. . . . His marriage was shattered."

Fon phoned Linda at her hotel and arrived unannounced with a picnic basket. Linda couldn't resist Fon's charm, and in fact once the affair started, she didn't keep quiet about it. For those who felt that Christian was using Fon, "Who cares?" he said with a shrug. She, for her part, was very much in love with Fon—but what woman wasn't? He took her to 40 avenue Foch, gesturing at the empty rooms. "As you can see, my wife took everything to New York but me," he said.

Portago hoped to retire from racing eventually and was reluctant to drive in the Mille Miglia, Italy's treacherous thousand-mile auto race. Adding to his discomfort, he was given an unfamiliar car at the last minute. He joked in a note to Dorian, who was always in his life, that premonitions of his early death might come true. At a checkpoint Christian darted out and, as mechanics worked on the Ferrari, kissed a helmeted, goggled Fon. The paparazzi of the day captured the soon-to-be famous kiss. It was Fon's last. Shortly afterward the Ferrari blew a tire and careened into the crowd, killing Portago, Nelson, and ten spectators. It was May 12, 1957, and Fon Portago, at twenty-eight, was dead. "It would be a flinty heart that did not mourn his death. . . . He was an adornment in the world, an excitement, a pillar of fire," the automotive journalist Ken Purdy noted.

In New York, Carroll learned of her husband's death when a reporter from *The New York Times* telephoned for a reaction. She was facing not only tragedy but a potential public relations disaster: Christian was telling every reporter with a notepad that Fon had planned to marry her; the actress was usurping the role of the grieving widow. With reporters buzzing around, Carroll flew to Paris, where she borrowed a black dress—she does not like to wear black and owned nothing appropriate for a funeral—and then flew to meet Fon's family in Milan. They were flying with Fon's body in a private plane to Madrid for the funeral. Christian had planned to fly with them but was bumped to make room for Carroll—Christian always insisted that Fon's family would have preferred to take her on the plane instead of Carroll and had chosen Fon's wife purely for the sake of appearances.

As the drama unfolded, Carroll was magnificent. Standing by the coffin that held Fon's mangled remains, Carroll dismissed rumors that she and Fon had been heading for a divorce and characterized Christian as "just another girl." She spoke of her abiding love for Fon. "You must understand," she said tearfully, "we loved each other, to the very end, the bitter end. And I still love him." Christian was still determined to attend the funeral in widow's weeds and sit with the family. Fon's sister, Sol, and a family friend spent hours trying to persuade Christian that this was "not the done thing." (It was for the sake of propriety, not prudery—Sol would later laughingly tell me that if all the women Fon had slept with had showed up, the church wouldn't have been large enough. Dorian, perhaps the most genuinely grief-stricken, did not attend.) Linda and Carroll arrived in church within a few minutes of each other. "My husband's aunt went over to her in the church in Madrid and said 'This is for the family,' " Carroll told me in an interview many years later. Linda was forced to kneel in an obscure place. Whatever the private emotions behind her thick black veil, Carroll McDaniel presented a portrait of nobility in grief not unlike the one Jacqueline Kennedy, behind her black veil, would project to the world a few years later. The widow draped in black was the counterpoint to Christian's kiss; it showed which woman was truly worthy to be the Marquesa de Portago. "I had a strong mother, and she was very wise. I think she had a strong role in how I handled it [the embarrassing scene at the church]," Carroll said. Many years later, as a wealthy New York socialite, Carroll would reminisce, on camera for a documentary on Portago, about the fabulous parties she had attended in Paris and insist, without missing a beat, that her marriage to Fon had been "very stable." I asked her about her husband's philandering when I went to see her while she was in her early seventies. "The way I saw it, I couldn't do anything about it," she said. "That was the nature of the man. At that time, most men in Europe did behave like that. Maybe my husband was more visible because he was a major personality. I married for life—that's the way I saw it. You can't just walk out over it the first time something you don't like happens."

Fon's death, as had her father's, put Carroll's fate in the hands of one powerful matriarch. Fon had no more than a decent income from a trust fund and his earnings as a Ferrari driver. Olga made a settlement on Carroll. It was, by all accounts, not lavish. Though Carroll also had use of a trust fund until both her children reached the age of twenty-one, she did not have enough money to maintain her in the style her beauty had won for her. This is the point at which most women, having faced down a rival but ended up relatively poor (at least by the standards of the world in which she lived), might have headed home to woo the local Rotary Club president.

All too many glamour girls setting out for New York with high hopes and great expectations find it more difficult to become a movie star or make a brilliant marriage than they'd anticipated. Flaubert's Madame Bovary also wanted to dance at balls, wear fine clothes, and be courted by well-born men, only to be undone. Carroll was hardier than Flaubert's heroine, who was sentimental and romantic whereas Carroll was romantic and clear-eyed at the same time. Carroll could be seen as more like Anne Welles, the heroine of Jacqueline Susann's *Valley of the Dolls* (dare one call it *Madame Bovary* for the 1950s?). No matter what happened, Anne was determined never to return to the claustrophobia of her hometown. Greenville, South Carolina, had a place in Carroll's heart, but she did not want to live there. She needed another rich man. "If you've lived a life like that, hanging out with the Duke and Duchess of Windsor, and suddenly you don't know where your next meal is coming from," said a close friend, "what do you do? The only thing you can do is marry money."

HONG KONG, NEW YORK, 1959–1974

Several times she seemed on the brink of another grand marriage. There were Carroll sightings in Europe and South America and in the South of France. As part of the legend, she was rumored to have had an affair with Manolete, the bullfighter, though his biographer says this is not the case. "I've followed her career," said a New York socialite, "and there were times when she was absolutely in need of money." "She [Carroll] was very good at getting money from men," said a titled detractor. Being strapped for cash, of course, is a relative thing: Carroll lived on Fifth Avenue and employed a French governess for the children. Charles Engelhard, the industrialist, was said to have helped Carroll live on Fifth Avenue. She told me that she and Portago had owned the Fifth Avenue apartment in the mid-1950s.

New York was always her base, but in the years following Portago's death Carroll went all over the world to hunt big game, both the human kind and the other kind—she went by yak to shoot a rare Marco Polo sheep, which occurs only at 175,000 feet above sea level, and a polar bear she killed with her custom-made Purdey rifle is now in the American Museum of Natural History in New York. She also went to live in Hong Kong, still an exotic outpost of the empire with Englishmen in pith helmets. There she met Dr. John Carey-Hughes, a Welsh physician, who fell madly in love with her. Carey-Hughes confessed to Nancy Holmes, another Powers Girl who was in Hong Kong, that he didn't think he was up to Carroll's standards. Carroll had once taken a boyfriend away from Holmes—now it was payback time. Holmes told Carey-Hughes to tell Carroll that Holmes was in love with him. Perhaps her competitive juices were flowing; Carroll soon accepted Carey-Hughes's offer of marriage, and they went to New York, where they wed at the Carlyle Hotel on April 12, 1964. They lived in Hong Kong, where Carey-Hughes, a ruggedly handsome man, owned a bungalow on Island Road, the exclusive enclave favored by well-to-do expatriates and home to some of the richest people in the world.

A doctor in Hong Kong could make a great deal of money, but Carey-Hughes was hardly a rich man. Carroll has maintained that she chose Hong Kong because it was a good place to raise children. But Andrea, then a teenager, lived with her governess at the Carlyle in New York, where she studied ballet. Tony was sent to boarding school in England at the age of six. "There was a lot of chemistry between them," said Andrea Portago, "but I think he was a very difficult man." The Carey-Hughes marriage did not last long—this time Carroll was not married for life. "I think he just bored her to death," said a close friend. Carroll refers to Carey-Hughes only as "the Welsh doctor." "I met him a couple of times, and he just was wild if you ever mentioned Carroll's name," said a socialite. Carroll returned to New York.

When asked what a single young woman in pursuit of a rich husband should do, one New York social wag, teased, "I'd tell her to become close to the wife. That way she'll be in his view more often." He added, "And she should give the wife some perfectly terrible recipes." According to the woman who claims to have made the introduction, Carroll asked to meet Jane Engelhard, a powerful New York socialite who was married to Charlie Engelhard, heir to the Engelhard Corporation, the largest metal-processing business in the world. Carroll and Jane Engelhard became good friends, and Charlie Engelhard fell head over heels in love with Carroll. "Carroll Petrie is awfully pretty," said an insider, "but she's also lots of fun. What Engelhard liked was highly entertaining women. The reason she landed this guy is she was full of laughs."

For the most part, the relationship with Engelhard took place after the Carey-Hughes divorce, though it may have had its beginnings in the period when Carroll lived in New York before Fon died. A portly man who always looked older than his age, Engelhard had started life with great wealth, which he had increased. He had used an ingenious ploy to get gold out of South Africa. It was illegal to export gold bars from the country, so Engelhard had the gold made into statues, often of a religious nature, and shipped to Hong Kong, where they were melted down. Engelhard was a racing enthusiast, the owner of Nijinsky II, the beloved Epsom Derby winner.

New York watched, fascinated, as Carroll seemed on the verge of capturing great wealth. "Everybody knew he wanted to divorce his wife and marry her. Even Engelhard said so," John Galliher recalled. Jane Engelhard knew it, too. "Carroll simply hadn't counted on Jane Engelhard," an anonymous source told the authoritative *W* magazine. "Jane was wild," said a senior socialite. "I mean, she had befriended Carroll, and here was her so-called best friend going behind her back." After Jane reportedly intercepted a telegram from Carroll to Charlie asking him to join her for safari in South Africa, she hired a private detective.

Carroll has always been given jewelry by men, and it was—according to the Carroll legend—a piece of jewelry that led to Carroll's downfall. A widely repeated story has Carroll trying to return a sapphire ring Engelhard had given her for the cash and getting caught in the act by Jane's detective. When Charlie was informed, he ended the affair. An intimate of Carroll's heard a somewhat similar story, but one with variations. He would not elaborate. Engelhard was so unhappy that his wife reportedly felt bad about her role in the episode. Engelhard seems to have taken his grief out by eating. Eleanor Lambert, the late fashion publicist, said he kept a cake by his bedside and nibbled through the night. It has been said that "the Engelhard women" (a formidable group that includes Annette de la Renta, Jane Engelhard's daughter and the wife of designer Oscar de la Renta) continued to "loathe and detest" Carroll many years later. A quite possibly apocryphal story had them passing around a dartboard with Carroll's face as the bull's-eye.

The end of the affair had a profound effect on Carroll's social standing in New York. Most people took Jane Engelhard's side. The socialite who claims to have introduced the two women confronted Carroll and told her, "[Unlike you,] I was born to be a lady." Even someone with a strong ego such as Carroll had to know that she had become one of the most unpopular women in New York. Some think that it was Carroll's need for "social protection from Jane" that led to her next marriage.

Richard Chadwick Pistell weighed around three hundred pounds and looked like a sumo wrestler—but he had money. Or so it seemed. Pistell was chairman of General Host, a $200 million company, and a bit of a buccaneer, the precursor of the modern merger kings. He was engaged in a much-publicized attempt to acquire Armour & Company, the meat-packing giant. According to *The New York Times,* Pistell had "perfected a daring and unorthodox approach to finance which drew the suspicion of traditionalists." "One of the things I go into a rage about is exclamation points," said John Ledes, one of several lawyers who represented Pistell's estranged wife in their divorce. "If you use exclamation points, it's be-cause you haven't written well enough to make your point. But Dick's life was a walking exclamation point." Like Carroll, he enjoyed big-game hunting and was recognized for his prowess.

At the time he was seeing Carroll, his divorce from Louise Pistell was making headlines. The *New York Daily News* reported in March 1969 that Louise had hired superlawyer Percy Foreman, wryly noting that the wife of the "big-game hunter" was "loaded for bear." Louise charged cruelty. Conjuring up a delicious image, the massive Pistell claimed that he had been terrorized by Louise's "ferocious, vicious" poodle. Two months after the poodle story, Suzy Knickerbocker, the social columnist, reported in a one-sentence lead item that the Pistells were "finally out of court and divorced." That same month Carroll married him in a brief ceremony in her 817 Fifth Avenue apartment. Richard Pistell Jr., then a little boy, remembers that the Duke and Duchess of Windsor refused to share the elevator with the Pistell children. "I think they just wanted to make an entrance instead of having three kids tag along," he said. "The duke and duchess were very nice but very aloof." Carroll and her new husband set off to the Central Republic of Africa to hunt antelope. "Boy, that Pistell was an unattractive-looking fellow. A real thug. For God's sake, if she'd been left well off, she'd never have married Pistell," said an old-money New Yorker.

Catty socialites dubbed her "the Pistell-packing marquesa." Eventually it became clear that Carroll, along with a lot of other Pistell investors, had made a huge mistake. Pistell's partner in a number of ventures was the notorious Robert Lee Vesco, a corporate looter who, in the words of his biographer, reached "the pinnacle of white-collar thieves." Pistell and Vesco attempted unsuccessfully to wrest control of Nassau's Paradise Island from Howard Hughes and turn it into a gambling haven. In 1974 Pistell was sued by court-appointed liquidators of four Vesco-plundered mutual funds who claimed that Pistell had fraudulently received $3 million. Pistell owed $500,000 in back taxes, and the federal government had put a lien on his property. "Pistell was a manipulative wheeler-dealer. He was just not Mr. Respectable. He was always needing money," said former *Wall Street Journal* reporter Stanley Penn, who covered the debacle. "The minute he lost his money, she took off. It's unbelievable, this woman," said a senior socialite. Another version has her trying to help Pistell by selling some of her jewelry. *W* magazine summed it up this way: "A page in the Carroll Petrie saga has her marrying Pistell in the belief that he had some dough; he thought the same of her. Two broke and disappointed people got divorced."

She owned an apartment on Fifth Avenue and a smallish, not fancy cottage in Lyford Cay, an expensive enclave in the Bahamas. But she did not have money. She could, of course, always go back to Greenville, where she now had inherited a few hundred acres. Carroll was forty-two and still beautiful—a knockout, in fact. But the clock was ticking.

NEW YORK, 1974 TO THE PRESENT

"Carroll always had the mantle of great wealth, but she didn't have the wealth," said a New York social observer. Fortunately, Carroll had friends willing to help her acquire the wealth to go with her mantle. They arranged a blind date with Milton Petrie, a ready-to-wear magnate thrice divorced with three grown children—and in his seventies. "My first thought was that no one had ever introduced me to someone I was supposed to get along with that I got along with," she said with what some might consider feigned innocence. But this was the exception. A Spanish grandee Milton Petrie was not, but Carroll liked him immediately. He had come up the hard way. He went bankrupt as a young man but through sheer grit managed to pay his debts in full. A gruff man, he smoked smelly cigars and still ran Petrie Stores, an apparel chain. He went to his drab office in Secaucus, New Jersey, daily. He looked so much older than Carroll that one New York socialite thought he was meeting Carroll's prospective father-in-law.

While they were courting, she introduced him to the social circuit, and he allowed her to indulge in one of her favorite pastimes: buying major-league jewelry. They made a trip to Harry Winston, the New York jeweler. An amused reporter described Carroll as she "dug through the diamonds with the vigor and expertise of a Korean grocer sizing up eggplants." Said a woman close to the couple, "Carroll introduced Milton to a world he never even knew existed." He seemed genuinely in love and impressed with her aristocratic history. A year after their blind date, in 1979, Carroll and Milton Petrie were married in a civil ceremony witnessed by a business associate of his and her lawyer. It was the fourth marriage for both.

"Marrying Petrie was a big 'fuck you'—it had to be. When they walk into the Metropolitan Museum, they can't avoid seeing the Carroll and Milton Petrie European Sculpture Court," said a close friend of Carroll's. "They" were the Engelhard women and those who'd whispered about Carroll over the years. The sculpture garden, a replica of a classical French garden, opened in 1990, joining the Charles Engelhard Court in the American Wing as a major attraction. Milton Petrie, though he looked like a caricature of a stingy, cigar-chomping millionaire, was a famously generous philanthropist who sent money to perfect strangers who'd endured hardship.

New Yorkers said that it was difficult to decide who the real Cinderella was—Milton or Carroll. She buffed his rough exterior, replacing his off-the-rack suits with Huntsman's of London. She took him to all sorts of exciting parties—he met Prince Charles at a White House dinner when Nancy and Ronald Reagan, Carroll's dear friends, lived there. He found that he quite liked the social circuit. A man who'd struggled with alcoholism, he was finally able to quit for good after meeting Carroll. For her part, Carroll "embarked on an occupation of opulence that [was] nothing short of splendid," according to a magazine, hiring a fleet of decorators—including Jackie O's—to redo the Southampton spread and the new co-op at 834 Fifth Avenue and buying a silver fur coat to go with the silver Rolls-Royce. "Milton was the king of the house," said a relative. "He gave her jets and jewels and enabled her to realize her dreams, and she loved him for that."

Carroll's marriage to Petrie brought her everything she'd sought, including love. "If you asked Milton 'Who do you trust?' he always said it was Carroll," her friend the author William Nathan Banks said. "When she married him," said a man who knew them, "he was a physical wreck. She was no Anna Nicole Smith. She kept him going for a long, long time." When he was a very old man, in a wheelchair, Carroll hovered about him. "Come talk to Milton, he loves pretty girls," she'd say. She was spotted spooning food into his mouth in Lyford Cay. The only discord *chez* Petrie was, alas, an implacable hatred between his pampered bulldog, Begin, and her perfumed, pearl-sporting poodle, Peaches. (Carroll has always loved tiny dogs. When a Southampton hostess asked Carroll to shush her dog, Carroll snapped, "This dog is better bred than anybody here.")

Petrie died in 1994, at the age of ninety-two, leaving Carroll a very rich woman. She inherited $5 million in cash, a trust fund of $150 million, a plane, cars, and houses, including the one at 834 Fifth Avenue and a large spread in Southampton. His three children and his grandchildren received relatively modest amounts, ranging from $2 million to $15 million, and there were numerous charitable bequests. But Carroll got the bulk of his estate. Those who thought she'd married just for the money noticed her obvious sense of loss. After a respite from society, she resumed her life, reigning as the queen of chic Southampton. She used some of her money to establish a scholarship fund in honor of her son at the United World Colleges (for which Tony, her son by Fon, had been a fund-raiser) and to build a $1 million music school at her alma mater, Converse College. In the end, she had gotten it all. "You can say a lot of things about Carroll Petrie," said an admirer. "You can say she's ambitious and that she's always wanted the better things of life. But she's always conducted herself as a lady." Her beauty, used wisely, had conquered all.

3

IF AT FIRST YOU DON'T SUCCEED . . .

A successful fortune hunter sometimes has to endure a lot of matrimonial karma before attaining that special nirvana that only a filthy rich husband can provide. Public humiliations that would permanently sideline most women are a mere bump in the road for her. She must be shameless, confident, and endowed with an indestructible belief that she is supposed to be rich. She does not fold when a marriage folds.

She is able to cut her losses and move on. If her husband is going to jail, she starts looking for a richer husband. She does not perceive a nasty divorce as a personal failure. Why cry over spilt milk? The adept fortune hunter concentrates on what really matters: alimony—enough to tide her over until Mr. Richer II comes along. But she doesn't just wait for her next husband to appear on the scene—she finds him.

A woman who is inclined to waste precious time on the "healing process" is not cut out for this line of work. Embarrassment must be an alien concept. Spunky Becky Sharp of Thackeray's novel *Vanity Fair* is the poster girl for the "if at first you don't succeed" crowd. She was a penniless adventurer whose marriage to the dim son of a baronet saves her from being a governess. "I'm no angel," Becky admits, and she isn't kidding. But she is smart, canny, and saucy. If women don't care for her, men do.

Study well the saga of Becky Sharp. No matter what, Becky Sharpe never loses sight of her objective: the financial and social ascent of Becky Sharp. She makes her first play for her friend Amelia Sedley's brother, Joseph, an official in the East India Company, "a stout, puffy man, in buckskins and Hessian boots, with several immense neck cloths that rose almost to his nose." He is a ridiculous man, but being Mrs. Sedley is better than being a governess. When the assault on Joseph fails (because of snobbish outside intervention), Becky goes glumly to the country to teach the daughters of Sir Pitt Crawley, an uncouth baronet. Becky fixes her attentions equally on Sir Pitt and his younger son, Rawdon, a military officer. When Sir Pitt finally proposes, Becky and Rawdon are already secretly married. She is devastated that she will not become Lady Crawley but is fond of Rawdon. "If he had more brains," she muses, "I might make something of him."

Through her connection to a well-born family—and by living on credit—Becky becomes a "smart and leading" member of Paris society and later a London hostess. If the staid elements of London society aren't drawn to her dinners and opera parties, she entertains such risqué personages as the wicked Lord Steyne, who uses his influence to have Becky presented to royalty at court. But living on credit has its limits, and with bailiffs at the door, Becky flees to the Continent and becomes a gambler. Once again, Becky, by now widowed, encounters Joseph. This time she catches him. Becky convinces the self-deluding Joseph that she has been pining for him. To condense, upon receiving a large inheritance from Joseph, Becky establishes herself in the idyllic English town of Bath, where she busies herself with pious works (the Victorian equivalent of serving on a benefit committee) and goes to church. Becky calls herself Lady Pitt and is embraced by "a very strong party of excellent people [who] consider her to be a most injured woman. She has her enemies. But who has not? Her life is an answer to them."

NEW YORK, 1980S

Although there were many stalwarts of Nouvelle Society—a term coined by a magazine editor to denote a glittering Vanity Fair of new money and conspicuous consumption that flourished in New York in the 1980s—the most dazzling creatures of the day were two women who'd surmounted formidable obstacles to get where they were and whose opulent parties raised eyebrows among staid elements of society. But nobody refused their invitations. Who could possibly turn down a hand-delivered invitation, tied with a perfect yellow rose, from the ebullient Susan Gutfreund? All agreed that Susan's "Proustian evening"—with the imposing gilt candelabrum on every table and the little bag of scents tied to the back of each chair—was a night to remember.

"It's so expensive to be rich," Susan was famously quoted as saying in John Taylor's article "How to Be Rich" in *New York* magazine at a lunch given by the late Malcolm Forbes. But nobody doubted that Susan Gutfreund, not a great beauty but an extremely attractive blonde with a large, brilliant smile, was having a lot of fun being rich. She once remarked to a reporter that New York was "like living in a fairy tale." A former Pan Am flight attendant, Susan had married John Gutfreund, head of the largest investment banking house on Wall Street and her second husband, in 1981. A somewhat dumpy man with black-rimmed glasses that make him look like the teacher he once aspired to be, Gutfreund was known on Wall Street as a "brutal" bond trader. He had become managing partner of Salomon Brothers in 1978, selling Salomon to Phibro, the big commodities trading firm, four years later and becoming chief executive officer of the new entity. He is seven years older than Susan. He was not a smoothie in the drawing room. The writer John Taylor reported that he once said to a dinner partner, "Well, you've got the name, but you don't have the money." The rude trader was (and is), however, as an associate put it, "ass over teakettle mad about Susan." He's miserable when she's in Paris and he's in New York.

As Mrs. Gutfreund, Susan charted a course of irrational exuberance, even by New York's Nouvelle Society standards. Dividing her time between New York and Paris (the designer Givenchy had the other half of the Paris duplex), she hired the famous French decorator Henri Samuel to do both residences. Samuel turned the New York apartment at 834 Fifth Avenue into an outpost of eighteenth-century France with trellises and painted panels. The estimated cost was $20 million. A writer described it as "a true palace for the very model of the modern prince of finance." "My wife has spent all my money," Gutfreund famously joked, "but it was worth it." Amenities at 834 Fifth Avenue include a refrigerator in Susan's bathroom to keep her perfume cool. *New York* magazine touted the apartment as "arguably one of the most sumptuous homes in the city."

There was, indeed, a fantasy element to the life of the rich Mrs. Gutfreund. New York's most Olympian socialite, Jayne Wrightsman, had taken Susan under her wing, tutoring her in all things French. Susan was pilloried mercilessly behind her back for her Francophile affectations, not that, if she knew, it tamped down her high spirits. There was high delight when Susan addressed Mrs. Reagan with the words *"Bonsoir, Madame"* or when the Gutfreund butler solemnly informed callers that Madame was in the *fumoir*. Susan reportedly claimed to have been born in a thatched house in England, though her father, a career serviceman, placed the blessed event in Chicago. "Her Achilles' heel is a certain amount of pretension," a socialite noted, with admirable restraint.

Few in New York society had trouble recognizing qualities of Susan in "Mrs. Gesternblatt," the new rich hostess in an article by Michael Thomas in the magazine *Vanity Fair*. "As a hostess," Thomas wrote, "Mrs. Gesternblatt has found her true vocation. The naysayers mutter that she got a lot of practice at 30,000 feet, but pay no mind to them. They need their daily ration of *Schadenfreude* the way health nuts need their granola. The fact is, Mrs. Gesternblatt and the age are made for each other; she fits contemporary life like a tiny foot in a glass slipper. If she didn't exist, we—or, more properly, Gesternblatt—would have to make her up."

But Thomas hit on something important about Mrs. Gesternblatt: Say what you might, but Mrs. Gesternblatt's parties (and, by extension, Mrs. Gesternblatt) were a huge success. Everyone had a good time. Depicting a Gesternblatt soiree—the apartment stocked with "more cymbidiums than in the Oahu Hilton," the Dom Pérignon flowing freely, and Henry Kissinger surrounded by fellow nabobs—Thomas concluded: "The distinguishing quality of Mrs. Gesternblatt's evenings is their imaginative vitality, which is why, I think, hers *work*, while better-heeled, better-bred women put on the dog and end up with mongrels [as guests]."

Gayfryd Steinberg, a stunning, whippet-thin, dark-haired geisha, is the other woman who best captured the opulence of Nouvelle Society, and two parties she gave were of such epic proportions that they entered social history. They arguably rank with Mrs. William K. Vanderbilt's fabled costume ball given in 1883 to celebrate the completion of her Fifth Avenue mansion, and with Truman Capote's Black and White Ball in 1966. One was Gayfryd's 1988 wedding reception for her stepdaughter, Laura, held at the Metropolitan Museum of Art; the tab for flowers alone was put at $1 million. The inevitable headline in the society magazine *W*: LET 'EM EAT CAKE.

The other epochal assemblage, the next year, rated three *New York Times* pieces exploring the sociological and economic ramifications of such wretched excess. It was a fiftieth-birthday party for Gayfryd's third husband, Saul Steinberg, a chubby corporate raider who, in formal attire, looked rather like a frog going to the ball. Steinberg had made himself a millionaire by the time he was thirty, and a billionaire by forty, with Reliance Insurance Company the flagship of his empire. Gayfryd and Saul lived in a thirty-four-room Park Avenue apartment filled with (in the words of Geoffrey Colvin) "paintings you studied in college." "Of all the new-money women making their mark on Manhattan," *Vanity Fair* magazine gushed, "Mrs. Saul Steinberg is the most likely to succeed."

Marie Antoinette herself might have been pleased with the expenditures and planning that went into Saul's birthday party. A socialite called Gayfryd "the most efficient human being in the world," and at no time was her attention to detail more evident than that evening. The setting was the Steinberg estate overlooking the Atlantic in Quogue, a trendy town in the Hamptons. Best remembered are the scantily clad actors recreating Old Master paintings. There were identical twins got up as mermaids in the swimming pool. Columnist Liz Smith, the only invited journalist allowed to write about it, was amused by the sight of the head of Warner Brothers dancing with the girl from Vermeer's *Woman with a Water Pitcher* during her "rest" period. Two hundred and fifty guests attended. "Honey, if this were a stock, I'd short it," Saul said in his toast. "With the help of party master Robert Isabell [a society florist and events planner]," Smith wrote, "Gayfryd has catapulted herself into the ranks of Charles de Beistequi's Venetian costume ball in the 1950s and Truman Capote's Black and White ball of the 1970s."

Gayfryd had come to New York and married Steinberg in 1983. She had blazed such a social trail that Tina Brown, then editor of *Vanity Fair,* heralded her as the Brooke Astor of the future. The revered Brooke Astor was the very pinnacle of New York society, spending old money to do good works. Mrs. Astor—the name said it all. Gayfryd was not warm in the Susan Gutfeund mold, though. "I found her cold and unemotional," Desmond Atholl, a controversial butler who worked for the Steinbergs, wrote in a tell-all book about his rich employers. "You don't call it cold as much as just without feeling," said a New Orleans woman. "I think she loves her children, but I doubt if she's capable of loving anybody else. I don't think she's ever loved anybody but her children and herself."

NEW ORLEANS, 1970S AND '80S

Moran's Riverside Restaurant was famous for its high-priced Italian cuisine and colorful clientele, a medley of rich oil-company men and not-quite-respectable types, some reputed to have ties to the city's thriving underworld. There was always a bevy of good-looking women at the front table. New Orleans restaurant critic Tom Fitzmorris sometimes wondered if they were paid to decorate the place. Located in a 1930s building on Decatur Street, the fringe of New Orleans's picturesque French Quarter, Moran's afforded a splendid view of the Mississippi River. The owner was Jimmy Moran, son of mythic restaurateur Diamond Jim Moran, so called because of the diamonds implanted in his glasses frames and teeth and the legend that there might be diamonds in the meatballs of another Moran family restaurant, La Louisiane. In the mid-1970s Jimmy Moran Jr. hired a pretty young woman with a curious first name. She was not a local girl but had come to town with her husband, a metallurgy engineer. She was so beautiful that heads turned. "She created so much excitement that you'd have thought she was up for bids," said a newspaperman who frequented Moran's. She would later describe herself as a consultant who designed costumes for the waitresses and on rare occasions filled in at the restaurant's small pasta shop. "She was working as the maître d' at Moran's when I first met her," recalled a New Orleans museum official. "She wore a bow tie and tux, and she had Elizabeth Taylor's eyes and reminded me of Delta Burke when Burke was on *Designing Women* and was so beautiful."

Norman Johnson, a millionaire in the oilfield pipe supply business, was a regular at Moran's. Johnson was "rough-and-tumble, oilfield-rough," said a friend. Despite his vast wealth, Johnson, a slight man with large jug ears, was socially ill at ease. Eager to be accepted, Johnson often picked up the tabs of people he knew in fancy restaurants. He was mesmerized by Gayfryd McLean. "Someone who looked the way she looked could have had a Hunt or a Murchison," said a New Orleanian who was close to Gayfryd. "But she was just in New Orleans, working at Moran's.

Supposedly, Johnson came in a fancy car and said to Jimmy Moran, 'I love her.' He was absolutely infatuated. Nobody knew much about her except that she was very beautiful."

She had been born Gayfryd McNabb in 1950 and had grown up in modest circumstances, rented houses, mostly in the mid-size Canadian town of Nanaimo in British Columbia. Her ambitious mother, Margaret, was a housewife, and her father, Ross, a clerk with the Canadian telephone company. Though there is a brother, David, three years younger, Margaret doted on Gayfryd, endowing her daughter with unshakable self-confidence. Ross went along with whatever Margaret wanted, and "Gay was Margaret's whole thing," said an uncle, George Kerr. "She was ambitious for Gay and promoted her whichever way she could." Margaret, a spotless housekeeper and excellent cook, made sure Gayfryd had ballet lessons. Gayfryd won several area beauty contests (including Miss Nanaimo). When she graduated from Nanaimo Senior Secondary School in 1968, the yearbook noted that she planned to be a dress designer. After a year at the University of British Columbia, she married John McLean, a metallurgy engineer whom she'd met at the university. He was twenty-two, and Gay was nineteen. They went to South Africa for his job. Gayfryd persuaded McLean, about whom very little is known, to return to the United States, and the couple ended up in New Orleans.

A magazine later wrote that Johnson had "J.R.-ed" into Gayfryd's life, a reference to the flamboyant J. R. Ewing on the TV series *Dallas*. "He was the first to show her that kind of [ultra-rich] life," said a friend. "Everybody knew that Jimmy got a Rolls-Royce to thank him for introducing Norman to Gayfryd," said a friend of the Johnsons. Though some maintain that the white Rolls-Royce was a gift to cement a business deal, not a thank-you for Gayfryd, the Rolls remains a prominent feature of the Gayfryd legend in New Orleans. "The joke," said a New Orleans blue blood, "is that Moran got a Rolls in exchange for Gayfryd." Johnson wanted to marry Gayfryd. He was divorced from Judy Holmes, believed to be his second wife, in 1975. (True to form, he had given Judy a Rolls-Royce with red trim the previous Valentine's Day.) In March 1976 Gayfryd went to the Dominican Republic for a quickie divorce. She married Johnson the next month. But there was a glitch: Her Dominican Republic divorce was not legal in Louisiana. McLean, out of the picture, doesn't seem to have protested. Still, the Johnsons weren't legally married.

After Gayfryd obtained a legal divorce in Louisiana, they were definitively married in October 1977. (It was not the last time Gayfryd would be accused of having overlapping marriages.) Their only child, Rayne Johnson, a son (who has since been adopted by Saul Steinberg), was born in December.

The Johnsons bought one of the biggest houses in town, an Italian Renaissance–style stone castle on tree-lined St. Charles Avenue, and set about a mammoth decorating project that took two and a half years and several million dollars, and ultimately merited a spread in *House & Garden* magazine. Meanwhile, Gayfryd launched what would be an unsuccessful assault on stodgy New Orleans society. New Orleans has always been one of the few places in America where it matters very much who your grandfather (if not your great-grandfather) was. Society—with a capital S—is dominated by the old-line krewes (men's clubs) that host exclusive balls at Mardi Gras and hold sway over the presentation of the season's debutantes (yes, that still matters, too). They have names like Comus, Momus, and Atlanteans, and they turn a cold eye on people like the Johnsons. For Gayfryd, the Big Apple would prove easier than the Big Easy. "They never got in with the 'society' people," said a friend of the Johnsons. Gayfryd was voted down by the snobbish Junior League of New Orleans. But what really amazed the Junior League ladies was that instead of hanging her head in shame, Gayfryd continued to show up at charity events they sponsored. Some harbored a grudging admiration for the gutsy outsider. One pillar of New Orleans society, however, did embrace the Johnsons: Muriel Bultman Francis, an art collector who was always on the lookout for people to support the arts. "Muriel liked a cross section of people, and she recognized that Gayfryd was lovely," said a kinder, gentler member of the New Orleans social elite. After Muriel Francis and Gayfryd became close friends, Norman joined the board of trustees for the New Orleans Museum of Art. The Johnsons gave generously to the local charities, including the New Orleans Philharmonic Symphony and the prestigious Isidore Newman School—Norman was on the boards of both, and Gayfryd also served as a trustee to the art museum board—and began collecting art themselves, relying at first on the advice of New Orleans lawyer and art collector Moise Steeg.

Gayfryd transformed herself from Moran's head-turning maître d' into a splashy St. Charles Avenue hostess. A local gossip column reported that Norman had spent a million dollars on her Christmas presents. Sheepish, he insisted it was only $100,000. "She looked like a child in her mother's jewelry, except it was real," said a New Orleans matron. "They were like Houstonians. Everything they did was splendiferous. The old-line money in New Orleans gets stodgy. So they were a real diversion," a Junior League member told the *Times-Picayune*.

A guest at a Johnson dinner party still savors the opulence—and what old-line New Orleans regards as social comedy—more than twenty years later. The rugs in the dining room had been woven to match the dinner plates. When Gayfryd pointed out that the marble staircase in the grand rotunda of her house had come from the old St. Charles Hotel, an old-line New Orleans snob whispered, "I think the hostess came from there, too." The only thing in the house that didn't sparkle was the host. "Johnson was just a nebbish," the guest said. "He wore little velvet slippers, even though nobody else was in formal clothes. He didn't have much to say." Gayfryd frequently overreached—to the sheer delight of society in New Orleans. At a birthday party Gayfryd threw for little Rayne Johnson, an elaborate, liqueur-filled baked Alaska–style concoction was served instead of a birthday cake. The children refused to touch it, and some were so disappointed that they left in tears. Gayfryd, said a New Orleans reporter, is "totally a made up construct."

When Johnson bought the house next to their palatial dwelling to build a tennis court for Gayfryd, a neighbor was astounded. "I'm just glad she doesn't play golf," Norman deadpanned. "He was totally obsessed with her and bought her a lot of jewelry," said a museum official. A subsequent tally of Gayfryd's jewelry would eventually take up five pages and list fifty-nine major pieces. Included were a 24-karat emerald-cut diamond ring and a diamond-sapphire-and-emerald-studded gold watch. "Norman was very possessive about Gayfryd," the official added. When the Johnsons weren't placed next to each other at a museum function, Johnson asked to be moved. "I always sit by my wife," he said.

Gayfryd wasn't a complete social butterfly. She impressed everybody by her dedication to being a good stepmother to Norman's three children by his second marriage, working hard to bring an element of stability into their chaotic lives. Gayfryd insisted that the family have Sunday dinner together and was the one to say no, you can't have a Mercedes—Norman was lavish with his children, too—you should have something less ostentatious. Gayfryd's parents, Ross and Margaret, also moved to New Orleans to be near her, and Margaret provided more stability for the children. Norman and Gayfryd had waged an epic legal battle for custody against Judy, an alcoholic. "Gayfryd was the leader of the fight to get custody of his children," said New Orleans superlawyer Jack Martzell. Judy ultimately lost by marrying a man with a criminal record. Norman used this as evidence that she was an unfit parent.

Ironically, the victory in the custody battle marked the beginning of the end for the Johnsons. They hadn't reckoned with Judy's bitterness. "After Johnson married Gayfryd, a friend of mine invited me to her house for dinner and introduced me to a woman who said she'd been married to Norman Johnson, and he'd divorced her," a New Orleans socialite close to Gayfryd said. "She was very homely. After dinner, my host—there must have been eight or ten people—said, 'Would you mind giving her a ride home?' She lived nearby. She was looped, and on the ride home she started talking. 'He may have her, and she may have him. Well, it's wonderful that they are happy now. We'll see how long it lasts. But it's not over with me yet.' There was a pause that indicated revenge. And then she said, 'Everybody has their way of taking care of things.' It was the bitter wife against the beautiful woman."

About the time of that conversation, somebody—believed by many to have been Judy—dropped the dime on Johnson. The IRS launched an investigation into his business affairs. The ensuing scandal was bizarre, even by New Orleans standards. Gayfryd realized something was up before she learned that her husband was the target of a federal investigation. "She told Muriel Francis that he had taken her jewelry and had it copied," said a friend. "He convinced her to give it to him to put in a [safe-deposit] box for her—he got these pieces and copied them, three or four major pieces. She was wearing copies and didn't realize it. She asked Muriel, 'What do you think about that?' They were good copies, not paste."

Johnson had evaded taxes on millions of dollars in income through a complex scheme involving offshore businesses. Johnson and an officer in one of his companies, a pipeline company in Houston, had formed two Bermuda companies and sold them pipe at below-market prices. The profits went into foreign bank accounts, which helped Johnson finance his lavish way of life. Johnson had not disclosed the $7 million income from these transactions or his interest in the foreign bank accounts on his income tax forms. The penalties alone accounted for half Johnson's massive tax liability. Those associated with the case maintain that there has never been any evidence that Gayfryd knew about her husband's illegal activities.

As the pressure mounted, Johnson was losing his tenuous grip on reality. He wanted to vanish—and he did for a while. Johnson flew to London, where he had a face-lift—part of his program to simply disappear with a new identity. Gayfryd, said a friend, begged Johnson to serve his time and let her run the business while he was in prison. He also contemplated suicide. From his hiding place in London, he wrote Gayfryd that most of the things he told her were lies. He wrote, "I know this hurts you and the children more than staying put, but my mind is so jumbled with pills that thinking clearly is past for months." He said not to bring his body back if it was ever discovered. Gayfryd and Jack Martzell flew to London to try to talk to Norman. Martzell had worked out a deal with the feds that if Norman came back willingly, they would make no attempt to bring him back. The trip was not a success. "We never saw him. We spoke to him. He called us finally."

Johnson changed his mind and returned the New Orleans a month after Gayfryd's fruitless trip to London. Shortly afterward, he was rushed to Ochsner Hospital with a drug overdose. Nobody knew whether he was trying to kill himself or had simply taken too many antidepressants.

Johnson survived and, having pleaded guilty in October 1982 to conspiracy to defraud the U.S. Treasury, was sent to prison camp at Eglin Air Force Base in Florida. He was handcuffed and led from the courtroom. His wife was not in attendance. Gayfryd had missed a plane back to New Orleans, but her brother and his wife were there to represent her.

Gayfryd had to struggle to preserve assets from the IRS. "Gayfryd is refined-looking, but when you get down to the nitty-gritty, don't cross her," said a New Orleans matron. Using her connections at the New Orleans Museum of Art, she stored nine valuable paintings at the museum, certainly a nervy approach to the problem. The cache included a Degas and a Picasso. When the IRS threatened to sue the museum, museum officials panicked at the thought that they may have done something illegal. Gayfryd quickly obtained an order from a New York court that authorized her to remove the art. She also claimed that jewelry in the Hibernia Bank belonged to her, not her husband. Fearing that valuable objects were leaving the Johnson house, IRS agents slapped a lien on the property.

Though, unlike Becky Sharp, Gayfryd hadn't been responsible for the financial ruin of her husband, the scene at the St. Charles Avenue mansion was reminiscent of the famous one in the novel when bailiffs surround Becky's London house—only worse. Federal agents padlocked the iron gates and swarmed the premises, literally snatching photographs from their silver frames.

"They grabbed everything," said John A. Mmahat, a friend of the Johnsons. "The feds can be awful, awful, awful. They took the chandeliers off the ceilings. Gayfryd prevailed in getting some of her stuff back, but they grabbed everything." IRS stickers publicized the coming auction of the house. Neighbors joked to a reporter that the guards were "not in keeping with the décor."

New Orleans had changed Gayfryd. "There had been a complete transformation," said an observer. "She dressed in a somewhat more understated fashion and even wore a strand of about a million pearls." Gayfryd looked like the lady of the manor, but the manor was gone.

With her husband in jail and her house on the block, Gayfryd moved into a small apartment not far from the site of her former glories. A sympathetic friend owned the property and allowed Gayfryd to stay there rent-free with five-year-old Rayne and two of the three Johnson children. Another woman might have begged for her old job at Moran's.

FORT WORTH, TEXAS, 1970S

What being a hostess at Moran's Riverside Restaurant was for Gayfryd McNabb, serving as a flight attendant for Pan Am was for Susan Kaposta: a way to get noticed. Flight attendants were notorious for finding rich husbands back in the days when they were still called stewardesses and only pretty girls need apply. Susan Kaposta worked for Pan Am, known for hiring especially personable young women. A passenger from Fort Worth named John Roby Penn, who had inherited a fortune in Texas oil money, found Miss Kaposta very personable. He met her on one flight, and when he learned that her next one was to Japan, he bought a ticket to Japan. Not everybody would have considered Penn Mr. Eligible. He could charm the birds out of the trees, as they say in Texas, but his marital history was colorful. "I have been at parties where Roby was there with the most recent wife, and three ex-wives were also there," chuckled Cissy

Stewart Lale, retired Fort Worth society columnist. The *Social Register* of Fort Worth lists Penn's widow—and three ex-wives. All in all, Penn married nine times. Two were flight attendants, and the others were Texas society girls. "The joke was that Roby loved to buy diamonds, and each wife got a bigger one," said a Fort Worth native.

Though it's hard to keep track of the merry wives of John Roby Penn, Susan was (by most accounts) number five. "Anybody who'd marry Roby was obviously looking for a rich husband," opined a Fort Worth socialite, "not that he didn't have personality all over the place. Roby would marry these young things, pay them off, but then the other eligible men ran away from them because the whole thing with Roby made them look like gold diggers."

Susan Kaposta had not grown up with wealth. A magazine profile written at the apogee of her social career in New York described her as "secretive" about her past. She was one of six children, and the only daughter, of Lewis, a career air force officer of Hungarian descent, and America Kaposta. The Kapostas had been stationed in Chicago, Shreveport, Los Angeles; and abroad. "You have to learn to make friends wherever you go," said her brother Eric. Susan helped in the kitchen and with the boys. The family once lived in a fifteenth-century thatched cottage in England, said Eric. But Susan was not born while her family lived there. She spent part of her high school years in Shreveport, where she attended St. Vincent's, a Catholic high school. She then went on to LSU, pledging Kappa Kappa Gamma, one of the top sororities. It was difficult in those days to pledge a top sorority in the South without family ties. But Susan had made friends in Shreveport. "She never smoked or drank, which was probably a world record for LSU," said an admiring college comrade, adding, "She's the product of an air force family and a Catholic family, and that has made her durable." Susan has kept in touch with people from college. She left LSU without graduating, and when her father was transferred to Paris, she took courses at the Sorbonne. She went to work as a Pan Am stewardess while living in Paris. It turned out to be a good career choice.

Susan Kaposta and John Roby Penn were married in 1970, at the house of Fort Worth socialites Elton and Martha Hyder. "Everybody used to tease Roby and say that he was just boot camp for Susan. You either really, really liked her or you disliked her," said one observer. Susan set about to make her mark on Fort Worth. "Susan cultivated people," said the observer. "She found out who the important ones were and sent them the most elaborate flowers you've ever seen on their birthdays. She did everything to endear herself to important people. The little people she didn't endear herself to." Susan's father granted an indiscreet interview to a Louisiana newspaper, bragging that Susan was, as they say down there, "in high cotton."

Susan and Roby divided their time between Fort Lauderdale, where they owned a house, and Fort Worth, where they rented an apartment in an exclusive neighborhood. Susan clearly wanted to establish a place in society. "Susan hadn't been around that much before she married Roby, but she is a quick learner," said a woman who didn't care for her. "She was around Martha Hyder and a lot of social people, and she learned fast. She learned the fine art of having a party. She made it a point to zero in on the [Fort Worth billionaire] Basses."

The Penns enjoyed sailing their yacht in Florida, where Susan took flying lessons, and traveling abroad; and Susan honed her skills as a hostess. "There's no one who entertains as well as Susan," said a stalwart (who happens to be rich). "It's very unfair to imply she had to learn—she was a young bride. She was sweet and dear and lovely as a young bride."

Susan was clearly having a good time and she was considered something of a flirt in Fort Worth—with men even richer than Penn. She batted her eyes at Charles Tandy, of the Tandy electronics family, but Anne Tandy—known as Big Anne—either didn't notice or dismissed it as Susan's way. When the inevitable divorce from Roby was imminent, "Big Anne helped her find a good lawyer. She said she didn't want Roby to clobber Susan." Brad Corbett, then owner of the Texas Rangers baseball team, was another man with whom Susan made eyes. "She blew smoke up her skirt on that one," said a matron, "because everybody liked his wife."

What happened to the marriage? Silly question. Eight of Penn's nine marriages ended in divorce. He was married to the ninth Mrs. Penn when he died of cancer in 1996. Penn inevitably tired of his wives. Given his penchant for verbal abuse, they probably tired of him, too. "Roby could beat you to death with his tongue," said one of them. One wife became so angry with Roby that she flushed her big diamond ring down the toilet. Roby had to go next door to borrow the Roto-Rooter to retrieve it.

Susan and Roby were married for five years and had one daughter, who died at birth. Susan insisted upon a Catholic burial for the infant. Penn attended to this, since Susan was still in the hospital.

Penn was intensely jealous. He would later insist that he'd had Susan watched by a private detective and had stashed the report in a safe-deposit box. If this was the case, no evidence shows up in the court papers. But the divorce was bitter nevertheless. Susan's lawyer was forced to write Roby's lawyer to complain that Roby was reading Susan's mail and to make arrangements to have Penn's clothes and other personal affects sent to him by taxi.

But what awed everybody—including Penn, who spoke of it later—was Susan's presence of mind in court. "You had to go to court and fight Roby," said an ex, "because when he was through with you, he was through with you." Susan was up to the task. When Roby made the big mistake of giving Susan a dirty look in court, the quick-thinking Susan seized the opportunity. "She said, 'I can't go on, Your Honor. My husband is intimidating me,'" according to a source close to the proceedings. According to this version, Susan mouthed the word *bitch,* indicating that this is what Penn had whispered in court. According to court papers, Susan had been receiving $6,000 a month in temporary support; it is believed that her settlement from Penn was around $350,000, a nice chunk of change but hardly enough to last forever.

After the Penn marriage was dissolved on February 18, 1976, Fort Worth expected Susan to head for greener pastures. "Everyone was surprised she stayed around attending all the parties," retired society scribe Cissy Lale told a reporter. "But she was out to catch a rich husband." As far as Fort Worth was concerned, however, some felt that her marital prospects had been tarnished by the marriage to Roby.

NEW YORK, 1980S

Susan might have wanted to test the waters in Fort Worth, but Gayfryd had been through a scandal, though not one of her making, in New Orleans—and besides, New Orleans, with its often stumbling economy, even then, wasn't as good a hunting ground as Fort Worth. Even before Norman went to prison, Gayfryd had been spending more and more time in New York. "The minute he [Norman] went down, she was out of there," said an old-line New Orleans observer. "As soon as she realized that Norman Johnson's portfolio had taken a plunge, she got the hell out of the marriage," echoed a newspaperman. Jack Martzell said that Gayfryd stuck with her husband until it became clear that Johnson had told her a pack of lies. "They had a serious telephone conversation that resolved things between them," he said.

Gayfryd met Saul Steinberg at a party in New York when her troubles in New Orleans had reached a desperate point. Tina Brown placed their meeting in November 1982—only a month after Norman pleaded guilty—at a dinner party given by Richard Feigen, the New York art dealer. Saul was intrigued, according to Brown's story, when Gayfryd announced, "I run a steel-pipes business in New Orleans." Saul felt that here was a woman capable of understanding his heady world of mergers and acquisitions. He might not have been as impressed if he'd known more about New Era Tubular, which Gayfryd owned with Arlene Mmahat— then-wife of John Mmahat, another New Orleans tycoon who'd end up doing time in a federal prison. New Era had been set up with minority set-asides from the federal government, and most people felt that Norman had "set the girls up and told them what to do." A business associate disputed this. Although still in operation when Gayfryd met Saul, the company folded in the mid-1980s. A curious Dun & Bradstreet listing for 1986 said, "Local authorities stated that this business has discontinued operations." Amoco, a New Era creditor, ended up putting New Era in a bankruptcies folder with a bad debt written off. Saul decided to bide his time when he learned that his "stunning dinner partner" was married.

There is another account of a dinner party, this time at Steinberg's and also in November 1982, by butler Desmond Atholl. Atholl wrote that he observed Gayfryd in action—covert action. "This provocatively attired creature sauntered around the table until she found her designated seat. She then exchanged her place card for one on Saul's left and strolled out of the room. During dinner I watched the social engineer engage in an obvious flirtation with my employer. Had he been one of the lamb chops we were serving for dinner she would have devoured him in a single bite." Saul invited her to go look at Old Masters. "Never was art appreciation so lucrative," Atholl wrote. No wonder Gayfryd occasionally missed her New Orleans–bound flight. "She had ambition of epic proportions," Atholl wrote. "Saul was the perfect solution to all her problems. She played her trump card: She gave him an ultimatum, and within weeks Saul proposed." (The Steinbergs made litigious noises when Atholl published an account of working for them, but nothing came of the threats.)

After a tortuous trial—Gayfryd and Norman's divorce actually ended up in both state and federal court for a while—Gayfryd was free (or so she thought) to marry Saul. In granting her divorce, on December 22, 1983, New Orleans District Judge Henry Roberts noted that Mrs. Johnson was guilty of adultery. Gayfryd married Saul the next day. She converted to Judaism to please her new family.

But Norman, increasingly irrational, wasn't quite done. In March 1984 he filed a suit claiming that Gayfryd was still married to him. This claim relied on a curious twist: Louisiana law allows a felony conviction as grounds for divorce; tax fraud, Johnson's lawyer argued, was "only" a misdemeanor. Ergo, Gayfryd had not had grounds to divorce Norman. WIFE IS BIGAMIST, TAX EVADER JOHNSON CHARGES, blared the New Orleans *Times-Picayune* headline.

Johnson's suit went nowhere, and this time Gayfryd didn't have to remarry her husband. She quickly rebuilt her life as a society hostess. Released from prison, Johnson checked into the Lincoln Park Hotel in Houston in July 1985, demanding a room on the top floor, and jumped to his death. To their credit, Saul and Gayfryd were spotted at the back of the room during his memorial service. Gayfryd kept in touch with the Johnson children for a while, sometimes having them stay with her in New York. Norman Johnson's children have since left New Orleans, and even people who were once good friends do not know where they are now.

Susan Penn had already launched herself in New York. Susan had begun making frequent use of a New York apartment that belonged to a wealthy Fort Worth family. It was on the fashionable Upper East Side. In 1980 Susan asked Sandy Lowenstein, wife of Hugh Lowenstein, a prominent investment banker, to introduce her to John Gutfreund. Sandy told her husband, according to writer John Taylor, that Susan had met Gutfreund casually and had been "intrigued" by him. The owlish Gutfreund, known as "the king of Salomon," was recently divorced. Susan was soon invited to an intimate dinner for four—herself, the Lowensteins, and Gutfreund. The evening was a huge success: not long afterward, Susan moved into Gutfreund's Park Avenue apartment and happily began spending his money, indulging in her passion for interior decoration. Their first Christmas tree is still famous because under it were nothing but Tiffany boxes, empty blue boxes there for decoration. She married Gutfreund in 1981 and the next year the couple moved into a duplex apartment at River House, one of New York's best addresses, a starter house before the Gutfreunds moved to 834 Fifth Avenue. The quintessential fortune hunter believes she has the power to be whoever she wants to be, and Susan, New Yorkers noticed, had reinvented herself as a Francophile with an aristocratic past. A magazine article wryly noted that if you commented on an antique in her apartment, she always replied that she'd "had it for ages."

*W*hy are some women able to triumph over defeat? Why do some stare down disasters of truly cataclysmic proportions to emerge victorious—with a new husband, a second collection of fabulous diamonds, and a string of even bigger new houses—while others are defeated by smaller disasters? The woman who doesn't feel up to shirking shame and spurning failure should consider marrying more humbly. No, there's not as much glitter and you won't be photographed for glossy magazines. But you probably won't have the feds snatching the chandeliers from your ceiling or a gumshoe on your trail.

"One of the things is the ability to have the energy not to be fixated on the past," said Dr. Carol Goldberg, a psychologist. Such a woman must be a "calculating optimist." In other words, you aren't mired in regret, because the opinions of others don't control you.

Some would argue that the fortune hunter moves on smoothly because the attachment was never that great in the first place—she is more focused on her own ambitions. Thackeray's Becky Sharp certainly fits the bill on all these qualities. Rawdon Crawley, her husband, is merely a means to an end—she would have married his father if he'd asked first, and she flirts with his older brother, who inherits the title and the money and from whom Becky wheedles diamonds. When Rawdon and Becky can no longer fend off their creditors, she thinks only of herself.

One need not be entirely lacking in feeling for others to succeed as a fortune hunter, though Becky is a monster. A prodigious resilience, not Sharpian narcissism, is often enough to armor the fortune hunter against defeat, allowing her to recover quickly even as others fall by the wayside. The pop psychology book *Dancing Backwards in High Heels* is about women and resiliency. A series of agree/disagree sentences is supplied to help assess your degree of resiliency, with "agree" being the "right" answer.

A few sample statements taken from the book:

- I make room in my life for my own needs.
- I do not make excuses for who I am.
- I make my own luck.
- I can take care of myself.
- I can learn from difficult experiences.
- I am flexible and able to develop new solutions to existing problems.

Aren't these just the sorts of qualities that might take a woman, cruelly ejected from her New Orleans residence by the IRS, to Park Avenue? Sit around and moan about a divorce? Susan Gutfreund made her own luck. Gayfryd didn't cross her fingers and hope to be seated by Mr. Richer—she switched the place cards to ensure it. These are women who made their own luck, who were flexible enough to take advantage of new opportunities, and who believed in themselves. Like Becky Sharp, who could forget the "duns round the gate" and walk into court to be presented "with the toss of the head that would have befitted an empress," they kept going no matter what. Dear Reader, who among us is free from at least a tinge of admiration for these women?

NEW YORK, LATE 1980S TO THE PRESENT

As the 1980s drew to a close, Nouvelle Society went into retreat. Some of its most visible members were felled by scandal. Saul Steinberg's fall was as dramatic as his rise. Reliance Insurance and junk bonds had made him rich. A federal investigation, however, revealed Reliance to be badly managed and heavily in bad debt. In 2001 Reliance filed for bankruptcy. Steinberg's income was drastically cut. "He reaped what he sowed," a Harvard professor told *U.S. News & World Report.* Gayfryd must have had a sense of déjà vu as the Steinbergs put their Old Masters, museum-quality furniture, and pricey baubles up for auction. The couple was forced to leave their Park Avenue apartment.

John Gutfreund's problems stemmed from illegal bids made by others, not himself, at Salomon Brothers. He did not participate, but when informed of the illegal activity, he failed to notify the Securities and Exchange Commission. He was forced to resign and agree never again to serve as chairman or chief executive of a securities firm without SEC approval. "Mr. Gutfreund's departure from Salomon marked one of the quickest falls for a Wall Street executive," *The Wall Street Journal* noted. Gutfreund's collapse was less complete than Saul Steinberg's. The Gutfreunds did not have to move out of the Fifth Avenue apartment or put their belongings on the auction block. Still, erstwhile mentor Jayne Wrightsman and others wanted to see less of her. People who'd vied for invitations were no longer such dear friends. New York is a hard town. It fawns on those who succeed and kicks those who fall. A cynical article on surviving scandals in New York once examined the options of the wife whose husband was in trouble. "If I were her," a canny socialite confessed to reporter Kevin West, "I'd say to everyone, 'Oh, I could never be married to a dishonest man.' That way if he doesn't go to jail, she's got nothing to worry about. But, if he does, she's got her excuse to leave."

Though neither Susan Gutfreund nor Gayfryd Steinberg was impoverished, both had fallen from great heights—but, in a way, it was their finest hour. "When John Gutfreund got in this trouble, a lot of people anxious to know them when they were riding high suddenly didn't know them," said Michael Thomas. "But, my God, Susan took it on the chin. Sometimes when a fortune is compromised, the wife moves on. Susan stayed with him. She ran with her pedigree. She didn't complain and she didn't try to bluff. The Gutfreunds lowered their visibility without slinking off the map." Thomas was so impressed that he now regrets the Gesternblatt piece. "She stuck her nose in the air and acted like a lady," said an old LSU friend.

After keeping a low profile for a while, Susan reinvented herself: she became a professional interior decorator. Her husband, who now works at a small investment house, loves to brag that she makes more money than he does. Susan has restored a Federal-style house on Philadelphia's Main Line for herself, a weekend retreat when she's not in Paris. It somehow just seems right that the house once belonged to the Main Line aristocrat whose life inspired *The Philadelphia Story,* a movie about high society. Susan's decorating scheme was not subdued. "It's grandiose, and we don't do grandiose here," a Main Line matron sniffed. Susan Gutfreund does, though.

The Steinbergs moved to a five-story brownstone on East Seventy-third Street, one of the highest-priced neighborhoods in the world. The property is listed in her name. After Saul had a stroke in 1995, Gayfyrd did not cut and run. She has been a faithful nurse to an ailing man. "There has to be a point when love takes over," said a woman who knows both Susan and Gayfryd well. "Their husbands were ousted and had lost power. They could have walked but they didn't." Susan Gutfreund and Gayfryd Steinberg—like Becky Sharp—have been embraced by "a very strong party of excellent people" who consider them to be most injured women. They have their enemies. But who has not? Their lives are an answer to them.

4

THE GREAT COURTESANS:
Their Simple Recipes for Riches

A fortune hunter often takes a perfectly ordinary skill and uses it as her recipe for riches. She may be a great cook, have a gift for sparkling conversation, or be a perfect hostess. She may simply be kind and understanding, have a cheerful personality, or exhibit the kind of limitless tact that is helpful when dealing with rich people who take deference for granted. Whatever her talent, she uses it to one end: pleasing her rich husband. She is, in short, a courtesan.

Though the word conjures up sexual aptitude, being a courtesan encompasses far more. Madame de Pompadour, mistress to Louis XV, knew better than anybody that this is a job done both in and out of bed. "She knew a hundred stories to amuse him," her biographer Nancy Mitford wrote. "She read the police reports from Paris, the equivalent of our yellow press, and told him the tidbits she found in them."

Like all great courtesans, Madame de Pompadour understood that allowing a man to be bored is fatal. Her task was "to rescue the monarch from the black slough of *ennui* which was perpetually threatening to engulf him, and, in so doing, to make herself necessary to his very existence," wrote her biographer H. Noel Williams. Before Madame de Pompadour, Louis had only one diversion: hunting. Realizing that Louis needed a project, she hit upon the ideal project, the same one that the wives of American multimillionaires use: buying and decorating houses. Believe it or not, interior decorating—or, in its more elevated form, art collecting—can be just as fascinating for the male of the species as for the female. "The king ran up her stairs," reported Mitford, "knowing that, in her warm and scented rooms, he would find some fascinating new project afoot, plans for designs waiting for his approval, bibelots and stuff for him to buy if he liked them."

She knew how to pick the right guests for small supper parties of eighteen or so. Most elaborately, she organized the famous *petit théâtre* at Versailles to amuse Louis. Courtiers vied for roles, and the scripts were written by prominent intellectuals of the day, with scenery from the best artists. Because of her ability to please the king, Madame de Pompadour acquired some of the most splendid houses in France (including the Hôtel d'Evreux, now the Elysée Palace), along with art, jewelry, and furniture beyond compare. "Few human beings since the world began can have owned so many beautiful things," wrote Mitford.

What worked for Madame de Pompadour also worked for Mercedes Bass, who, in 1986, after fourteen years of marriage to a diplomat, hooked the biggest fish of all, billionaire Texas oilman Sid Richardson Bass, provoking the most gossiped-about society divorce of the eighties. It also worked for Marylou Whitney, who became the fourth Mrs. Cornelius Vanderbilt Whitney only one day after Whitney was—or wasn't, depending on what state you were in—free from his third wife.

THE EXECUTIVE ASSISTANT

The Watergate in Washington, D.C., was still just a fancy apartment building and not yet the name of a scandal. Its dragon's-teeth architecture was distinctive, and the hub of upscale shops and restaurants nearby made it an enclosed world of the well-to-do. It was here during the Nixon administration that Mercedes Tavacoli, an Iranian-born party girl in her twenties, lived with Ambassador Francis Kellogg, Princeton class of 1940, a special assistant to Secretaries of State William Rogers and Henry Kissinger. Mercedes was waiting for Kellogg to marry her. Friends knew she was worried that he would not. They had met in Geneva when he was on a diplomatic mission to advise a U.S. delegation to the United Nations. Mercedes, who had been sent to Europe for a convent education, worked as a personal assistant to a high-ranking U.N. official. The woman who would one day be known in New York society as "the Iranian firecracker" was already the life of any party, having been linked, according to *Vanity Fair,* to the financier Sir Jimmy Goldsmith and to Swiss baron Hans Heinrich Thyssen-Bornemisza. She came from a family with connections. "When I was ambassador in London, she was young and beautiful and studying in England," recalled Ardeshir Zahedi, the shah's last envoy to Washington. "She would come to the embassy with her mother and stepfather."

Her father—who had named his daughter after his favorite car—had died when she was a child, and her mother then married Abolhassan Diba, an uncle of Queen Farah Diba, the shah's third wife. The shah had yet to be toppled by the mullahs, and the Diba tie still counted in international circles. Mercedes's stepfather owned the Park Hotel in Tehran, and the Dibas also had a villa in Lausanne. Mercedes was close to her mother, whom she called Mummy, and loved to talk of her mother's friendship with couturier Hubert de Givenchy. "Her mother was considered one of the most beautiful women in Iran," said Kellogg.

While not as great a beauty, Mercedes, who was heavier than she would be in later life, made an impression on Kellogg. "We hit it off immediately and I remember [having] long conversations with her on the telephone," Kellogg said several years before he died in 2006. "She had an apartment across the lake and from my room I would call her." He was also impressed with her achievements. "She was a career person and executive assistant to the top person in the labor organization at the U.N.," Kellogg recalled. "I said, 'Well, I don't believe you can take shorthand.' And she said, 'Try me.' It came out perfectly. She had an important job that required French and English."

A gentlemanly diplomat who had had a string of girlfriends, Kellogg was married to Fernanda Munn Kellogg, scion of the Wanamaker department store family. It was not a perfect match. "My wife and I had been married for thirty-five years," Kellogg said, "and I always wanted to work. I had a work ethic. She lived in Palm Beach, and I'd go down. It was separate lives."

Tavacoli came to visit a friend who lived in New York's posh River House. She loved going to the "21" Club, and she spent time with Kellogg. "That seemed to solidify a feeling of friendship and warmth and ultimately love and affection," he said. "I invited her to come to Washington with me when I was special assistant to Rogers and Kissinger."

Newly arrived in Washington in the late 1960s, Tavacoli found herself living in bachelor digs, sharing the Georgetown house of Kellogg and Fitzhugh Green, a wealthy CIA agent with Newport connections. It was a big house with a garden and a view of the Potomac, but eventually they decided that three was a crowd. Mercedes found a small apartment in the Watergate. "She was a wonderful hostess even in a tiny apartment that she managed to make so attractive. You'd go there and it was perfection," said Nuala Pell, wife of the senator Claiborne Pell. "I just remember being frightfully impressed."

Pell added: "First time I met her she was brunette, and then she was blond. I think Fran wanted her to be blond. Whoever she is married to or with, she is totally immersed in what she can do to make them happy. She has the attributes of a great courtesan."

Madame de Pompadour would have been proud of Mercedes, who left sweet little notes on Kellogg's pillow at night and made sure that his friends enjoyed coming to their apartment. "Everything she did, she did well," said Pell. "The apartment was lovely. The flowers were lovely. She has an up personality. I've never seen her down, except when she was worried that Francis wouldn't marry her. That was the only time I've ever seen her not totally up, and that was only in flashes. She made any party go."

"She was pretty nearly perfection," Kellogg recalled. "She loved to keep the house in tip-top shape. She did all the cooking. She'd say, 'If you're unhappy with what I've cooked, there's a great restaurant next door.' She has total charm, a wonderful disposition, wonderful laughter, and she enjoyed life a great deal."

Not surprisingly, Kellogg succumbed. They were married in Geneva on October 12, 1972, first in a civil ceremony performed by the chief registrar and then in a Muslim ceremony at the Diba villa, though "Mercedes was never a practicing Muslim," said Kellogg. Zahedi served as Kellogg's best man. They settled in New York, where Mercedes became a popular adornment of the social circuit. She was "a hearty, vodka-drinking extrovert whose dark looks [were] compared by *Women's Wear Daily* to those of Minnie Mouse."

She brought a zany element of fun. At a birthday lunch she gave for

Venezuelan heir Reinaldo Herrera in 1983, she wore a SAVE CLAUS T-shirt, to the delight of Mercedes's dear friend European charmer Claus von Bülow, whom she loyally supported during his 1982 trial after he was charged with putting his wife, Sunny von Bülow, the oil and gas heiress, in a coma.

During the eighties Mercedes gave two lunches a week. "She has all the fashionable ladies," a regular guest once told writer Steven Aronson, "and the usual men you have around fashionable ladies—the fun fellas, the wits. At lunchtime, you know it's not going to be the head of a corporation."

She remained the perfect courtesan. For example, Kellogg—whom she referred to as "my stallion"—loved the opera. "Before going to the opera," said a friend, "Mercedes always got the cheaters' guides and listened to records so that she could whisper into his ear, 'Ahhh, this is the most wonderful part.' Mercedes has the geisha thing down pat. 'What are you interested in? Oh, that's what I'm interested in, too.'" She served as a board member of the New York City Opera.

Mercedes, a daring dresser who made the best-dressed list—she once showed up at a party in a tuxedo, bow tie, and wing collar—loved the social whirl, but Kellogg had become a stay-at-home husband. Ironically, this may have happened because Mercedes had done her job too well. "He got so he didn't want to do anything or go out," said Pell. "He just wanted her to take care of him. She used to complain about this. After they were divorced, of course, he went out all the time."

Another friend detected discontent in Mercedes. She was walking with Mercedes when they noticed a jewelry ensemble in a store window. The price was $28,000, and Mercedes wanted it badly. Why not just ask Fran for it? Mercedes glumly said that she was certain that her husband, well off but not one of the richer members of the famous cereal family, would not buy it for her. "I want to be rich," she said.

THE COOK

Marylou Hosford's recipe for riches was—quite literally—her recipes. She used her culinary talents, that most quintessential of womanly skills, to reel in Cornelius Vanderbilt Whitney.

She was born Marie Louise Schroeder in 1925 in Kansas City, one of the four daughters of Harry R. Schroeder, who had attended night school to get his law degree, and Marie Jean Schroeder, a housewife who sang in the choir and at weddings. Her father was prosperous, but "she was not a debutante of the city," said a Kansas City arbiter of her vintage. That sort of thing mattered then, and Marylou blamed this lapse on World War II's effect on social life. But she had something better: a happy childhood. "I had a warm home life," she once told a journalist. "My parents were always laughing and singing." Her mother made sure that the four Schroeder girls could cook.

Marylou graduated from Kansas City's Southwest High School in 1943 and went to the University of Iowa, where she hoped to study drama. Her father died, and after her freshman year she returned to Kansas City and became a disc jockey at station KCKN. "I created a show for servicemen called 'Private Smiles,'" she once said. "We played Tommy Dorsey and Frank Sinatra, and it was very popular and made me a kind of star. In those days, there was something called the Hooper Rating, and I had a higher Hooper Rating in that area than Bob Hope."

After a year the ambitious disc jockey, still toying with the idea of being an actress, was ready to take on New York. "She walked into '21' on the arm of Ted Howard, the theatrical agent, and three men at the bar were instantly interested," said Palm Beach socialite Richard Cowell, one of the three. "She was unquestionably glamorous." Frank Hosford, a pudgy, easygoing, hard-drinking John Deere heir from Moline, Illinois, was also at the bar. A recent Yale graduate, he was known as Fink A. Dink.

Under the tutelage of Howard, a former Ed Sullivan copyboy who helped people get their name in the society pages and the first in a long line of public relations counselors who would toil for Marylou, as she now called herself, she was presented in the media as the daughter of a Midwestern cattle magnate. "Even the most minor performer realized that publicity, not necessarily talent, was the way to fame, fame the way to success, and a press agent was the first step along the way," Walter Winchell biographer Neal Gabler wrote.

In a colorful, ink-garnering moment in 1947, Marylou rode up to the exclusive nightclub El Morocco on a horse, which she hitched outside while she went inside and partied. Howard later quietly claimed credit for the stunt. "She has five press agents on her payroll, and they're all busy," somebody said after she became Mrs. Whitney. "Tell them everything," she said of her theory of press manipulation, "but don't tell them anything."

She shared an Upper East Side apartment with a girlfriend. "She was a fun-loving girl at all the parties," said Brownie McLean of Palm Beach, another fun-loving girl of the day. She worked as an "idea girl" for a soap opera writer. She was popular with the boys, but the one who was most taken with the fun-time gal was Hosford. "She married Frank Hosford when her Prince Charming didn't come along," said somebody then on the scene. In 1948 they eloped for a civil ceremony in Brooklyn and then returned to El Morocco for a celebratory meal. "He had some money, and I think that mattered," said a friend.

On the surface, it looked like a good marriage. The Hosfords bought a sprawling three-story house with two towers and impressive grounds in Greenwich, Connecticut, and named it Deere Crest. Marylou had her critics, one of whom described the "Texas whorehouse pink" she used in decorating. Four children, two boys and two girls, were born in rapid succession, and Marylou launched herself as a hostess, later reminiscing about cooking chicken Marengo for two hundred. When Hosford invested in a car dealership, "she informed him," according to columnist Charles Ventura, "that his business was much too plebeian for her tastes."

After the car dealership, Hosford went into the insurance business. "I loved the guy, but he was a terrible investor," said a friend. "He invested in Jaguars when nobody wanted Jaguars and TVs when people didn't want TVs." He was drinking heavily. In 1953 Marylou moved, without enthusiasm, to Phoenix. Frank hoped to start afresh. "I always did what a man wanted to do," she recalled to a reporter in 1994. "He wanted to start a new life out west. All right with me. He didn't know. He was drinking. What do they know? He wanted to goof off and go to bars at night. He'd end up in jail. I'd pick him up off the street."

They renovated a house in a fashionable Scottsdale suburb. A smiling Marylou was shown with her hair swept back in a headband, hugging her two little boys in a *Look* magazine article on M'Lou, the oldest, who was the only girl at an exclusive boys' school. Marylou was forced to get a job as a part-time TV cooking show hostess on a local station and to obtain a real estate license to keep the family afloat. "You do what you have to do. You get two jobs to support your family," she would tell a reporter.

There are several versions of how Marylou met Cornelius Vanderbilt Whitney. Whitney placed the encounter at the Backstage Club, a popular Phoenix hangout. When Marylou walked in, "I said, 'Who's that woman?' She'd be perfect for the role of Anna Love Price in *The Missouri Traveler*." "Sonny," as Whitney was called, had invested in the movie. Marylou has claimed that they met through an arranged tennis date when (she has meaningfully noted) her divorce was already in progress. ("I thought I'd turn around and go home. Then I thought 'Oh, don't be silly.'") An article in the English *Tatler* magazine related a rumor that Zsa Zsa Gabor introduced them. "Mrs. Whitney was not in any sense 'recommended' to Mr. Whitney by Zsa Zsa Gabor," the magazine subsequently apologized, adding that Mrs. Whitney had never been "a showgirl" or enjoyed a "secret life."

Whitney was fifty-seven; Marylou was thirty-two. He was married to Eleanor Searle Whitney, a former receptionist at Pan Am, the airline he cofounded. A man with a receding chin, blue eyes, and a patrician demeanor, Whitney had been born rich and made himself richer, developing mining interests and investing in movies (he was a backer of *Gone With the Wind*). His nickname may have been Sonny, but he was a man of such bleak moods that he once became convinced that his wife and the butler were in cahoots to poison him. According to his authorized biography—which was financed by Marylou—he was so miserable in his marriage when he met Marylou that he spoke of suicide on their first date. She said she'd never see him again if he continued to entertain such thoughts. But he was fascinated by Marylou's job—cooking on TV. "Oh, I've never seen a woman cook before," he said.

Marylou was soon in a house in Los Angeles's fashionable Bel-Air section. When columnist Sheilah Graham, interviewing her about her acting career and matrimonial prospects, asked her if Sonny had bought it for her, she was miffed (but not terribly). "If he'd bought it, I wouldn't have such a big mortgage," she said. But what if Whitney wanted to pay the mortgage after the wedding? "I'd be delighted," said Marylou. (She was more miffed later, in the 1970s, when Graham published in *How to Marry Super Rich* that Marylou was the daughter of a butcher and had been a soda jerk. Whitney lawyers made sure that this allegation did not appear in subsequent editions.)

Marylou's was an uncontested divorce in which she charged cruelty, granted in June 1957, eight months before she wed Whitney. Sonny's divorce was a horror story. Described as a home wrecker in the press, Marylou shot back, "There wasn't any home, not when I knew him."

For Whitney, making headlines with a messy private life was nothing new. While a Yale undergraduate, he had to flee the country when a *Ziegfeld Follies* dancer sued him, claiming he reneged on a promise to marry her. Living in Paris as the suit, which he eventually won, dragged on, Whitney married Marie Norton, an old family friend (and the future Mrs. Averell Harriman). Marie got a Reno divorce from Whitney on the grounds of mental cruelty and incompatibility in 1929. Next was Gee Hopkins, a Main Line horsewoman. This marriage of ten years ended after Sonny spotted Eleanor Searle. Sonny and Eleanor had a thirteen-year-old son, Searle Whitney.

Eleanor, living at Sonny's Old Westbury estate in Long Island, was determined to fight for her marriage. Telling friends he was going to Paris, Sonny went to Nevada, home of the quickie divorce, and established legal residence at the El Ranch-O-Tel Motel in Carson City. Eleanor filed for separation in New York, a move intended to block a Nevada divorce. Sonny outwitted her by filing secretly for divorce in out-of-the-way Lovelock, Nevada, where media scrutiny was unlikely. There he appeared in court, trembling with anger, and read from notes in his own handwriting. "She used ugly language, went into frequent outbursts of rage, abuse, insults, arguments, and discourtesies that deprived our marriage of beauty and meaning," he said of Eleanor, adding that she "made a great show of religion" but "never practiced it in the home." (She eventually joined the Billy Graham crusade.) Sonny's divorce was granted on the spot, and he was driven to Carson City for his second big event of the day: his wedding with Marylou (whom he always called Mary).

Sneaking off the plane to avoid detection, Marylou had flown in from California. The wedding took place in the Indian Treaty Room of the El Ranch-O-Tel on January 24, 1958. Marylou wore a suit and a corsage. Sonny, still handsome at fifty-eight was extremely nervous, fearing emissaries from Eleanor until the final "I do." Then he said, "I'm happy now," and the newlyweds took off for a trip to Flin Flon, Sonny's Canadian mining camp near the Arctic Circle, as Marylou eagerly waited to see how the press would react to her marriage.

Upon receiving word of the wedding, Eleanor, back in New York, said, "He's still my husband," and a headline blared, SONNY WHITNEY BEATS NO. 3 TO DRAW IN RENO. It was an interesting legal situation—Sonny was married to Eleanor in New York, while elsewhere he was married to

Marylou. Eleanor managed to have Whitney's New York assets frozen. Sonny was legally forbidden to set foot in New York, facing arrest if he did. He took actions to ensure that Eleanor's funds would be tight, too. "Even a self-respecting wolf might not care to hang around her door," the popular *Cholly Knickerbocker* column declared, "since her phone, gas and heat have been shut off. Eleanor's butler, touched by her straitened circumstances, offered her a loan to tide her over."

After months of headlines about his novel marital status, Sonny was granted special permission to go to New York to negotiate. As Marylou waited in Bel-Air, Sonny and Eleanor reached an agreement. The *New York Post* reported on February 21, 1958, that Sonny had agreed to pay Eleanor $5 million in tax-free dollars, then the second-largest divorce settlement on record. (Bobo Rockefeller's was the first; hers was around the same, but not tax-free, the newspaper noted.) Sonny and Marylou had a second wedding in Bel-Air. At last, Marylou was free to go to New York as Mrs. Cornelius Vanderbilt Whitney. She threw a small luncheon at Ciro's, a restaurant in Saratoga, New York, where the Whitneys owned a house (the Whitneys liked to own houses near racetracks). Columnist Doris Lilly noted that "Sonny's chief adventure these days is sampling the various recipes Marylou runs up on the stove." Lilly speculated that the new Mrs. Whitney might be too busy in the kitchen to make use of her late mother-in-law's fabulous jewels. Marylou published some of her recipes in *Missouri Traveler Cookbook,* which came out in 1958 and did not eschew the humble canned soup or processed cheese as ingredients and ended with the words "The sky is blue, my heart is full, and the future looks bright and Sonny."

The former Marie Louise Schroeder had married into the upper reaches of the American plutocracy. She could now claim a duchess of Marlborough, the lovely Consuelo Vanderbilt, as a relative. Novelist Edith Wharton, who personally liked many of the Vanderbilts but deplored the wretched excess of their age, modeled the Van Osburgh family, whose "crushes," or masked balls, were famous in her fictional New York society, on the Vanderbilts. "Marrying C. V. Whitney was like standing before the world in your underwear," said literary agent Marianne Strong. "Everybody was waiting for this new trophy wife to make a mistake." "She was very common but smart," said someone who knew Marylou at this juncture (echoing the Marquis d'Argenson's comment that Madame de Pompadour was "excessively common, a bourgeois out of her proper place"). "She has very common bone structure," Harry Whitney sniffed on meeting his future stepmother. "The Whitney children found her excessively vulgar," said a friend of the family.

Marylou, who was, according to a Whitney relative, "infatuated with the names Vanderbilt and Whitney," was optimistic—and determined. "I am the fourth Mrs. Cornelius Vanderbilt Whitney, and I'll be the *last* Mrs. Cornelius Vanderbilt Whitney," Marylou vowed. There was ample reason to regard this as an impossible undertaking. Sonny was one of the unhappiest rich men in America.

THE EXECUTIVE ASSISTANT

As all followers of society lore know, one of the greatest love affairs of the mid-1980s began with the toss of a dinner roll at the Black and White Ball, a charity event at Blenheim Palace, the ancestral home of the dukes of Marlborough. Food fights, indeed, would be the principal motif of the courtship phase of this unlikely romance. The hurler of the dinner roll was none other than Mercedes Kellogg, who was simply trying, in her own uninhibited way, to liven up the evening. Sid Richardson Bass, the handsome Yale-educated Fort Worth oil billionaire and one of the richest men in America, was seated next to Mercedes, while not too far away at another table, placed beside Prince Michel de Bourbon-Parma, was his wife, Anne Bass. Known in some circles as the Ice Princess, Anne Bass was a serious-minded patron of the arts and the ballet, though many in Fort Worth felt, as *Texas Monthly* would put it, that Anne was "better at running things than taking orders." The magazine noted that many ascribed to her domineering personality the high administrative turnover at the Modern Art Museum of Fort Worth, where people spoke of the "Bass body count." Anne had married Sid, whom she'd known since childhood, after she graduated from Vassar and worked in New York, and they had become Fort Worth's ideal couple. Anne parted her blond hair in the middle and pulled it back in barrettes, which some considered too schoolgirlish. Her dignified demeanor could not have been in starker contrast to what one observer called Mercedes's "vampy vitality." The regal Anne would not dream of tossing a dinner roll. Sid Bass, however, seemed to like the vivacious Mercedes. It was also noted that, once she had caught his eye, Mercedes seemed in no hurry to go home. Before leaving, Sid wrote her number on a napkin. Gossip columns would report, without details, that they lunched together the next day.

Two weeks after the Blenheim ball, the Basses and the Kelloggs ended up at socialite Elizabeth Fondaras's Bastille Day party in East Hampton. The Kelloggs were her weekend guests. The Basses were brought to the party by decorator Mark Hampton, with whom they were spending the weekend. There were about 125 guests, including Lee Radziwill, Lauren Bacall, and Kurt Vonnegut. Somehow Mercedes found a seat next to Sid. And somehow a food fight broke out among the giddy socialites, with Mercedes and Fernanda Niven playing notably active parts. It was such fun. "Maybe Mercedes already suspected how much bread she'd soon be tossing around," a witness later told journalist Steven Aronson.

The next food fight occurred a few nights later at dinner in Southampton, another one of the fashionable little towns known as "the Hamptons." The dinner was given for the Basses, who were houseguests of Jamie and Fernanda Niven. Sid and Mercedes were not at the same table, but when the hostess suggested that her guests change places for the dessert course, Mercedes was seen to spring with alacrity from her seat to one at Sid's side. "Then Jamie Niven and Mercedes started in [with] the rolls," a guest told Aronson. "I particularly noticed because I couldn't believe she was throwing bread around again." "Sid and Mercedes connected that night," said a New York friend of Anne Bass's, "and soon I began to get calls and letters from Anne asking if I'd seen anything. That was the night that so disturbed Anne. They may have connected before, but it didn't register with his wife."

There were no further public developments on the Sid-Mercedes front until September. Saying that her mother, Madame Diba, was sick and that she had to go to France to see her, Mercedes left New York. She actually joined Sid in a suite at the Hôtel Plaza Athénée in Paris. As fate would have it, French socialite Sao Schlumberger spotted them, and the cat was out of the bag. Anne Bass reportedly called Sid to ask him what was going on at the Plaza Athénée, and Mercedes phoned Francis Kellogg, famously telling her sixty-nine-year-old husband, "Good-bye, darling, I'm marrying Sid."

Social columnist Suzy broke the story of Sid and Mercedes's affair, and suddenly nobody in New York or Fort Worth could talk about anything else. "Sid Bass and Mercedes Kellogg stun society," *New York* magazine proclaimed. The article was headlined THE BOLTERS. The financial ramifications of Sid's decision to bolt his twenty-three-year marriage were mind-boggling. According to a March 2002 *Vanity Fair* article detailing the Bass family finances. Sid and his brothers presided over a fortune that had been worth $14 billion at its highest point. The brothers had inherited $2.8 million each from their great-uncle, Sid Richardson, a Texas wildcatter, and through shrewd management and investments, they had turned this inheritance into one of the great American fortunes. Sid Bass was a major force at Disney, where he owned about a quarter of the company's stock, according to *Vanity Fair*, before a sell-off several years later. The Basses at the time of the divorce owned 51 percent of Famous Amos Cookies; a sizable chunk of the old Alexander's, the department store; and 10 percent of Texaco. In the end, the divorce was rumored to have cost him in excess of $200 million, plus the Bass apartment in New York and a clutch of important paintings by Rothko, Degas, and Monet. "Sid Bass paid $200 million for a used Mercedes," columnist and bon vivant Taki quipped. Sid and Mercedes were married seven weeks after the divorce became final in an elaborate affair at the Plaza Hotel. It was an exuberant occasion. When Sid kissed Mercedes, the Texans erupted with the cry "Yee-haw!"

For the most part, New York society seemed enchanted by Mercedes's good fortune. Her old friend Claus von Bulow set the tone when he impishly remarked that "Mercedes Bass sounds so much better than Mercedes Benz." But what about Fort Worth? Would Sid's hometown welcome his new wife? And would Mercedes, the most European of women, like Fort Worth?

The Basses were synonymous with Fort Worth, a town that mixed big oil fortunes with a cowboy heritage, sophistication with down-home charm. It's been described as the sort of close-knit community where people reach for the local social register instead of the phone book when they want to make a call. Fort Worth was part of the package.

Sid, low-key with WASPy good looks, had always been the dutiful son. He had wanted to be an artist, but his father, Perry Bass, had put him in charge of the family's financial empire shortly after he returned to Fort Worth in 1968 having earned an MBA at Stanford. "If I'd been like a lot of fathers," he once told a financial reporter, "Sid would have gone off and been an artist. I had to give him a big assignment." It was widely known in Fort Worth that Nancy Bass, Sid's revered mother, regarded Anne as the role model for her other daughters-in-law.

THE COOK

As Mrs. Whitney, Marylou had an extensive supply of places to live—five houses in the United States and two in Spain. Sonny had been planning to sell Cady Hill House, a former stagecoach inn purchased by a Whitney because of its propinquity to the famous racetrack at Saratoga, New York, but Marylou fell in love with the twenty-one-room, self-contained world of Victorian gardens and tennis courts. "I said, 'Sonny, this house smiles at me. It beckons me to come. I know I am going to be happy here because it has good vibes,'" she recalled. Marylou's "social office"—where she planned elaborate parties—was set up in a converted carriage house, with her party clothes stored in trunks with identifying tags.

She also fell in love with Sonny's 540-acre stud farm outside Lexington, Kentucky, adding a classical facade to the rambling antebellum house. She turned a slave house into a guesthouse where Princess Margaret and Anthony Armstrong-Jones stayed when they attended the Kentucky Derby in 1974. Her Kentucky Derby party became famous. She once remarked in an interview that she'd been a sickly child who lay in bed and daydreamed about throwing parties. Her grown-up parties were a little girl's dream come true. She would send her plane to New York to fetch such luminaries as designer Arnold Scaasi, Robert Higdon of the Prince of Wales Foundation, and gossip columnist Richard Johnson. One year a prominent Kentuckian dropped dead at the dance. But perfectionist Marylou ordered the ambulance to turn off its sirens, and most guests never even knew what happened.

In Saratoga she threw costume parties inspired by the Vanderbilt fetes of the Gilded Age. They were minutely choreographed productions. When she threw a *Gone With the Wind* party, the dimity for her Scarlett O'Hara costume came from the same factory in France that supplied the material for Vivian Leigh's frock in the movie. She was spoken of as the queen of Saratoga, and there's even a song with the refrain "Marylou, Marylou, come and see our Marylou," which is likely to be played whenever she strolls into a restaurant. A local radio station sponsored a Marylou look-alike contest, which drew dozens of contestants, not a few of whom were gay men. Mrs. Whitney dropped in and thoroughly enjoyed herself.

Of course, Marylou's parties had a benefit beyond her own insatiable love of the spotlight: Her parties kept Sonny amused. They were part of a two-pronged strategy for being the last Mrs. Whitney: She never let him get bored, and she never let him out of her sight for too long. Sonny loved to paint, so Marylou took up painting, and soon the Whitneys were having a joint show. As Madame de Pompadour had to amuse a monarch born bored, Marylou had to amuse a bad-tempered multimillionaire. "Sonny loved projects," said Marianne Strong, explaining that a project might be planning a trip or buying a piece of property (which sounds not unlike Madame de Pompadour's schemes).

Marylou put an oversize calendar in her office at Cady Hill and planned the year with Sonny's happiness in mind. "She fussed over Sonny like a mother cat over her kittens," Strong has been quoted saying. Sonny's day began with a love letter on his breakfast tray. "She had a tough life, in a way, with Whitney," said Marylou's old beau Richard Cowell (who eloped with Whitney's daughter Gail the same day Marylou and Sonny wed), "but she helped him a lot. He became much more outgoing." Said Gertrude Connor, "Uncle Sonny was difficult, demanding and spoiled, and none of his other wives made him happy. But Marylou did." Even so, Sonny sometimes erupted in uncontrollable rage with the words "I own you!" He once shocked guests at a dinner party by announcing that Marylou had been "grounded" for doing something to displease him. "I never saw them have but one argument in thirty-four years of marriage," said Bud Calesch, her longtime press agent. "I cater to him," she admitted to journalist Jane Lane. "If I didn't look after him, some other woman would, and I'm not going to let that happen."

A special attitude toward the male of the species sustained her in this challenging job. "All men—fundamentally—are little boys," she added to Lane. "Women are stronger than men, but even though they may have big jobs and run corporations, they can't forget to take care of their men, or they'll lose their marriages. At times, you've got to act weak, but it pays off."

Despite his wealth, Sonny had missed one of the great advantages of life: the sort of happy childhood that Marylou remembered. Sonny's parents spent little time with their son, who knew of their comings and goings from reading the society pages. Both his parents had indulged in extramarital affairs, his mother with both men and women. Marylou once said that Sonny had been raised by servants who were mean to him. "In terms of affection," she once told a reporter, "Sonny was not spoiled. I decided to spoil him."

Marylou had never realized her girlish ambition to go on the stage, but in a way she became a great actress. "I thought of every day with Sonny as a performance," she once said. "All right, the curtain is going up. I want to be as perfect as I can be. When I went to bed, I'd think, 'The curtain is going down. What kind of performance did I give?'" Sonny and Marylou liked to pretend they were strangers. Sonny, it seems, got a bang out of being picked up in public places by his wife. "It was a way of keeping him busy," a friend told *People* magazine.

As years came and went, it became clear that Marylou had figured out how to do the impossible: be the last Mrs. C. V. Whitney. In 1981 Sonny published a little book entitled *Live a Year with a Millionaire!* It was a hymn of praise to Marylou for the happiness she had brought him. Sonny loved to brag that the best investment of his life had been the two dollars he spent for the license to marry Marylou. (He gallantly refrained from mentioning the expensive divorce required to make the marriage legal.) The book is replete with blissful descriptions of fried chicken, green peas, and freshly baked cakes. "She wooed him through her cookbook," said an amused member of the Whitney family. "She played the role of the simple girl from the Midwest who loved to cook, and C. V. wanted to be fussed over."

Both the queen of Saratoga and Madame de Pompadour knew that, as we moderns might put it, it's always best to be yourself (or at least to pretend to be yourself). "Madame de Pompadour never became a courtier in her manners," wrote Mitford, perhaps her most sympathetic biographer. "There was no nonsense about her. She gave herself no airs; on the contrary she hardly bothered to change her bourgeois ways at all."

Marylou began to affect the upper-class, lockjaw accent of Sonny's milieu, and she can be very Mrs. Whitney. But like Madame de Pompadour, she knew it wasn't a good idea to change too much. "She knows that corn sells better than caviar," said Marianne Strong. Marylou never became too stuffy to dress up as Little Bo Peep for a party or too jaded to arrive for the Whitney Gala in Saratoga in a hot-air balloon or write a cookbook with popcorn recipes.

During the last ten years of Sonny's life, when Alzheimer's combined with his already severe mood swings (Marylou would reveal after his death that he had bipolar disorder), Marylou supervised his care with devotion and attention to detail. She arranged matters with such grace that once, when a visitor noticed an attendant nodding off in chapel, Marylou changed the guard so efficiently that nobody else noticed. At the end, Sonny was afraid to go to sleep at night unless Marylou was there (though one profile would report that sometimes there was a "substitute arm" so Marylou could take care of various obligations). "Up until the end," said Gertrude Connor, "we used to love to watch Uncle Sonny gaze at Marylou with complete adoration."

Whitney died on December 13, 1992, at the age of ninety-three, leaving almost his entire estate to the fourth and last Mrs. Whitney. It was valued at around $100 million and included land Marylou would later sell to the state of New York for $17.1 million.

She had done it, been true to her word to be the last Mrs. Whitney. But the next act of Marylou's long life would prove the most startling of all.

THE EXECUTIVE ASSISTANT

As Mercedes settled into her role as Mrs. Sid Richardson Bass, people began to notice something curious—she was no longer so much fun. The change was so pronounced that *W* magazine did an infamous article on "the two Mrs. Basses," suggesting that Anne and Mercedes "seem to have traded personalities." The article noted Mercedes's metamorphosis from "uninhibited and fun-loving to tense and chilly," while former Ice Princess Anne Bass was "now the outgoing one, the one you want to sit next to." *W* called the personality transfer "kind of spooky."

One friend of both Mrs. Basses has attributed the change to Mercedes's stunning realization of just how rich the Basses were. "She realized where she was, what she'd done, the sense of power," he said. Mercedes was also "growing thinner by the minute," and more than one observer noted her increasing resemblance to the pencil-thin Duchess of Windsor. "Don't think she didn't read about the Duchess of Windsor and make this her Bible as to how to marry a wealthy person," a friend opined. "It's almost as if Mercedes is channeling the Duchess of Windsor. She does the duchess by having a little silver pen and notebook beside her plate to make notes during dinner [Wallis Windsor did this in case a servant made a mistake that needed to be corrected]. The Duchess of Windsor is her goddess."

While Mercedes's new personality merited an article in a magazine, it wasn't the only thing that had changed. Everybody noted that Sid was blissfully happy. He was pleased with his new wife and his one unfilial act of rebellion in ending his "perfect" marriage to Anne Bass. "Good Sid, who always did what he was supposed to do, *finally* did what he wanted," a friend told *Vanity Fair* writer Suzanna Andrews. Unlike Anne, Mercedes is touchy-feely with Sid, whom she praises constantly. "Anne was cool to the point of cold," said a mutual friend. "I've seen her lash out at him. That probably got tiring. Mercedes is the ultimate courtesan. 'Oh, darling let me bring you that pen.' 'Oh, darling, does your drink need freshening?' The complete geisha."

There is one aspect of the geisha's job in which the great Madame de Pompadour was apparently bested by Mercedes (and Marylou). Oddly enough, one of the greatest courtesans in history didn't care for one facet of the calling—the sex part. Though she adored the king, Madame de Pompadour was what used to be called frigid. For a while she tried all sorts of quack cures, such as living on truffles and celery, to correct this inadequacy, until Madame de Brancas threw her assortment of drugs into the fire. "You must make yourself indispensable to the king by always being nice to him. Don't rebuff him at those moments, but just let time do its work and in the end he'll be tied to you forever by force of habit." The king and de Pompadour's love eventually evolved into a deep friendship, with her living in a grand apartment in Versailles and the king seeking sexual pleasure with young women installed in the notorious Parc-aux-Cerfs, a private brothel for the king. "It is his heart I wish," she said over and over again.

Though it's never possible to know about a couple's intimate moments, this doesn't seem to be an area in which Mercedes is remiss. While frantic executives tried to get calls through to them, Sid and Mercedes holed up in the Carlyle Hotel in New York during important Disney negotiations, giving the impression that they had even better things to do than managing their portfolio.

Mercedes has taken up shooting and fishing because that's what Sid likes, and she's become a popular member of Forth Worth society, having cultivated mother-in-law Nancy Bass, who bragged at a function sponsored by the Assembly, which brings out Fort Worth debutantes, that she was sporting a handbag given her by Mercedes. It is said in Fort Worth that she "lets Sid call the shots." The Bass family has always been notoriously shy about publicity, and Mercedes's close friends tend to honor her request never to speak about her to the press. She graciously turned down a request for an interview for this book, saying that she was "most flattered" by the request but that she and Bass have a policy of not granting interviews. "I will be the first to buy your book, and I think it is a brilliant concept," she wrote.

They divide their time between Aspen, Fort Worth, and New York. Even by Texan standards, the Forth Worth house is lavish. The Basses bought four lots in the best part of town, leaving only one house standing that Mercedes transformed into a Georgian manor of cut sandstone. "Mercedes would say, 'I don't like that wall. Remove it.' There were horror stories from the builders," said a source. "If that house cost less than fifty-five million dollars, I'll eat my hat."

A DESSERT MORSEL

Shedding her pretense of weakness, Marylou emerged as a tough businesswoman, ready to take control of Whitney Industries, the entity that manages the assets and sprawling property in the Adirondacks. After a few years on her own, however, Marylou decided she'd prefer to have a man do it. She wanted more than a business partner, though. She wanted romance. "Marylou loves men, and men love her," a friend said. Marylou had always obeyed the Golden Rule: He who has the gold gets to make the rules. Now she had the gold.

She was as flirtatious as a teenager. According to a delicious item in *W* magazine's October 1995 "Uncensored" column, Mrs. Whitney had spotted a handsome ex-Marine in his thirties walking into a Saratoga party. She sprinted across the room to plant herself beside him, declaring, "He's mine." She was dangling several men at the time, according to the *New York Post*'s "Page Six" column.

Marylou's choice for her third husband was almost as smart as her second. Once again, true love was not blind. On a trip to Alaska she met him: John Hendrickson, thirty-nine years her junior. He was an aide to her old friend, then governor Wally Hickel, whom she'd known since the Nixon administration. Hendrickson ended up driving that evening. "I'm looking through the rearview window, and I'm thinking, 'Wow! This is a beautiful woman,'" he recalled.

"That was the day my life began again," said Marylou. They went halibut fishing, and pretty soon Marylou was cooking steak and her famous apple brown Betty in his two-bedroom condo.

Nobody who's seen them together believes this is the relationship of an older woman and a walker. But true love had not been blind. Marylou asked Hendrickson to take over Whitney Industries as president, and he turned out to be her not-so-secret business weapon. He was crucial in the lucrative sale of part of the Adirondacks land to the state and developing plans for swank estates—he even renegotiated royalties on *Gone With the Wind*. "We worked together," Marylou said. "And, yes, John did some of the dirty work. But isn't that what a man does?"

They were married on a mountaintop in Alaska in October 1997. During an interview at Cady Hill House, Marylou and her husband—"Mrs. Whitney and John" to the four secretaries—behaved like lovestruck teenagers. They could not stop touching each other.

"Where do you want my hands?" asked the cherubic Hendrickson, a pleasant young man in a charcoal blazer, newly laden with love handles born of his wife's cooking, as they posed for a photographer.

"You can put them anywhere you want to," Marylou responded in a whispery society-girl accent.

"You're perking up, aren't you, baby?" he said, giving her rump a playful slap. A few minutes earlier Marylou, running a temperature of 103 degrees, had been wilting. But if anybody knows that the show must go on, it's Marylou. Plucking her pink spiked heels from the hands of a hovering secretary, she became suddenly animated, flashing a dazzling smile. "Santa," she said, perching on her husband's knee, "bring me something good."

Santa? Marylou Whitney had made her own fate. She may have been the only Mrs. C. V. Whitney to prepare tuna noodle casserole with a can of cream of celery soup or serve "hors d'oevres Honolulu" made with a jar of hickory-smoked cheese. Simple? Corny? Ingredients that Martha Stewart would spurn? You bet. But in the right hands, worth millions.

5

BRINGING DOWN THE HOUSE

*A*fter the wedding, the fortune hunter's real work, the day-to-day grind, begins. What beckoned as an eternal holiday of sunshine, shopping sprees, private jets and yachts, parties, and designer clothing can quickly turn into the nightmare of incompatibility. The predicament is all the more painful if Mr. Rich happens to be Mr. Rich *and* Famous: Then his wife's every move is subject to scrutiny by the tabloid hacks, always alert for a whiff of discord. As wonderful as it is to be rich, it's important to be rich with the right person.

It's homework—not housework—that defines the smart fortune hunter. Before taking the plunge, she does her research. Is this the right Mr. Rich? An important part of the fortune hunter's preparation is taking stock of herself: Can I really do this job? *How to Marry Super Rich* author Graham asked herself if she wanted to marry super rich. "I'd rather scrub floors," she insisted in the book.

Neither of the women in this chapter was going to end up scrubbing floors. But both would have done well to familiarize themselves with the job requirements. Neither possessed that most old-fashioned of virtues: a sense of duty. A sense of duty sustains the fortune hunter long after the excitement has faded, enabling her to find fulfillment in a grueling job.

Lady Diana Spencer and Carolyn Bessette did not ask what would be expected of them until it was too late. Both, in a way, made royal marriages. "A royal marriage is the princely edition of a universal fact, and as such, it rivets mankind," Walter Bagehot wrote in the nineteenth century. But these deluxe editions afford insights for less regal marriages.

DIANA

On the night before the wedding, which took place on July 29, 1981, of Charles Philip Arthur George, Prince of Wales, heir to England's throne, and Lady Diana Spencer, the English rose, bonfires were lit all over England. The impending wedding was, as gossip columnist Nigel Dempster and Peter Evans noted, "the greatest ceremonial event ever mounted in the history of the British monarchy." It has been estimated that 750 million people watched on television. In all the world, it appeared that only two people were doubtful that this marriage would be "the stuff of which fairy tales are made" (in the words of the archbishop of Canterbury, who performed the rite): Lady Diana and Prince Charles.

"The night before the wedding, I was calm, deathly calm. I felt I was the lamb led to the slaughter. I knew it and couldn't do anything about it," Diana would recall.

The groom was in "in a contemplative mood," according to Jonathan Dimbleby, his biographer. Vetted by Charles, Dimbleby's book may be regarded as the most authoritative expression of Charles's views. According to Dimbleby, the prince was "not at all elated, but aware that a momentous day was upon him." He was "concerned about his duty and filled with concern for his bride at the test she was to face."

Prince Charles was thirty-three, and Diana was barely twenty, until recently a nursery-school aide and the sort of upper-class, young girl-about-London known as a Sloane Ranger. Charles had been under intense pressure to marry and secure the succession. He found Lady Diana "exquisitely pretty, a perfect poppet," but he also viewed her as "a child." Was this young woman ready for the obligations of a marriage that would rivet mankind?

Princess Diana was a woman who, had things gone well, would not be in this book. Though she wanted to marry Charles, she was too much of a romantic to be a genuine fortune hunter. She was taken with the glamour of a royal marriage and giddy at the prospect of being the Princess of Wales. It was the breakdown of the marriage that would transform her into a brilliant schemer. Had Diana lived and gone on to marry Dodi Al Fayed, son of one of the world's richest men, she would have gone down in history as a great fortune hunter. All that, of course, could hardly have been anticipated when Shy Di rode through the streets of London in a gold-encrusted horse-drawn royal coach to her wedding at St. Paul's Cathedral.

Lady Diana Frances Spencer was the first English girl to marry the king or the heir to the throne since the reign of Henry VIII—the Queen Mother, Elizabeth II's mother, was Scottish—and (like the Queen Mother) one of the few not born royal to take on the job. In 1464 King Edward IV had stunned England by marrying an English woman and a commoner, Elizabeth Woodville, the daughter of Sir Richard Woodville (and, adding to the novelty, a widow). Edward announced that he was going hunting but instead secretly wed Elizabeth with only her mother and a gentlewoman present. No king of England had ever wed so humbly.

A member of one of England's great noble families, however, Lady Diana has been characterized as almost the girl next door. Her father, the eighth Earl Spencer, had been an equerry (personal assistant to a royal) to King George VI and later to Queen Elizabeth. Althorp, home of the Spencers—which dates from 1508 and houses an art collection that features work by Rubens, Van Dyck, and Caneletto—is near the royal estate of Sandringham. Lady Diana's older sister Sarah had dated the prince.

As arguably the most eligible bachelor in the world, Charles had played the field, always with the shadow of choosing the next queen of England hovering over him. The jug-eared prince would not have been regarded as wildly eligible had he not been who he was. "He has all the makings of a curmudgeon," a friend once said. "If he doesn't find a suitable wife soon—and, my God, what exacting standards have to be met—even the Prince of Wales may have a serious problem on his hands."

Seemingly out of the blue, Lady Diana Spencer, whom Prince Charles knew but not well, received an invitation to his thirtieth-birthday party at Buckingham Palace. She assumed it was because of the prince's past relationship with her sister. Sarah sensed that her pretty younger sister had made an impression on the heir to the throne. She must have made another at the birthday party. Shortly afterward, the three Spencer sisters—including Lady Jane Fellowes, whose husband, Robert Fellowes, was assistant private secretary to the queen—were asked to a shooting party at Sandringham. Royal biographer Penny Junor has written that "that weekend was the beginning of Diana's relationship with the Prince of Wales. . . . Diana still nurtured a schoolgirl crush on him, which she had ever since their meeting in November 1977, which he cannot have failed to notice and been flattered by."

Charles and Diana began seeing each other frequently, though generally as part of a group. "Charles found himself strangely attracted to her," wrote Junor. "He found Diana fun to be with. . . . She did liven up the party."

A sympathetic remark at a weekend house party held at New Grove, the Sussex residence of Commander Robert de Pass, a polo-playing friend of the royal family, paved the way for a proposal. As Charles and Diana sat on a haystack, she told him she had been touched by his obvious sadness at the funeral of Lord Mountbatten, Charles's "honorary grandfather," assassinated by the IRA, in Westminster Abbey. "It was the most tragic thing I've ever seen. I thought: It's wrong, you are lonely, you should have somebody to look after you," she said. According to Sally Bedell Smith, Charles confided shortly afterward to Lady Susan Hussey, a lady-in-waiting to the queen, that he had met the girl he would marry. Diana, in a show of compassion, had almost closed the deal.

As the courtship progressed, several of Charles's close friends became alarmed. Penny Romsey, wife of Norton Romsey, Mountbatten's grandson, felt that Diana had "fallen in love with an idea rather than a person" and seemed to be "auditioning for a central role in a costume drama" without understanding the "enormity" of taking on the heir to the throne. "During the relationship," wrote Smith, "she seemed enchanted mainly by the idea of becoming a princess." Her giddiness was obvious at a picnic luncheon at Balmoral Castle, the royal estate in Scotland. There was linen, heavy silver, a menu card, and other accoutrements not found at every picnic. "Oh! This is the life for me! Where is the footman?" an excited Diana asked. Sally Bedell Smith would judge the remark "endearingly refreshing, yet ominously childish."

Royal princesses such as Charles's great-grandmother Queen Mary, born Princess Mary of Teck and called Princess May, and his great-great-grandmother Queen Alexandra, a Danish princess who married the future Edward VII, had known the score before they married. Romance in a royal marriage was fine, and indeed many royals, once married, fell warmly in love—but it was a bonus. Romantic love was not what mattered in a royal match. Loyalty to the institution of the monarchy, personified by her husband, was what counted. Having watched their relatives' thrones swept away by revolution, royal princesses understood that personal sacrifice was required to keep royalty going. When Edward VIII abdicated to marry Wallis Simpson, it was said that he had done so because of a "craving for private happiness." Royals must overcome such cravings.

Queen Mary had an almost religious reverence for royalty that enabled her to perform her duties. A great-granddaughter of King George III, Mary of Teck was born at Kensington Palace, where Diana would suffer so much. Despite their lineage, her parents had often been forced to live abroad to avoid creditors. Princess May was first engaged to marry Prince Eddy, heir to the throne, a simpleton, and most likely a homosexual—he was implicated in a raid on a notorious gay brothel—and a candidate for the honor of being Jack the Ripper. When Eddy died before they married, Queen Victoria promoted a match between Princess Mary and the new heir, Prince George. Mary, something of a Cinderella herself, was amenable, and a more dedicated consort there never was. "[S]he was consumed by one single abstract passion, which ruled her life, and dictated her whole conduct. . . . This was her passion for the British monarchy," her biographer wrote. "I must remember that my husband is also my sovereign," said Queen Mary.

Diana the Sloane Ranger was not consumed by a single abstract passion for preserving one of the last standing royal houses. Her notions of the role of a wife, even a royal wife, were founded more on the trashy novels of her stepgrandmother, Barbara Cartland, than on the steely courage of Queen Mary. "[Diana] had a romantic view of life," a friend told Smith, "but Barbara Cartland books didn't prepare you. They were cloud cuckooland, all very romantic escapism, and she was very impressionable."

Meanwhile, the press took up her cause, egging Charles on with headlines such as TO DI FOR or CHARLES: DON'T DITHER. Diana posed for the photographers but wisely she said little. Her way of peering shyly at the camera won her the nickname Shy Di. The impression was just right, and the world fell in love with Lady Di. The staid *Sunday Times* of London found her "serious but not boring, sweet but not too sweet."

On the day the press ferreted out the name of the new girl in Charles's life, Diana had accompanied the prince to the River Dee to fish. She remained on the bank. Veteran royal watcher James Whitaker, observing Diana through binoculars, was astonished to realize the clever young woman was also watching him—with her compact mirror. She was already press-conscious.

The media played a major role in the courtship. A story in the *Sunday Mail* may have precipitated a proposal. On November 16, 1980, the *Mail* broke a salacious story headlined ROYAL LOVE TRAIN. Quoting an unidentified policeman, the article reported that Charles and Diana had spent several nights alone together aboard the royal train. Buckingham Palace broke with precedent—it was charged with responding only to stories about royals—and called the story "absolutely scurrilous and totally false." Nevertheless, Prince Philip took the story seriously. "[Philip] counseled his son that he could not delay a decision much longer," wrote Dimbleby. "That to do so would cause lasting damage to Diana Spencer's reputation. The prince interpreted his father's attitude as an ultimatum."

The question of what to do weighed heavily on the prince during a skiing trip to Klosters in Switzerland. "No matter how he tried to be funny, a sense of foreboding kept breaking through," a friend confided to Dempster and Evans. Charles made up his mind and phoned Lady Diana, asking her to meet him at Windsor Castle, telling her he had "something important" to ask her. The meeting took place on February 6, 1981, in the nursery of Windsor Castle. When the Prince of Wales proposed, Diana's first response was to giggle, but Charles reminded her of the gravity of the situation. "Yes, please," she said, accepting the proposal.

Had she thought about what would come after the hoopla of courtship and wedding? If her family had doubts, they did not confide them to her. Indeed, one of the strangest aspects of Diana's story is that nobody in her family—a family that had a tradition of being around royals for hundreds of years—bothered to worry about what, at the age of nineteen, Diana was agreeing to do with her life. The tabloids presented Diana's grandmother Lady Fermoy, a lady-in-waiting and loyal friend of the Queen Mother, as someone who conspired to bring about the marriage. In reality, Lady Fermoy felt it was a mistake but failed to say so. The writer A. N. Wilson has written that Lady Fermoy, in a position to know that "British royal personages are different from the rest of mankind," should have told her granddaughter, "It is not difficult to be married to any member of the royal family. It is impossible."

"The royal family are not like us," a friend of the queen's confided to Sally Bedell Smith. "They cannot be, bless their hearts. It is difficult to find yourself in that world and have your wings clipped." Smith quoted

Diana's friend Roberto Devorik as saying, "For Diana, royal life was like a movie. She thought royalty was one thing when she was growing up. Then she opened the back door of royalty and found she could not cope with it."

The night before the engagement was announced, Diana was whisked from Coleherne Court, where amid her girlfriends she lived the life of a Sloane Ranger, to Clarence House, residence of the Queen Mother. When her Scotland Yard bodyguard reminded her that "this is the last night of freedom in your life," Diana felt that his words were "a sword through my heart."

Finding himself engaged to a woman thirteen years his junior, a woman he hardly knew, Charles was worried. According to Dempster and Evans, he took the unusual step of seeking counsel from his sister, Princess Anne, to whom he was not close. Pregnant and almost ready to give birth, Anne

> could not take seriously her brother's lugubrious litany of reasons why he feared that Diana would not be a suitable bride for him. . . . [B]ut no sharpened sisterly senses detected the subtext, that really dangerous undercurrent of his concern, that anticipated the biggest crisis the Royal Family had known since the abdication of Edward VIII. . . . He was too stuck in his bachelor ways, she chided; and told him to grow up. . . . She added slyly in tones that had so often angered and motivated him as a child, and now evoked and mocked the Windsor insularity they still shared: "Just close your eyes and think of England, Charles."

Diana's appreciation of the enormity of what she had done grew as she moved from Clarence House to Buckingham Palace, where she would live until the wedding. The palace seemed cold and the courtiers distant to a young woman used to a gaggle of girlfriends. She fretted that Charles wasn't paying enough attention to her. "She felt trapped and frightened," according to Dimbleby. Unschooled in royal ways, she was distressed that Charles left her behind for a five-week tour of Australia and New Zealand. When she cried saying good-bye at the airport, the delighted hacks ate it up. In reality, it was not a good sign.

Like any bride, she wanted to be cosseted and petted by her bridegroom. But she was not any bride. "She went to Buckingham Palace and then the tears started," her friend Carolyn Bartholomew would later recall. "The little thing got so thin. I was worried about her. She wasn't happy, she was suddenly plunged into all this pressure and it was a nightmare for her."

Diana's raw emotions and obvious misery, so bewildering to royals, alarmed Prince Charles. Diana became obsessed with something a royal princess would have found a way to ignore: Charles's relationship with Camilla Parker Bowles, the horsey, jaunty woman whom the prince loved. Camilla had married Andrew Parker Bowles, an army officer and godson of the queen, when a proposal of marriage from Charles was not forthcoming. Lady Diana discovered a bracelet that bore the monogram "GF," for Girl Friday, Charles's nickname for Camilla. It was supposed to be a farewell gift for Camilla, and Charles felt it was only right to present it in person. Diana was distraught. "I asked Charles if he was still in love with Camilla Parker Bowles, and he didn't give me a clear answer. What am I to do?" an anguished Diana said to a courtier. It is impossible to imagine such behavior from Queen Mary or Queen Alexandra, whose husband, Edward VII, carried on a long-standing affair with—oddly enough—Camilla's great-great-grandmother Alice Keppel. ("My great-grandmother was the mistress of your great-grandfather, so how about it, then?" Camilla is supposed to have said the first time she met Charles.)

A few days before the wedding, Diana made an attempt to tell her sisters about her misgivings. They had come to lunch at Buckingham Palace. "Well, bad luck, Duch [for Duchess, a nickname]," they said, "your face is on the tea towels, so you're too late to chicken out."

Instead of running for her life, Diana walked up the aisle of St. Paul's Cathedral, visibly shoring up her feeble father, the Earl Spencer, who had suffered a stroke, to become Diana, Princess of Wales. Years later, while listening to land-mine victims describe the gruesome details of their accidents—it is said that the time and date are etched forever in their minds—Diana would say, "My accident was on July 29, 1981." That was the day of her wedding.

CAROLYN

Although the Kennedy family isn't an ancient dynasty like the House of Windsor, the woman who married America's Prince Charming would face almost as many obstacles as the one who wed England's Prince of Wales. The burden of history would be as heavy, the press scrutiny as ruthless. But Carolyn Bessette—like Diana Spencer—was blinded by the glamour of the job. She seemed the perfect choice, though.

An old boyfriend of Carolyn Bessette's wrote that she "oozed class." She had grown up in the affluent suburb of Greenwich, Connecticut. Like Jacqueline Kennedy Onassis, Carolyn was a Catholic with WASPy polish.

Unlike Diana, Carolyn was one of those women who are born worldly. At St. Mary's High School—where she was voted "Ultimate Beautiful Person"—she was already practicing the art of driving men crazy. Eugene Carlin, a jock who became a stockbroker, told a reporter that Carolyn "would make you jealous and if you tried to do it back she'd ignore you. Then you go completely crazy." "She's passionately sexy," he elaborated. "Use your imagination. Beautiful. Sophisticated. Tough. Driven. She can drive you nuts."

She enrolled at Boston University, where she was involved with John Cullen, a future pro hockey player with the Tampa Bay Lightning, and his roommate at the same time. "Cullen was crazy about her," a classmate told Christopher Andersen. "But Carolyn was sort of known as the campus man eater—she dumped him, broke his heart and moved on to the next victim."

Although Carolyn majored in elementary education, she chose a job doing public relations for Boston nightclubs. She moved on to become a saleswoman in Calvin Klein's Boston outlet, and a Calvin Klein talent scout offered her a job in New York. She quickly became close to Calvin Klein and his wife, Kelly. She had a brittle wit that goes over well in New York showrooms. "Calvin just flew in on her broom," she teased. Bessette's innate sense of taste and blasé attitude about celebrity made her a perfect personal shopper for VIP clients. Soon assigned to public relations, Bessette worked comfortably with actress Annette Bening, New York socialite Blaine Trump, and TV personality Diane Sawyer. A journalist captivated by Carolyn told *Newsweek,* "I remember what she was wearing the first time I saw her: penny loafers, no socks, black leggings, a white T-shirt, and a jacket. I think the jacket was the only item that could have been by Calvin Klein. She looked fantastic. You wanted to look like that."

Carolyn hung out at hot nightspots with names like Rex, MK, and Buddha Bar. It is uncertain how she met John F. Kennedy Jr. Some insiders say that they met at a club, others that they were jogging in Central Park or that Kennedy was one of the celebrity shoppers she met through her job. John Kennedy had never met a girl like Carolyn.

He was accustomed to having women throw themselves at him. Actress Sarah Jessica Parker, with whom John had a fling, once met him at the airport naked under a mink coat. He was devastatingly handsome, in looks more like his maternal Bouvier ancestors than the all-hair-and-teeth Kennedys. He had graduated from Brown University, where he showed talent in university theatricals, but Jacqueline Kennedy Onassis regarded acting as an unsuitable profession for the son of a president. John enrolled in New York University's law school and upon graduation took a job as a Manhattan district attorney, the ideal stepping-stone for the political career his mother seemed to want for him. John, who suffered from dyslexia, flunked his bar exam—twice. "THE HUNK FLUNKS, blared a *New York Post* headline. He passed on the third try.

In 1988 *People* magazine named the twenty-seven-year-old DA "the sexiest man alive." Friends thought that John secretly loved the spotlight. The little boy who imprinted himself on the consciousness of a nation when he saluted his father's coffin had grown up to be the most glamorous of the second generation of Camelot. While still in his thirties, John had been linked to Julia Roberts and Melanie Griffith. He had even had a minor fling with Madonna. John's on-again, off-again girlfriend was the actress Daryl Hannah, who was believed to be eager to marry him. Mrs. Onassis, who'd been debutante of the year back in the days when ladies didn't go on the stage, did not approve because of Daryl's profession.

As with Prince Charles, the press grew impatient with John's bachelorhood. I was working for the New York *Daily News* in 1990 when John turned thirty, and I ended up with an assignment to write a "Why isn't he married?" story. It was, of course, impossible to get an interview with John. So late one afternoon I went downtown to the DA's office and sat on the steps near where John's bicycle was chained. I was wondering how he would treat yet another stranger with a notebook when John Kennedy emerged from the building, wearing the most beautifully cut suit I'd ever seen, with a faint lavender shirt and patterned tie. He couldn't have been nicer. He'd heard a story was in the works, he said pleasantly. No, he

didn't tell me why he wasn't married, but we chatted quietly as he un-
locked his bicycle, and stopping for just a moment before climbing onto
his bicycle, he asked gently, "Any more questions?" Good manners, I
thought, paying silent tribute to Jacqueline Kennedy Onassis. He glided
off into the Manhattan traffic.

A couple of years later I was working as a gossip columnist for *The
New York Observer* when Calvin and Kelly Klein gave a huge party around
their penthouse pool. Celebrating publication of her coffee-table book on
swimming pools, it was the sort of party known as a "rat fuck"—a collection of boldfaced names and hangers-on. John Kennedy stepped off the
elevator, sending a bolt of electricity through the party. But the press
missed a tiny drama that evening. Carolyn Bessette was there, as was her
sometime boyfriend, Michael Bergin, an aspiring model and doorman at
the trendy Paramount Hotel. Bergin was one of the shapely young men
circulating in loincloths with trays of canapés. Before leaving, Kennedy
walked over to Carolyn and gave her a quick peck. Bergin and Carolyn
were estranged, but she waited for him at the elevator. Ashamed of being
"a fucking cabana boy" that night, Bergin taunted her about Kennedy. "I
told you," Carolyn insisted. "He's not my type. He's not for me. I'm not
interested in him or the life he leads." According to Bergin, they went to
Bessette's apartment and made love. The party was in September of 1992,
before Bergin attained fame as the Calvin Klein underwear model.
Kennedy was still publicly involved with Hannah, the last of his girlfriends
his mother would know.

Throughout her courtship, Carolyn would hold on to Bergin as a
valuable weapon. "Carolyn was like, 'Fuck you, I am going to go off,'" a
member of her inner circle told reporter Rebecca Mead. "I don't think
anybody but John believed for a minute that she meant it—like she was
going to turn in John for Michael Bergin, or something—but it played on
his ego."

Carolyn and John were first seen together in the tabloids at the New
York Marathon in 1993. Her relationship with Bergin began earlier. They
met at an Upper East Side hangout called Joe's Café. A boy from a
working-class family in Naugatuck, Connecticut, Bergin was fascinated by
Carolyn's seemingly effortless elegance. "A simple dress, simple shoes, the
tiniest hint of makeup—everything about her was pared down. She
wasn't about noise or flash. She was about beautifully understated ele-

gance." She was also about hot sex. One day Carolyn stopped by the Paramount, where Bergin was opening doors in his doorman's uniform, to say hello, and they went to get lunch. "Before we made it to the hotdog stand, she grabbed my hand and pulled me into an alley—where no one could see us—and kissed me very hard. 'Meow,' she said." Still, Bergin was troubled by her refusal to reveal much about herself, and the picture frames in her tiny apartment were all empty.

On the same morning Carolyn informed Bergin she was pregnant, according to his book, *The Other Man,* they were rushing to the subway when somebody cruising by on a bicycle called out her name. "Was that who I think it was?" the staggered Bergin asked. Carolyn admitted that it was Kennedy and that she had been to Martha's Vineyard several times to see him. "It was really nothing," Carolyn insisted. "I went as a friend. Let's drop this. Nothing happened. It was no big deal." Bergin claims to have accompanied Carolyn to have an abortion.

Although Jacqueline Onassis probably never heard about Carolyn Bessette, who would later be likened to her, John was in the initial stages of his romance with her when his mother died in May 1994. John and Daryl were still involved, though, as were Carolyn and Bergin.

At first, John and Carolyn dated secretly—John's old friend from Brown Rob Littell felt that John enjoyed the mystery of it. Littell was at John's apartment one night, however, when John kept begging him to stay just a little longer—he had "a surprise." Littell waited around, wanting to leave, until the buzzer rang. "John became uncharacteristically jumpy," Littell recalled. "Bam! In walks the hottest girl I'd ever seen in my life. Tall, bright blond, in loose-fitting jeans and a big blue shirt, she literally glowed. She said hello and turned to John. From somewhere, he pulled out a cigarette—a sure sign he was a wreck because he rarely smoked." Carolyn lit John's cigarette with a Zippo with the words "Blue Eyes" engraved on it, the gift of an old boyfriend. "I asked her, pretending fear, 'What happened to him?' She laughed sweetly."

When he called John the next day, Littell said, "I feel bad for the dudes who got blinded by her light! Wow . . . what *was* that?" "Pretty wild, huh?" John replied. "That's why I had you stay over. I wanted you to meet her." "Meet her? I could barely look at her!" Littell said. He realized that John had met the girl he wanted to marry. "The qualities John always liked in women—irreverence, mystery, drama, and beauty—she had in abundance. John knew he'd hooked the big one right away, though she put up a sporting fight."

While Hannah was available, Bessette—who also wanted to marry John—played hard to get. Carolyn was frequently called a "Rules Girl," after the bestselling book *The Rules: Time-Tested Secrets for Capturing the Heart of Mr. Right,* which came out while they were courting. The book laid down such rules as "Be a 'Creature Unlike Any Other,'" "Don't Call Him and Rarely Return His Calls," and "Don't Open Up Too Fast." There is no evidence that Carolyn read the book—she didn't need to. "She's a natural Rules Girl," Ellen Fein, one of the coauthors, told *Newsweek.* "She would tell people, 'I'm not waiting around for him,' knowing it would get back to John," a friend told the magazine. "But in fact she would stay home and wait for John to call."

Georgette Mosbacher, whose "Ten Proven Techniques for Turning a Moment into a Lifetime" include "But *never* play hard to get unless there's a very good reason for it," was not a Rules Girl. She would probably have advised Carolyn on a different course of action, but John Kennedy, who had grown up as "the most famous boy in the world," as his uncle Teddy would put it, was in a class by himself. Used to women flinging themselves at him, John Kennedy was challenged by Carolyn.

John not only had a new girlfriend, he had a new magazine. *George,* John's political magazine, was launched in September 1995, with the backing of Hachette Filipacchi, the French publishing group. Because of John it received unprecedented media attention. While the first issue was in preparation, John asked Carolyn to marry him. Instead of jumping at the chance, Carolyn told John she couldn't give him an answer yet. Carolyn had moved into John's TriBeCa loft in April 1995, but she was still keeping him dangling. She waited a month, or more than a year, to give him a definitive answer, depending on who's talking.

While involved with Kennedy, she showed up at Bergin's apartment with a large pea green bird, a sun conure, similar to one Bergin's mother owned, as a gift. "She seemed to have reached a breaking point: she could only go a few months without seeing me," Bergin wrote. "We're just friends," Carolyn continued to insist of her relationship with JFK Jr., even though Bergin had seen tabloid pictures of them kissing in Central Park. Once, before she moved in with John, she invited Bergin over. When the buzzer rang, she said to Bergin, "Would you mind taking the stairs, sweetie?" Another time she stopped at Bergin's to announce that she had had a miscarriage and ended up spending the night. This time the buzzer went off at seven o'clock in the morning; it was Carolyn's friend the designer Gordon Henderson, frantic that John was on the way over to check on Carolyn. Bergin ran off half-dressed, with his shoes in his hands.

As he once had with Daryl Hannah, John engaged in a very public spat with Carolyn. They were walking their dog, Friday, on whom both doted, in Washington Square Park when the couple started yelling at each other. "What's your problem?" Carolyn fumed. John grabbed her hand and pulled off the engagement ring. John sat on the curb and began to sob. She demanded that he return the ring, which he did. She sat down and began to sob. When she tried to take Friday's leash, John shouted, "You've got my ring. You're not getting my dog." "It's our dog," Carolyn yelled, pulling at the dog's leash. After resisting, John gave up and they headed in different directions, Carolyn with Friday. Bessette turned and took John to a bench, where they talked. They finally walked away together, holding on to each other. Unfortunately, the spat had been videotaped for the *National Enquirer* and a TV show without their knowing.

One of the few milestones in the too-brief life of John Kennedy Jr. that was not a media circus was his wedding. It took place in a church built for slaves on a barrier island off the coast of Georgia. John left the *George* offices carrying golf clubs to give the impression that he was leaving for a weekend of golf. "She's the best shot I've got," he had whispered to Rob Littell a few months earlier as the two friends walked off the racquetball court at New York's Downtown Athletic Club.

There was one awkward moment at the rehearsal dinner. When it came time for Carolyn's mother, Ann Freeman, to make a toast, she spoke candidly about her misgivings. "I was surprised by her bluntness and felt bad for John, who was visibly stung by her remarks," wrote Littell.

The wedding took place at dusk in the First African Baptist Church, which was lit by candles—there was no electricity. Carolyn was two hours late because her makeup was ruined and had to be redone after she tried to put her slinky $40,000 Narciso Rodriguez gown over her head. When she finally did arrive, walking across the sand dunes in four-inch heels, with her corn-silk hair swept back from her face, she was more dazzling than ever. The priest used a flashlight to read the service, and everybody cheered when he pronounced them man and wife. It seemed such a perfect choice for John to have made. Letitia Baldridge, Jackie's former social secretary, supposed that "Jackie must be smiling in heaven."

DIANA

There was never a honeymoon for the Prince and Princess of Wales—or rather, Diana and Charles's unsuitability for each other was already manifest on their honeymoon, two days at Broadlands, the Mountbatten estate, and a two-week cruise on the royal yacht *Britannia*. The trip to Gibraltar and along the Algerian and Tunisian coasts, with stops at isolated beaches and along the Greek islands and ultimately to Egypt, should have been a happy time. But it was not. Charles had brought along his books, suggested by the aged philosopher Laurens van der Post; Diana, who'd packed six sexy lace teddies and several sheer nightgowns, wanted her husband to pay attention to her. A thank-you note that Charles wrote from *Britannia* is revealing. "All I can say is that marriage is very jolly and it's extremely nice being together in *Britannia*," he wrote. "Diana dashes about chatting up all the sailors and cooks in the galley etc. while I remain hermit-like on the veranda deck, sunk with pure joy into one of Laurens van der Post's books." On the wedding trip, Charles discovered Diana's bulimia, a binging-and-purging eating disorder brought on by stress; he witnessed more of the mood swings that had alarmed him at Buckingham Palace.

After the cruise came a long holiday at Balmoral, the estate in the Scottish Highlands that Queen Victoria had purchased with a legacy from a besotted admirer, the eccentric John Camden Nield, who had never actually met the queen. Like Victoria, Charles loved Balmoral. There the royal family hunted grouse, fished for salmon, wore kilts, and was serenaded by bagpipes. There Diana realized that she had made a terrible mistake. "This was going to be her life," a courtier told Smith, "spending wet days shooting, and she hated it."

Their first royal tour together was to Wales for three days. Charles was solicitous of his wife, asking the lady-in-waiting to stay close to her. Diana talked with children, and she looked beautiful. Between appearances, however, she sobbed. Diana wasn't the only one having adjustment problems. The prince found himself overshadowed. "Over here, Diana, over here," people would say, obviously disappointed if the prince was working their side of the street. Diana showed her empathy for ordinary people.

When a little boy shouted, "My dad says give us a kiss," the princess gave him one, a gesture that was highly unusual for a member of the royal family. "There's the person you came to see," the prince said in his self-deprecating manner as he grew accustomed to—but not entirely happy with—hearing the Welsh shouting. "There she is." Diana wanted praise from the royal family when she carried out her public obligations, but none was forthcoming. The royals understood duty as a way of life and performed theirs without seeing it as anything out of the ordinary. "Duty is the rent you pay for your life," the Queen Mother said.

Charles would say later, in a disastrous televised documentary, that the marriage had "irretrievably broken down" by 1984. In fact, it never had a chance. Except for the public adulation, which was her drug, Diana hated royal life; there was no breakdown because there was nothing to break, except for the fragile princess.

The princess suffered intensely. One courtier would later recall devoting an entire day to trying to comfort her. "During her bouts of unhappiness, the Princess would sit hunched on a chair, her head on her knees," wrote Dembleby. "When it proved impossible to cajole her from this state, those around her concluded yet again that the stress of her new life was more difficult for her to overcome than they had expected." Diana's bulimia returned and she became "sick as a parrot."

Shortly after their first Christmas as husband and wife, the princess, who was pregnant, either tripped or hurled herself down the stairs at Sandringham. She was unhurt but would later claim it had been a suicide attempt. Her friends would insist that Charles was a cold husband. Others who saw the couple at close range said that Charles "had become accustomed to spending much time at her side, haplessly trying to soothe her back to cheerfulness."

Diana refused to believe that her husband had severed his ties to Camilla. Most shockingly for a royal wife, Diana confronted Camilla at a birthday party for Camilla's sister, Annabel Elliot, in 1988. Diana told Parker Bowles that she wanted to speak to her in private. Looking Parker Bowles in the eye, she said, "Why can't you leave my husband alone?" Royals don't behave this way, and in doing so, Diana was blazing a dangerous trail with possibly fatal consequences for the House of Windsor. Queen Alexandra, Charles's great-grandmother, loved Edward VII, but she would never have dreamed of a public confrontation with Alice Keppel.

When Edward VII was dying, Queen Alexandra sent for Mrs. Keppel and took her to his bedside. In other words, Queen Alexandra knew how to behave like a queen.

Charles did eventually resume the affair, though probably not before 1984, when he felt his marriage was beyond repair. Unlike Diana, Camilla bolstered Charles's ego. ("You're a clever old thing. Awfully good brain lurking there, isn't there?" she said in the infamous recorded telephone conversation between them.) But if Camilla worked to sabotage the royal marriage, she was not being true to the spirit of Mrs. Keppel. Like a royal princess, a royal mistress knows her job, and Mrs. Keppel was hailed as a perfect royal mistress. In a possibly apocryphal remark, she said, "A royal mistress should curtsey first, then leap into bed."

On June 21, 1982, Prince William, second in line to the throne after his father, was born. Both parents were overjoyed. But it was clear that Diana had grown strikingly thin and that royal life was difficult for her. Charles blamed himself because he had brought her into a position she found intolerable. It was clear to his friends that he felt both tender toward and bewildered by his desperately unhappy wife. But he was not always solicitous. Though Charles's paternal grandmother, the deaf and beautiful Princess Alice of Greece, had undergone psychoanalysis, no member of the royal family was capable of handling somebody who, it increasingly appeared, had serious psychological problems. Nevertheless, Charles arranged for Diana to see a psychiatrist. "The trouble is," he wrote to one of his friends, "one day I think steps are being made uphill only to find that we've slid back one and a half steps the following day."

Unlike Queen Mary, the princess did not revere her husband as her future sovereign—indeed, she began to take a dim view of the entire royal family. "Because her family looks down on the royal family, she thought of them wrongly as German parvenus," Andrew Roberts, a historian, once said. In a breathtaking act of lèse-majesté, Diana referred to the royal family as "that fucking family." It was inconceivable that the future queen of England should express such thoughts.

The sovereign is also the titular head of the Church of England, which until recently did not sanction divorce. But in two public, precedent-shattering acts, Diana made the unthinkable—a divorce for the heir to the throne—conceivable. The first was her secret cooperation in a revealing 1992 book, *Diana: Her True Story,* by journalist Andrew Morton, "a humiliation of almost unendurable proportions" for the prince. Based on interviews with Diana's friends and taped interviews with her smuggled out of the palace, the book portrays Charles as faithless and cold and inadequate as a father. It reveals the princess's bulimia and apparent suicide attempts, including the Sandringham incident. Diana denied any part in the book. But then she gave it her seal of approval by visiting Carolyn Bartholomew, a source, and kissing Bartholomew outside her house, where photographers caught it. The Morton book set the stage for an official separation. Charles had dithered until his wife abruptly decided he was not to have a planned outing with the children. On December 9 Prime Minister John Major announced on the floor of the House of Commons that the Prince and Princess of Wales had decided to separate. He pointedly said they had no plans to divorce.

Diana took the second irrevocable step two years later when she sat for an interview with Martin Bashir of England's *Panorama* show. The BBC crew filmed the segment on Guy Fawkes Day, when Diana's staff would be away from Kensington Palace. The show aired two weeks later. While admitting her struggles with bulimia and her adultery with James Hewitt, an army officer, Diana was critical of Charles and the royal family. She made her famous (and utterly prepared) charge that there were "three of us in the marriage." She challenged her husband's fitness to be king— "I would think the top job, as I call it, would bring enormous limitations to him, and I don't know whether he could adapt"—and said that she felt she would never be queen but wanted to be "a queen of people's hearts." Referring to herself in the third person, Diana threw down a gauntlet to the royal family: "She won't go quietly, that's the problem," she said, and, reverting to the first person, added, "I'll fight to the end."

Diana's performance was without precedent in the history of the monarchy. A Gallup poll may have shown that immediately after the broadcast a majority of viewers had reacted favorably, but Diana had lost the audience that really mattered: the royal family. The source of her prominence was royalty, and she was questioning her husband's fitness to be king. The innocent Spencer girl, the former nursery-school aide, the Sloane Ranger who loved children, was causing more harm to the monarchy than anybody since a brittle divorcée from Baltimore named Wallis Simpson. The interview forced the queen to step in and attempt to protect the crown. Queen Elizabeth wrote to Charles and Diana, asking them to agree to a divorce. The divorce became final on August 28, 1996, leaving Diana a very rich woman (she received a settlement of about $26 million to be paid over five years and an allowance of $600,000 a year for staff and supplies) with a residence in Kensington Palace. She would be styled Diana, Princess of Wales, but—like Wallis Simpson—she was not permitted to retain the HRH (Her Royal Highness). Shorn of her real royal title, Diana still aspired to her fantasy title, Queen of Hearts. To win it, she launched the kind of all-out campaign that would have done Napoléon proud. Diana had wanted not only a royal marriage but the fairy-tale romance of which the archbishop of Canterbury spoke at her wedding. Thwarted, Diana turned viciously on her husband and the royal family in a way that must have made them long to be able to bring back the Anne Boleyn solution (colloquially known as "off with her head") to deal with troublesome royal wives. It is tempting to speculate on what would have happened if Diana had bolted before the wedding and made those tea towels into collector's items.

Diana Spencer, both before and after the divorce, fought the War of the Waleses brilliantly and on two battlefields of her choosing. The first was the media. She made the media the third partner in her marriage, much more than Camilla Parker Bowles was. The media have always been a presence in celebrity marriages, but Diana invited them into the palace in an unprecedented way, turning a royal marriage, with constitutional ramifications, into a celebrity marriage pure and simple. The press was not the only combat zone. Like any society lady with an image problem, Diana knew the best place to fight back: the charity circuit. In waging her war, Diana was ruthlessly willing to employ, in the words of her private secretary Patrick Jephson, the "guerilla tactics" of press manipulation, "calendar rivalry"—planning her schedule to upstage Charles. She also used the young princes, cards too tempting not to play, to engage in emotional blackmail.

Diana began to branch out from traditional charities and focus on causes that highlighted suffering or death and dying. AIDS and the eradication of land mines were her most prominent ones. "I have to do it, Patrick. Nobody else understands the rejection they feel," she said of her involvement with AIDS patients. She had become painfully aware of the toll of AIDS when her friend Adrian Jackson, an art-world figure, was dying of the disease. She carried a beeper when he was in the last stages of the disease; it was then, wrote Jephson, that the princess found "a chance to focus enormous reserves of compassion, as well as a particular fascination with this disease, which appeared to draw its victims principally from the beautiful and the talented." She became convinced that she had a healing power, curiously reminiscent of the power ascribed to the medieval kings of England, who had been thought to cure scrofula by their touch.

CAROLYN

On her honeymoon Carolyn was sitting in a café in Turkey when she overheard a group of vacationing New York magazine editors saying that John Kennedy's new bride simply wasn't attractive enough for him. It was a minority opinion but nevertheless stinging to a woman who put so much stock in dazzling everybody who saw her.

Carolyn was further traumatized when the couple returned from their honeymoon to find a mob of photographers waiting for them at the entrance to their TriBeCa loft. For John, it was old hat; but for Carolyn, who had given insufficient thought to what being married to John would be like, it was deeply disturbing. John made a plea for understanding and privacy for his frightened wife. "This is a big change, and for a private citizen even more so," he told the assembled paparazzi. "I ask you to give Carolyn all the privacy and the room you can spare."

But Carolyn was New York's newest celebrity, and the paparazzi were not going to go away. She was mobbed only a few days later when Caroline Kennedy Schlossberg threw a party for the newlyweds at her apartment on Park Avenue. "I can't see," Carolyn complained as the flashbulbs went off in her face. John knew how to give the press tidbits of information to make their jobs easier and to be pleasant. Carolyn, on the other hand, regarded the press as the enemy and snubbed them. She refused to stop for a second and dole out a few details—who designed her dress or something similarly inconsequential—at a benefit at the Whitney Museum and was booed by the photographers. John had never been booed. To make matters worse, Carolyn had quit her job and now had nothing to do all day but hang out in the loft and think about how miserable she was. Because there was no back door, Carolyn had a choice between being stuck at home and running the press gauntlet. Carolyn once stayed inside for two weeks in a row. John spoke to a lawyer, who said there was no way to banish the paparazzi at the door.

John was distraught about Carolyn's failure to accept her situation. "John was patient and he wanted her to adjust," a friend told author Laurence Leamer. "There were great things in their love regardless of what anybody says. She was strong, and she had some wonderful qualities, but the question was whether she was going to get beyond this obsession with the paparazzi."

On John and Carolyn's first wedding anniversary, Rob Littell and his wife, Frannie, invited the couple to dinner. Rob arranged for a limousine to pick up the couple so that Carolyn would be spared the necessity of standing in public while John and Rob hailed a taxi. "We got to their apartment on North Moore Street [in TriBeCa]," recalled Littell, "and they came down when we buzzed. John started to climb into the limousine, but Carolyn turned away and walked over to the stoop, where she sat down. She told John she couldn't do it, she couldn't go. The limo was a mistake. It made her feel more ostentatiously 'famous.' I felt horrible. She began to sniffle, and I said to John that we'd do it another time, no big deal." But John put his arm around his wife and talked to her quietly. She regained some color and got into the limousine. Carolyn enjoyed herself at dinner until the subject of the paparazzi came up. "They're out there *every* day. It's horrible," Carolyn insisted.

DIANA

Unless Prince Eddy, Queen Mary's hapless first fiancé, really was Jack the Ripper, it is safe to say that no member of the royal family ever prowled the streets of London in search of prostitutes quite as intently as Diana did. Unlike Jack the Ripper, she sought them out as beneficiaries of her good works. Diana's butler, Paul Burrell, wrote of accompanying the princess, who piloted her BMW, to find prostitutes. When the princess stopped her car, two tottered over in their high heels. "Hi, Princess Di. How are you?" said one of the women. "I'm fine. Have you been busy?" the princess said. "The Boss reached into her pocket and got out two crisp fifty-pound notes. 'Look, girls, have the night off on me. Go home to your children.'" Diane asked about one of their children. He had been sick. Was he better? "Oh, Paul," she told her stunned butler, "lighten up. Those girls need help, and that's all I'm doing—helping them." Burell could imagine the headline: DI AND BUTLER CAUGHT KERB-CRAWLING.

Most of Diana's good works did not go unrecorded—and this was not by accident. As every troubled socialite knows, a photogenic charity doesn't just help the designated beneficiaries. "Patrick [Jephson]," she said on the phone, "I'm so sorry to bother you when you're away on your hols, but I think it's really important we go to Calcutta to see Mother Teresa for Christmas. She'd love it. It would be a marvelous way of using all this wretched publicity of mine to draw attention to the wonderful work she's doing." When Jephson told her that Mother Teresa felt she could be more valuable visiting the order's less spectacular alcohol rehab center in suburban London, "there was a long, hurt, and unloved silence at the other end of the line before the train plunged into a tunnel and the phone mercifully went dead. I am afraid the alcohol projects never did get their visit." But the princess did visit so many people in charitable institutions that a London newspaper carried a slip of paper that could be cut out and carried in one's wallet like an organ donor card. It read: "In the event of an accident I do not wish to be visited by the Princess of Wales."

Most people, of course, would have been delighted by a visit from the beautiful Princess of Wales. She remained an immensely popular public figure, at ease with AIDS patients and able to put land-mine victims, drug addicts, and mental patients at ease. "They can talk to me because I am one of them," she told Jephson. He wrote that Diana rationalized the use she made of her charities with the belief "not unreasonable, that she was a pretty good cause in her own right . . . Her intentions were sharpened by her wish to draw a distinction between the perceived idleness of her in-laws and her own tireless dedication to the needs of her constituency."

In a way, Diana tried to kill Charles with kindness—her kindness to other people. She wanted to be chosen as the member of the royal family to visit—and show kindness to the Parry family, whose young son Tim had been killed in the Warrington bombing (1993). When the queen sent Charles instead, Diana upstaged him by writing directly to the Parry family. The letter meant a great deal, and when reporters showed up, the family spoke of the princess in glowing terms. They were more moved by the letter with its air of spontaneity than the poor prince's visit. "The kindness of her gesture," according to Jephson, "was as genuine as the tragedy of the circumstances deserved; it was just that there was a further, secondary agenda to the one presented more or less artlessly to the public."

Diana was the first major royal personage to deal directly with the press, talking to them off the record, often initiating contact, and alerting them to something she wanted in the public domain. She entertained members of the media at small lunches at Kensington Palace, including such luminaries as Barbara Walters and Oprah Winfrey. It was a dangerous game, but the campaign did make her a more sympathetic personage than the prince. A case in point was a 1993 piece in *Vanity Fair,* headlined Dı's PALACE COUP, that portrayed the divorce as "a moment of triumph" for Diana and a "crushing defeat" for Charles. She also knew how to stage a brilliant photo opportunity for the press, as she had in 1992 when she posed forlornly in front of the Taj Mahal, the monument of a Mogul emperor's love. The next day she turned her head just as Charles was trying to kiss her cheek—just the right moment to make Charles look ridiculous before the world.

Her affection for her sons was beyond doubt, but she was more than willing for the cameras to capture her outings with the princes. When she took them to Thorpe Park, an amusement park, Jephson noted, "significantly, she seemed unsurprised when the photographers turned up to capture the touching scenes as she put on a display of unstuffy modern motherhood." Another photo opportunity was her emotional reunion with the princes onboard the royal yacht *Britannia* in Canada. "Less visible but no less sincere," wrote Jephson, "was their father's greeting, which followed in private."

Diana found great pleasure in the company of celebrities such as Elton John, who became a close friend, and John Travolta, with whom she swirled around the dance floor at the White House. She began to become more like a movie star than a princess, dangerous to the monarchy because, when all is said and done, it rests not on glitter but on an unwritten constitution and on events that took place in the mists of history. In becoming, in effect, a movie star, the princess brought the monarchy down to a level heretofore unimaginable. Nowhere was this more blatant than when her speaking coach, Peter Settelen—she had told him about her marital infidelities—praised her performance at a public engagement with the words "Not bad—for a whore!" Far from wanting to behead him, she loved the compliment.

Four years before her death, the attention-craving princess used the occasion of a charity luncheon in London for the ultimate publicity stunt—her announcement that she was withdrawing from public life. She requested "the time and space that has been lacking in recent years." Diana had begun dropping hints that such a move was imminent. The queen and Prince Philip, wrote Jephson, "appreciated her need to withdraw but urged her not to use a public platform to do it." They obviously didn't know their princess. Jephson, who urged her not to make a public announcement, realized she wanted to use the opportunity to create drama to portray herself as a victim and—always on her mind—to make her ex-husband look bad. Over a *Daily Mail* story—for which the reporter had been "well-briefed by its royal subject as always"—the headline was CHARLES DROVE HER TO IT. Her withdrawal was markedly brief. Upon her return, she began to "cherry-pick" her causes even more carefully. "I sometimes wanted to attach to my office door an agent's sign saying, 'Anything Overseas or Photogenic Considered,'" wrote Jephson. Diana soon became a crusader against land mines, one of her best publicity-garnering causes.

Diana was tantalizing the press with hints of another shock announcement in the months leading up to her death—was the unpredictable princess going to withdraw again, perhaps to live abroad? Adding to the suspense was her romantic involvement with Dodi Al Fayed, the son of Harrods owner Mohamed Al Fayed. A Muslim stepfather for the future king of England? Diana's mischief was more inspired than ever before. Mohamed Al Fayed, the real promoter of the Diana-Dodi liaison, was a blunt-talking billionaire who had been denied British citizenship. He was involved in a scandal about bribing Tory MPs. Dodi, whose real name was Emad, lived on the fringes of Hollywood and international society. Despite his $100,000-a-month allowance, Dodi frequently got into gossip columns for not paying his debts. He had a bad cocaine habit for a while. But Dodi was sweet in a feckless way, with boyish good looks and a hint of a Middle Eastern accent that some found charming. He was engaged to Kelly Fisher, a fashion model. But Dodi knew that if he were to marry the Princess of Wales, he would earn his father's undying approbation—and unlimited access to the family funds.

Al Fayed introduced Diana to Dodi in St.-Tropez. They spent time on Mohamed Al Fayed's yacht, *Jonikal*. Not given to understated elegance, Dodi rented a disco for William and Harry. Dodi then returned to Fisher. Diana and Dodi were next together in Paris, where they took a midnight walk along the Seine and visited the restored residence of the Duke and Duchess of Windsor. Then there was a six-day cruise together on *Jonikal*.

The relationship with the Al Fayeds was the ultimate way to stick it to Charles and "that fucking family." But beyond a few glimpses, nobody knows enough to render a final judgment on the relationship. Sally Bedell Smith has noted that Dodi and Diana were "damaged in similar ways." Butler Paul Burrell believed, however, that given the vulgar way the Al Fayeds flaunted their wealth, "a niggling doubt wrestled with the Princess's excitement. It was all becoming a bit too much."

The relationship would cost Diana her life. Eager to slip unnoticed out of his father's Hotel Ritz Paris, Dodi hatched a plan to use a car as a decoy. Dodi allowed Henri Paul, the chauffeur who had passed the afternoon drinking, to drive the the princess and himself. When the paparazzi spotted them, Dodi ordered Paul to outrun them. "Don't bother following—you won't catch us," Paul shouted. When moments later the car crashed in Paris's Pont d'Alma tunnel, the life of the most colorful royal spouse since Eleanor of Aquitaine in the twelfth century came to an end.

Her death may have saved the monarchy. To endure, the monarchy must have pageantry, but not Hollywood pageantry. Royal pageantry is that of the church and of history. Diana had brought the monarchy down to the level of a cheesy movie in which she starred. "When people no longer venerate the monarchy, they will see us as their equals—and then the illusion is over," Louis XIV said. Diana had shattered the illusion.

Diana had not fully shattered the beautiful illusion. That was left to somebody born royal—Prince Charles. When in 2005 Charles wed the woman he loved, Diana's hated rival, Camilla—now Her Royal Highness, the Duchess of Cornwall—he had done that for which his great-uncle Edward VIII was forced to renounce his throne. For the first time, a future king of England was married in a civil ceremony, necessary because the duchess still has a living ex-husband. It was nice to see a middle-aged couple, united and happy at last, of course, but Louis XIV would have known that such a marriage was, in the long run, a very bad thing for the other-worldly prestige required to sustain a monarchy.

CAROLYN

After Princess Diana's death, Carolyn Bessette Kennedy became obsessed with the ill-fated princess. She identified with Diana, regarding her as a fellow sufferer at the hands of the paparazzi. "Poor woman," she said again and again to Michael Bergin, with whom she allegedly had resumed an affair.

Bergin, who had landed a role on *Baywatch,* was living in Los Angeles. Carolyn called him in the summer of 1997, less than a year after her magical wedding on Cumberland Island, and asked, "How much room do you have in your apartment?" "Plenty," Bergin replied. "Why?" Carolyn said that she and her friend Gordon Henderson were coming to visit.

On the third night of Carolyn's visit, Bergin says that the couple found the flesh was weak and ended up in bed together. "We shouldn't be doing this, should we?" he said. "I think John's having an affair, too," she said. Asked why she thought that, Carolyn replied, "I don't know. I just do."

She was probably wrong—if John was unfaithful at all, it certainly wasn't at such an early stage in a marriage he desperately wanted to work. For the next three days, according to Bergin's book, Bergin and Bessette Kennedy, along with Henderson, were holed up in Bergin's apartment, having an idyllic time, with Carolyn and Gordon walking on the beach before Bergin came home from *Baywatch.* Somehow they eluded the paparazzi. At Carolyn's request, Henderson returned to New York two days before she did, giving her time alone with Bergin. They next saw each other when Henderson's mother died, and Carolyn accompanied the designer to the West Coast for the funeral. One morning when Carolyn woke up in bed with Bergin, looking particularly lethargic, Bergin asked what he could do to help her. "Save me," she replied.

As time went on, it was clear that Carolyn was not learning to cope with her celebrity status. One particularly sensational report had John returning home from work at *George* to find his loft filled with Carolyn's friends from the fashion world and his wife in a coked-out stupor. They would fight, but they also made up and looked like people who loved each other. Rich Blow, a *George* editor who wrote a book about Kennedy, found her refreshingly candid. "I can't believe that I had to sit by that thug Puffy Combs all night," she whispered to Blow.

John had not given up on his marriage, and the couple saw both a professional marriage counselor and New York's Cardinal O'Connor in an attempt to save it, according to Ed Klein's *The Kennedy Curse.* O'Connor had been enlisted by John's uncle Teddy, who knew a divorce would be harmful if—or when—his nephew finally decided to enter politics. John wanted children—he was going to name his son Flynn and save him from the burden of being JFK III—but Carolyn said she couldn't bring up children with all the paparazzi around all the time. John had grown up just that way and turned into a decent man. But Carolyn was adamant. According to Klein, John told a friend two days before his death on July 16, 1999, "I want to have kids, but whenever I raise the subject with Carolyn, she turns away and refuses to have sex with me."

When John uttered these words, he was sitting on his bed in the Stanhope Hotel, where he had gone for a respite from the marital discord that made the loft in TriBeCa such a hellhole. Two days later, in an attempt to reconcile, John and Carolyn and her sister Lauren Bessette, an investment banker, would climb into his Piper Saratoga to fly to Martha's Vineyard for the wedding of his cousin Rory Kennedy in Hyannis Port. They would drop off Lauren on Martha's Vineyard. John would be flying with an injured foot. According to Klein, Carolyn delayed the flight, causing them to fly with lower visibility, because she insisted on having her nails done and redone to match the purple of a swatch of material she liked. Author Christopher Andersen has all three travelers heading to the airport by six-thirty in the evening. Earlier in the afternoon Carolyn had told a salesperson at Saks Fifth Avenue, where she bought her outfit for Rory's wedding at the last minute, that she wasn't looking forward to flying with her husband because she wasn't convinced her husband was ready to fly so soon after being hurt.

When it became inescapable that John's plane had crashed and that they were all dead, many thought of Jackie Kennedy and were grateful she had been spared. It had turned out that Carolyn had not been like her at all. Jackie had witnessed her husband's assassination and gone on to become a symbol of dignity; Carolyn couldn't even cope with paparazzi. Ed Klein thinks that had she lived longer, Jackie would have seen through Carolyn before it was too late. "Jackie was a shrewd judge of character," wrote Klein, "and would have seen Carolyn Bessette for what she was—a flirtatious, seductive, psychologically unstable young woman who had set her cap for the Prince of Camelot. Jackie would have been gravely alarmed that in a marriage to such a woman, John would inevitably come to harm."

6

GOLD-PLATED GODMOTHER:
The Duchess of Windsor

*A*n aspiring fortune hunter should be a student of history—not just enough art history to sound vaguely knowledgeable when buying a Renoir for the boudoir, but the history of the gold-plated godmothers who have gone before her and whose stories light the path: the Duchess of Windsor, the most daring of them all, the Mrs. Simpson from Baltimore who set her cap for a crown and became instead the most famous duchess in the world. For a fortune hunter in training, studying the lives of the paragons is like Napoléon poring over the maneuvers of other military geniuses. No university offers a course in Fortune Hunting 101, but we don't need one—we've got inspirational biographies of the godmothers instead. There is much to be learned from their campaigns. What were their special strategies? What kinds of mistakes did they make? Did they find happiness in their Midas marriages? And, the $64 million question: Can a really nice person succeed in this line of work?

The Duchess of Windsor is a fortune hunter who did everything right until she began doing everything wrong. She did not fail to make King Edward VIII fall in love with her—she made him love her too much, and he refused to be king unless she could be crowned queen.

She would have made a strange queen of England. She grew up shabby genteel, as Southerners call it. Her roots were old Maryland and

Virginia, but her parents were practically penniless. The combination gave her the kind of scrappy, clawing eagerness for not just the good things of life but the very best: it reminded those who met her of the social-climbing Becky Sharp of *Vanity Fair.* Teackle Warfield, her sickly father, and Alice Montague, her vivacious mother, were married in an Episcopal rector's parlor. There were no flowers, guests, or organ music. The wedding date was November 19, 1895. Wallis moved up the date by five months: the future Duchess of Windsor was born on June 19, 1896, seven months after her parents wed. She was named Bessie Wallis Warfield. Because of his tuberculosis, Teackle saw only a photograph of his daughter. He died shortly after she was born.

Alice Warfield was forced to move into the house of her domineering mother-in-law, Anna Emory Warfield. The older Mrs. Warfield wore widow's weeds, though her husband had been dead for two decades. Anna Warfield presided over a dignified house on Baltimore's East Preston Street, and Wallis would have warm memories of it for the rest of her life, perhaps because it was an oasis of relative tranquility in chaos. Solomon Davies Warfield—Uncle Sol—a well-to-do bachelor who also lived at East Preston Street, reluctantly provided financial help for Alice and Wallis. Since his donations varied from month to month, they actually added to their sense of uncertainty. When Solomon became infatuated with Alice, Alice and Wallis moved to a double room in the run-down Brexton Residential Hotel.

One of the rumors about her past that most upset the Duchess of Windsor was that her mother had run a boardinghouse. This undoubtedly came from their sojourn in a suite of rooms in the Preston Apartment House, a move up from the Brexton. Alice supplemented their meager income by renting rooms to relatives. She also hit upon the idea of providing home-cooked dinners for the other residents (Wallis helped serve), but since her taste ran to prime rib, crab cakes, and terrapin, this experiment put her in debt. Wallis would put the best face on the venture, gamely describing it as "the finest dining club in Baltimore history."

Alice eventually had a suitor. Fat, badly educated, and fond of alcohol but having a modest inheritance, John Freeman Rasin whiled away his days smoking cigars. "Free" was from a fairly established family, leading Baltimoreans to joke, "Nothing is wrong with his background, but his foreground is *awful!*" Ten-year-old Wallis objected in vain to the marriage. He gave Wallis a French bulldog that she named Billy, and she remembered her stepfather never "hitting a lick of work."

She grew up knowing that she was always the poorest girl at the dance, though her mother's sewing skills ensured that she would always be immaculately turned out. "Here," wrote biographer Michael Bloch, "was the root of her ambition—a desire to avenge early struggles, to prove herself in the eyes of rich and snobbish cousins, to restore herself to a social and material level that, in her heart, she felt to be rightfully hers."

Wallis attended the prestigious Arundell School for Girls and Burrland summer camp, run by the legendary Miss Charlotte Noland, later the famous headmistress of Foxcroft. After Arundell came Oldfields in Glencoe, Maryland, an expensive boarding school—really a finishing school. Wallis made her debut at the Bachelors Cotillon (it is misspelled on purpose), Baltimore's best.

After her debut, Wallis went to visit a relative in Pensacola, Florida, and soon wrote home that she had met "the world's most fascinating aviator." Earl Winfield Spencer was a lieutenant and a graduate of the U.S. Naval Academy—he ranked 115th in a class of 131 but had been popular. "Two facts were in the back of my mind: I was a burden on my mother and I was in love," she noted many years later. They were married almost immediately, on November 8, 1916, in Christ Episcopal Church in Baltimore.

On their honeymoon to White Sulphur Springs, a resort in West Virginia, Wallis discovered that she had married a drunk. Win Spencer was also insanely jealous, and he tied Wallis to the bed or locked her in the bathroom. Still, as a naval officer's wife, Wallis, who always wanted to know the right people, made many new friends. When Win was stationed in San Diego, she became friendly with diplomat Benjamin Thaw, who was married to Consuelo Morgan, one of the glamorous Morgan sisters. The others were Thelma, Lady Furness, and Gloria Vanderbilt.

Wallis had made a bad marriage in a day when ladies simply did not get divorces. Her announcement that she planned to divorce Win Spencer left her family reeling from the disgrace. Nevertheless, the couple separated in 1921. Wallis moved to Washington, D.C., where she lived for six years and had a fling with an Argentine diplomat, Felipe Espil. When Wallis asked Espil to get her invited to a society hostess's house, he replied, "I can't ask Mrs. Townsend to invite my mistress! *Ça ne se fait pas!*" Wallis gave Spencer a last chance, reuniting with him in Hong Kong, where he was serving as commander of a gunboat. It would later be said that in the Orient Wallis learned sexual skills with which to beguile a king, one of the many strange rumors that would follow her.

She returned to the United States, and her divorce from Win Spencer was granted on December 10, 1927. An old school chum, Mary Kirk, introduced her to Ernest Simpson, a half-English and half-American businessman. He lived in London. The aptly named Ernest was eight years her senior, a Harvard dropout who proudly belonged to the prestigious Coldstream Guards. Ernest wore the mustache and bowler hat and carried the rolled umbrella associated with the Guards. "I am very fond of him, and he is kind, which will be a contrast," Wallis wrote. "Also, 32 doesn't seem so young when you see all the really fresh youthful faces one has to compete against." Like Wallis, Ernest was recently divorced. They married on July 21, 1928, in a London registry office. Simpson's father owned a successful ship brokerage firm with offices in London and New York.

The Simpson marriage brought Wallis the financial stability she craved. For the first time in her life, she had the means to buy antiques and have a cook, a Scottish maid, and a part-time lady's maid. She hired Syrie Maugham, the fashionable decorator and former wife of the novelist Somerset Maugham, to help her with the couple's flat at 5 Bryanston Court. Mrs. Simpson soon became known as a hostess who eschewed the stuffy or dull in favor of the sparkling.

Consuelo Morgan Thaw, Wallis's old friend from her San Diego days, was supposed to chaperone a house party in Melton Mowbray, Leicestershire. It was in 1930 or 1931. Consuelo's sister Thelma, Lady Furness, was the mistress of the Prince of Wales. A chaperone was required for the sake of propriety. Needed elsewhere, Consuelo turned to Wallis and Ernest. When the big day came, Wallis had a terrible cold. She nursed her cold and played cards with the prince but, by her account, exchanged few words with him. Of course, she was not immune to what the historian J. H. Plumb called Prince Edward's "foolish, harlequin charm." On that first meeting, Wallis "judged the Prince an altogether charming and remote figure, not quite part of the workaday world—a figure whose opportunities and behavior were regulated by laws different from those to which the rest of us responded." "You Americans lost something when you dispensed with the British monarchy," Ernest told Wallis.

In *A King's Story,* the Duke of Windsor's autobiography, Edward gave Wallis a bigger speaking role in that first meeting. It was cold, and the prince mentioned that she must miss the central heating of her native land:

> A mocking light came into her eyes. "I am sorry, Sir," she said, "but you have disappointed me."
>
> "In what way?"
>
> "Every American woman who comes to your country is always asked that same question. I had hoped for something more original from the Prince of Wales."
>
> I moved away . . . but the echoes of the passage lingered.

Could such a conversation really have taken place? If so, it was a shockingly bold way to address a member of the royal family. True or false, that is how Edward recorded it.

After the house party, Wallis began to follow the prince's activities in the newspapers, with, as she would admit in her autobiography, "more than a casual interest." There had never been a more golden prince than Edward Albert Christian George Andrew Patrick David, with his golden hair and limpid Hanoverian eyes, with his love of dancing at London nightclubs, with his ability to wear clothes like no other man alive. "Every woman who saw that sad little face felt she had just the shoulder for him to cry on," said Freda Dudley Ward, the first important love of his life. Freda Dudley Ward and Thelma Furness were both married women. In fact, Prince Edward seemed to gravitate toward other men's wives.

A smart fortune hunter befriends the women who might introduce her to the men. Lady Furness was to prove invaluable—inadvertently. Wallis and the prince next saw each other and exchanged pleasantries at a party Lady Furness gave in her Grosvenor Square residence. "She did not have the chic she has since cultivated," Furness later recalled. "She was not beautiful; in fact, she was not even pretty. But she had a distinct charm and a sharp sense of humor."

Although Wallis professed to find England's hierarchical social structure "something of a joke," she was delighted to be presented at court, a ritual carrying immense social cachet. To be presented, Wallis had to provide divorce papers from the Virginia court proving that she was the injured party. Wallis was impressed "to the point of awe" with the grandeur as she came forward to curtsy first to King George V, then to Queen Mary. As the royal family walked out in a slow procession, Wallis chanced to hear a casual remark the Prince of Wales made to his uncle the Duke of Connaught. "Uncle Arthur, something ought to be done about the lights," he said. "They make all the women look ghastly." After the presentations, Thelma Furness held a small party, and the Simpsons were asked to drop in. The prince commented admiringly on Wallis's gown. "But, sir, I understood that you thought we all looked ghastly." Startled, Prince Edward then smiled. It was another one of those saucy replies royals never heard from any but their intimates.

He left soon after the conversation—royalty has the prerogative of leaving a party first. The Simpsons stayed only a few moments longer and were surprised to see him standing by his car, engaged in conversation with an aide. When he dashed forward to offer a ride, they accepted with alacrity. "Chatting easily and obviously in high spirits," Edward told them about his country place, Fort Belvedere—always called simply the Fort— of which he was proud and where he was to spend the night. As the prince helped Wallis from his car, she invited him up for a drink. Declining, he said that he had been told that their flat was "charming" and asked permission to call at a later date.

"That is how it all began," Wallis wrote, "to lead in five short years to a terrible conclusion of which I had not and could not have had the slightest intimation." Wallis was soon planning to have the prince over for cocktails, "but you have to work up to those things gradually and of course through Thelma," she wrote to her aunt, Bessie Merryman. But he made the next move.

Out of the blue, the Simpsons received an invitation to a house party at the Fort. It was early in 1932. Built for a son of George II and enlarged for George IV when he was Prince of Wales, the Fort was, in the words of Lady Diana Cooper, "an enchanting folly." For Wallis, the Fort would always be "the most romantic house I have ever known." Writing about it as a woman in her sixties brought "a lump in my throat." As the Simpson car halted in the drive, the Prince of Wales came outside to greet his guests. Thelma Furness waited for them inside. The Simpsons couldn't have failed to be impressed with the cozy elegance of the pine-paneled octagonal drawing room, with its Chippendale furniture, baby grand piano, and Canalettos. One surprise: when Wallis, dressed for dinner, entered the drawing room, she found the prince busily working on a large piece of needlepoint. Queen Mary taught all her children to do needlepoint. He coached Wallis at Red Dog, a card game, and when she began winning, said with a smile, "I don't think you need any more instruction from me. I'd better look after myself." "It was the first notice he had taken of me that could be described as other than a formality," Wallis wrote. The Simpsons were sporadically invited to tea and several weekend parties at the Fort. "Isn't it a scream!" Wallis wrote to Aunt Bessie.

When Wallis sailed for America on the RMS *Mauritania,* the prince sent her a bon voyage cable. She was consequently accorded all sorts of special treatment. On the return trip she used her celebrity to get a better cabin. The Prince of Wales began to drop in unannounced at the Bryanston Court flat, frequently staying for dinner. Sometimes he didn't leave until four in the morning. Thelma Furness continued to regard Wallis as a dear friend, one who could amuse the prince. It may have been her suggestion that the Prince of Wales throw a surprise thirty-seventh-birthday party for Wallis—she was two years older than Edward—at Quaglino's, the society restaurant. He gave her an orchid plant as a "pezzy."

Looking to reciprocate the royal hospitality, Wallis invited Edward to a Fourth of July party at Bryanston Court to celebrate his ancestor's loss of the colonies. She served classical American dishes such as fried chicken, grilled lobster, black bean soup, and raspberry soufflé (he requested the recipe). Thelma Furness was one of the ten guests. Though Thelma continued to be regarded as Prince Edward's mistress, Wallis, with Ernest in tow, now spent weekends at the Fort and went to London nightclubs with the prince.

There's one thing a smart woman never says to the fortune hunter: "Darling, won't you look after Freddy or Billy or Bobby Rich while I am out of town?" The hapless Thelma Furness not only chose to make what the author Michael Thornton has described as an "ill-advised departure in January 1934," to America, where her sister Gloria Vanderbilt was involved in a custody battle, but compounded the fatal mistake over a pre-departure lunch at the Ritz with Wallis. According to Thelma's version, Wallis brought up the subject of her imminent departure, saying, "Oh, Thelma, the little man is going to be so lonely," to which Thelma replied, "Well, dear, you look after him while I'm away. See that he doesn't get into any mischief."

In the duchess's memoirs, it is Thelma who broached the subject, saying over coffee, "I'm afraid the Prince is going to be lonely. Wallis, won't you look after him?"

While Thelma was away, Edward hosted a party at the Dorchester Hotel. As Edward and Wallis sat quietly at a table, he began talking about his duties and his ideas about the role he envisioned for a more up-to-date monarchy when he became king. "But I am boring you," he said. "On the contrary, I couldn't be more interested. Please, please go on," replied the enthralled Wallis, who, like most fortune hunters, was an excellent listener. "Wallis, you're the only woman who's ever been interested in my job," said the prince.

The prince was now at Bryanston Court "most of the time," and when he was not there, he was "telephoning two or three times a day," Wallis wrote Aunt Bessie Merryman. Wallis took care to dismiss rumors about her position. "It's all gossip," Wallis wrote. "I'm not in the habit of stealing my girlfriends' beaux."

Thelma Furness returned to England in late March. "Something had happened between her and the Prince," Wallis would innocently observe. That something was Wallis. Thelma had also been courted by Prince Aly Khan, the rich and notorious playboy, both in New York and on the ship returning to England. Wallis probably knew about this and might have alerted Edward. Thelma, however, sensed the real source of the threat and went to Bryanston Court to talk to Wallis. "Thelma, I think he likes me. He may be fond of me. But, if you mean by 'keen' that he is in love with me, the answer is definitely 'no,'" Wallis said. The phone rang as they were speaking, and Wallis chastised the maid for the interruption. "But, madam, it's His Royal Highness," the maid said. Wallis excused herself to take the call, and Lady Furness heard the words "Thelma is here," but no more.

A few days later the full import of what had happened in her absence sank in when both women were at the Fort. Wallis did something unheard-of: she publicly corrected the table manners of the heir to the throne. The prince had picked up a lettuce leaf with his fingers, and as Thelma "watched in horror," Wallis administered a playful slap of the royal hand and ordered him to use his fork. Far from being offended, Edward was obviously pleased. "Wallis looked straight back at me," Thelma remembered. "I knew then that she had looked after him exceedingly well. That one cold, defiant glance had told me the entire story." Thelma left early the next morning.

Wallis quickly took over running the three residences of Prince Edward: the Fort, York House, and St. James's Palace. She knew that even a royal prince likes to be fussed over, and she also knew, as most American girls of her day did, that food is not irrelevant when pursuing a man, be he heir to a throne or a self-made millionaire. She planned menus—the prince had been impressed that she knew how to make sauces and personally oversaw the preparation of food at Bryanston Court. The royal servants were not pleased. The butler at York House made his displeasure clear and lost his job. Another butler who apparently happened onto the couple by the pool said, "My sovereign painting a woman's toenails. It was a bit much . . . I gave notice at once."

Like any good fortune hunter, Wallis set about to find out what was lacking in her man's life and then fill that void. Wallis's intuition told her something very important about the prince: he wanted to be bossed around by a woman. Freda Dudley Ward, his first mistress, knew this but did not act on it. "I could have dominated him," she said. "I could have done anything with him! Love bewitched him. He made himself a slave of whomever he loved and became totally dependent on her. It was his nature; he was a masochist. He *liked* being humbled, degraded. He *begged* for it."

Wallis gave him what he wanted. One night at the opera Mrs. Simpson rebuked the prince for having a cigar in his pocket. "It doesn't look very pretty," she said sternly. "One has only to visualize Mrs. Keppel [the mistress of Edward VII] pulling at the King's cigar, and ordering him about to realize how little Mrs. Simpson knew about English ways," observed Frances Donaldson. But Edward VIII wasn't Edward VII, and he loved being dominated by Mrs. Simpson. She could give him something that no English girl, born to look up to the monarch, could. Lady Diana Cooper was horrified when Wallis ripped her gown on a chair, and Edward (by then King Edward VIII), got down on all fours to repair the damage. Wallis was irritable with him. But he loved it. Wallis treated Edward "as a man first, as a Prince second," Dudley Forwood, a royal equerry, told biographer Greg King. That may well have been the secret of her success.

Thelma's trip to America provided the opportunity for one turning point in the relationship, and a cruise provided the second. It was one of the couple's first excursions without Ernest—he grumpily begged off, citing business obligations. Wallis's aunt Bessie went along as chaperone. The *Rosaura,* a yacht owned by Lord Moyne, was barely seaworthy, and the atmosphere was not improved by the presence of Lord Moyne's terrifying pet monkey. Yet for the prince and Wallis, there was magic. He wore shorts and sandals even when they went ashore, much to the chagrin of his aides. Wallis and David—the name he was called by family and friends—strolled alone on romantic beaches. "Perhaps it was during those evenings off the Spanish coast that we crossed the line that marks the boundary between friendship and love," she recalled. Traveling with the Prince of Wales was intoxicating. In a revealing passage in her autobiography, *The Heart Has Its Reasons* (an odd title for somebody as calculating as Wallis), she explained:

> Over and beyond the charm of his personality and the warmth of his manner, he was the open sesame to a new and glittering world that excited me as nothing in my life had ever done before. . . . Trains were held; yachts materialized; the best suites in the finest hotels were flung open; airplanes stood waiting. What impressed me most of all was how all this could be brought to pass without apparent effort: the assumption that this was the natural order of things, that nothing could ever possibly go awry.

Wallis had done everything right so far, but she was about to overreach. Unlike the discreet Mrs. Keppel, who knew what being a royal mistress meant, Wallis began to glory in her position, flaunting the magnificent jewelry that the besotted prince bestowed upon her. There were disturbing rumors that some of his gifts were crown jewels or had belonged to his grandmother, Queen Alexandra. Diarist Chips Channon noticed that Wallis had changed in two months' time from "a nice, quiet, well-bred mouse of a woman," to somebody quite grand: "She already has the air of a personage who walks into a room as though she almost expected to be curtsied to."

She was not alone in her delusions. The prince wanted to marry her.

It was unthinkable—not because Wallis was an American but because she was a divorcée. The Church of England, of which the sovereign is titular head, did not permit divorced people to remarry in the church. Still, Wallis did "undeniably" flirt with the notion of being queen of England, a historian wrote. As one author on royal subjects has said, she imagined that she and Edward would transform the monarchy of stodgy King George VI and Queen Mary into something more modern and that she and Edward would be "an impossibly chic king and queen, a royal version of William Powell and Myrna Loy in *The Thin Man* films." She also realized that the prince could change his mind about her, and she seemed eager to solidify her position in London society before that happened. She apparently was able to envision a future as a royal favorite still married to Ernest. (A joke in a revue called *The Unimportance of Being Ernest* had Ernest saying that he regretted that he had but one wife to give for his country.) It was the sort of arrangement that had worked for the royals in the past. Edward wanted something else, however, and Wallis didn't know enough about the English Constitution to know that the man for whom yachts and trains were held had limited power in other ways. A fortune hunter is daring, but she is also a realist, and Wallis's realism deserted her. She wanted to be queen of England. She had no clue of the nature of the impediments.

Although terrified of his father, Edward had possibly planned to speak to George V about marrying Wallis. He was willing to renounce the throne. George V took a dim view of his oldest son, predicting, "After I am dead the boy will ruin himself in twelve months." Edward never managed to broach the subject with his father. In January 1936 Edward received a letter from Queen Mary informing him that the king's physician, Lord Dawson, was concerned about the state of the king's health. Five days later the world heard Lord Dawson's famous bulletin: "The King's life is moving peacefully to its close." Wallis, attending a movie put on by a charity, heard the bulletin. Shortly after midnight Edward called her and said, "It's over." "It was only when I hung up that I realized that David was now King," she wrote.

At the opening of the new reign, few people really believed that the king was planning to marry Mrs. Simpson, according to Frances Donaldson—and, of course, only a handful of people in England were even aware of the affair. The English press observed a respectful blackout. As Wallis watched her lover proclaimed King Edward VIII by the Garter

King of Arms, she reflected that things would be different now. "Wallis," said Edward, who had broken precedent by watching himself proclaimed king—by tradition, kings did not observe this ceremony, but he joined her in St. James's Palace as a spectator to the ancient ritual—"there will be a difference, of course. But nothing can ever change my feelings towards you."

Wallis did not yet realize what was at stake. "I am implored on all sides not to leave him as he is so dependent on me and I am considered to be a *good* influence believe it or not and right in the things I try to influence him to do," she wrote Aunt Bessie. Those imploring her never imagined that she could even consider being queen. Wallis asked Aunt Bessie to send her a family history. "I hope the histories of the [Warfields and Montagues] will stand up against these 1066 families here," she wrote.

From the moment the prince became king, Wallis and Edward—they called themselves WE in their letters—seemed to live in a dream world. Their love letters are filled with almost childlike fantasy—the letter writer who referred to himself as "a boy" was King Edward VIII of England. "Hurry here please as a boy is longing to see a girl," he wrote on mourning paper. In the letters, a boy is always holding a girl tight. There were made-up words: *eanum, ooh,* and *pooky demus.* The beloved cairn terriers were collectively "the babies" and individually "your eanum dawg." In a note that purports to be from "your loving babies," His Majesty the King wrote, "Please say you are sorry for that impulsive gesture of throwing us so far into David's shoes. Please put us back on our chairs where we belong and David says for you to come down quickly." Edward admitted in a letter before he became king that he was "just going mad at the mere thought (let alone knowing) that you are alone with Ernest."

The king seemed to believe that he could launch Wallis in society and make her acceptable to the establishment as his queen. Even if this were possible, it would have required keeping the public in the dark about Mrs. Simpson until the time was right. A second cruise, on *Nahlin,* shipwrecked the plan. It was to be a glorious holiday. "It was to give the girl from Baltimore a foretaste of the excitement, the adulation, and the luxury that go with a royal progress abroad," J. Bryan III and Charles J. V. Murphy wrote in *The Windsor Story.* The king and Wallis strolled arm in arm in public and made a quasi-official call on Kemal Atatürk of Turkey. Another time hundreds of peasants in a small fishing village came out with torches to serenade them. "It's all for you—because these simple people believe a King is in love with you," Edward told her. The writer Michael Thornton has called the voyage of *Nahlin* "the most bizarre royal odyssey since the Prince Regent's wife, Caroline of Brunswick, cavorted through Europe with her Italian chamberlain, Bartolomeo Bergami."

The mood of the voyage changed abruptly after Edward and Wallis paid a friendly call on his relative King George of the Hellenes, whose mistress was present at lunch. Back on the *Nahlin,* the clueless Wallis asked why the king didn't just marry his mistress. There was an awkward silence. It was explained that a king couldn't marry a commoner who already had a husband. Edward's buoyancy suddenly vanished. But Lady Diana Cooper, one of the guests, felt that Wallis now wanted out of her predicament anyway: "Wallis is wearing very, very badly. Her commonness and Becky Sharpishness irritate. . . . The truth is she's bored stiff by him, and her picking on him and her coldness towards him, far from policy, are irritation and boredom."

While the English press still maintained silence, the world press went crazy over the *Nahlin.* Even a distressed Queen Mary heard about it. The publicity surrounding the cruise destroyed any hope of Wallis's divorce being granted before anybody realized the king wanted to marry her. Wallis went so far as to suggest, in a letter from Paris, where she had stopped off on the way back to England, that they end the affair.

Wallis was still acting as if she might become queen of England, however. It had been the custom of King George V to invite leading people of the realm, including the archbishop of Canterbury, cabinet ministers, and admirals, to Balmoral in the Highlands for the final days of August. Instead of doing this, Edward, at Mrs. Simpson's suggestion, removed these stodgy personages from his guest list, inviting instead more stimulating guests. Wallis was installed as hostess in the house so beloved by Queen Victoria. The Duchess of York, the king's sister-in-law, pointedly brushed past Mrs. Simpson and her extended hand, saying she had come to see the king. Wallis did introduce the American triple-decker club sandwich, which the servants detested.

Edward hated stuffy events that intruded on what he thought of as his private life. When new buildings at the Royal Infirmary in nearby Aberdeen, were being dedicated, he refused to attend on the grounds that he was still in mourning. He dispatched the Duke of York in his place, not explaining why one brother was in mourning and one wasn't. On the day of the ceremony the king was spotted meeting Mrs. Simpson's train. On the ride to Balmoral, the car broke down and Wallis cajoled the irritated monarch into a better mood by singing, "King's Cross! King's Cross! The King is Cross! The King is Cross!"

Soon Edward and Wallis would have much to make them cross. Ernest arranged to meet the king at York House and tell him that Wallis had to choose between them. He really seemed to want to know if the king's intentions toward Wallis were honorable. "Do you really think I would be crowned without Wallis at my side?" Edward said. With the coronation set for May 12 the next year, he did not have much time to manage his two projects: Wallis's divorce and her social promotion. Since the king was in official mourning, the second was difficult. Two top London hostesses, Emerald Cunard and Sibyl Colefax, took up the job of introducing Wallis to important people at dinner parties.

Though the English press refrained from writing about the king's romance, Mrs. Simpson's divorce proceedings meant that it was just a matter of time before the story broke in England. Prime Minister Stanley Baldwin and Cosmo Gordon Lang, the archbishop of Canterbury, an old friend of George V's who, as primate of England, would preside at the coronation, were bitterly opposed to Edward's marrying Mrs. Simpson. Lang balked at the thought of having to crown a divorced woman queen of England. At ten in the morning on October 20, Baldwin called on the king, by appointment, at the Fort. It must have been a trying morning. "May I have a whisky and soda, please?" Baldwin said upon entering the Fort. Once fortified, Baldwin begged the king to ask Mrs. Simpson to halt her divorce proceedings. Edward took the position that the divorce was her business, and she should not be penalized merely because she was the king's friend.

Edward felt that he had to be the one to introduce Wallis to Baldwin. "It's got to be done," he told Wallis. "Sooner or later my Prime Minister must meet my future wife." "David, you mustn't talk this way," she responded. "The idea is impossible. They'd never let you." He told her he would "manage it somehow."

Meanwhile, Wallis planned the menu for the dinner. Lord and Lady Mountbatten and the Charles Lindberghs—he was the hero of the moment—were also invited to dinner at St. James's Palace. "Mrs. Simpson has stolen the Fairy Prince," Lucy Baldwin noted after observing the king and Mrs. Simpson together. Ernest was also present, the last time the Simpsons appeared in public together. In July the ever gentlemanly Ernest took a woman to the Hôtel de Paris at Bray, making sure they were observed and thus allowing Wallis to divorce him on the grounds of adultery.

Anticipating Diana, Princess of Wales, Wallis throughout the crisis seemed to regard the matter as a public relations issue. Almost until the bitter end, Wallis felt that the king could save himself—and her—by making a broadcast to the nation. She had been much impressed on her visits to the United States by President Franklin Roosevelt's "fireside chats," and she was certain Edward could do something similar. The king agreed and began to work on a speech. It informed the people of his realm that he loved Mrs. Simpson—her divorce was not yet final, and such a public admission might have indicated collusion and made the granting of a divorce problematic—and planned to marry her. She must have a status "befitting my wife," but he was not adamant that she be queen. After the address he would leave the country for a while, to allow the people to come to a conclusion "calmly and quietly, but without undue delay." Edward did not reveal how the people were to make known their collective judgment. But it didn't matter. Unlike a prince or princess of Wales, who would go on TV without telling anyone in advance, a king is a constitutional figure who requires permission from the government to address the nation, which Stanley Baldwin had no intention of giving.

Like Edward, Wallis was living in a world of delusions. "Nothing in her character, background, or experience enabled her to see beyond hotel suites and yachts to the realities of power or to recognize that the choice was not between being Queen of England or the King's mistress but between being mistress of the King and exile," wrote Frances Donaldson. It wasn't entirely her fault. Edward, reared in the shadow of the throne, should have been the realistic partner. He encouraged Wallis to think that she could be queen of England, though, wrote Donaldson, "whether he believed it himself no one will ever know."

Wallis knew nothing about the English Constitution. In her grab for the biggest of all prizes, she had abandoned that flinty realism that is the hallmark of the successful fortune hunter. And, more than Edward, she was the one making the decisions. "I feared for him," said Walter Monckton, his lawyer, in a biography by J. Bryan III and J. V. Murphy. "Outwardly, he remained charming, polite. But he was like a man who had taken leave of the real world. He was seldom alone at this stage. One or another of us was always rushing in and out. And whenever anything arose requiring a decision, or some action, he would hurry off to ask what *she* thought. She was his reality. We were shadows." Of course, for her part, Mrs. Simpson was depending on a man who was so besotted with love that he would do anything to marry her. She lost control of him because of the intensity of her hold over him.

Ironically, what brought matters to a head and doomed them was an attempt to find a compromise. Sometime in November Esmond Harmsworth, son of Lord Rothermere, owner of the *Daily Mail,* invited Mrs. Simpson to lunch at Claridge's (the locale of the luncheon has been disputed) and put forth the idea of a morganatic marriage. A morganatic marriage would allow her to marry the king but not become queen. Like Camilla, Duchess of Cornwall, Wallis would have a grand title—perhaps Duchess of Lancaster, since one of Edward's minor titles was Duke of Lancaster. Her children would not be in the line of succession. The English royal house frowned on such marriages, but Wallis embraced Harmsworth's proposal. She had returned to a moment of apparent realism but lacked the constitutional knowledge to see where this compromise would take them. Frances Donaldson believes that Wallis accepted it as a way out of a situation into which she and the king had "so lightheartedly drifted." Edward did not care for the idea, but Wallis persuaded him. "Mrs. Simpson," he told an adviser, "preferred the morganatic proposal over any other solution to the problem." In asking for a morganatic marriage, the king had put his head in a noose, or on the chopping block. Such a union changed the line of succession, and it therefore required legislation and approval of the dominions. The dominions said no. The cabinet also voted against the morganatic proposal. On the same day as the cabinet vote, an adviser to the king learned that *The Times* of London would have an editorial on the "King's Matter" in the morning—the provincial press had already broken the embargo.

The press reaction shocked Wallis, who now realized the enormity of what she had done. One of the harshest editorials came from the *Daily Telegraph,* an establishment paper: "Queen Mary, Queen Alexandra, Queen Victoria—these have been the Queens of England whom this country and Empire have known for a full century, and they will not tolerate any other or different standard of Queenship." Edward could not shield her any longer. He tried to hide the papers, but she had already read them. Edward decided to send her abroad while he tried to straighten out the mess at home. Lord Perry Brownlow, a friend of the king's, agreed to accompany her to Villa Lou Viei, the home of Katherine and Herman Rogers, old friends of Wallis, in Cannes. Brownlow wanted to avert a crisis, and he tried to persuade Wallis to leave Edward for good; she halfheartedly issued a statement saying she would do so—a public statement approved by the king, who had no intention of letting her go but wanted her to look like the injured party. Pursued by the press, Wallis was still blindly issuing orders to the king. At one stop she left her notes behind in a telephone booth—it would be obvious to anyone who found them who this "Mr. James" who should not quit was. (A chivalrous soul found the notes and saved Wallis from further embarrassment.)

But one can't fail to be shocked at the hectoring advice she sent the king, tottering traumatically on his throne. Still unable to believe he couldn't save the day with a radio address, she wrote, "I can't support you, unless you tell the country of the two proposals." (She was referring to the morganatic proposal and either abdication or the alternative idea that he could go abroad while his subjects made up their minds.)

She begged him not to abdicate and, always more interested in herself than in him, complained that abdication "is going to put me in the wrong light to the entire world." But it was too late. Edward had signed the papers. When Edward read his immortal speech renouncing the throne because he "found it impossible to carry the heavy burden of responsibility and to discharge my duties as King as I would wish to do without the help and support of the woman I love," the woman he loved was at that moment listening on the radio and sobbing at Lou Viei. It had taken Edward VIII eleven months to make a mess, one less than his father predicted. He would now be known as the Duke of Windsor, a title bestowed by the new king, George VI.

Could there have been a different denouement to the abdication crisis? She had been perfect in the first phase of her romance, the phase in which she made him love her. But in the climacteric moment, the world's greatest fortune hunter found that she simply cared too much what people thought of her, a most un-fortune-hunter-like trait. The king had settled money on her and she had a truly fabulous collection of jewels, including possibly

Queen Alexandra's, yet she could not bring herself to escape the entanglement. How can you jilt a man willing to renounce his kingdom for love and not look bad? And, of course, she was right: Wherever she went, the king would follow her. No, there was probably not a better ending. She did not quite grasp at first that they would be outcasts as far as the royal family was concerned. She browbeat the duke to prevail upon the king to grant her the style of Her Royal Highness; the duke was HRH the Duke of Windsor, but Wallis was merely Her Grace the Duchess of Windsor, a noble (but not a royal) duchess. The king refused to make his brother's wife a royal duchess. The royal family also refused to announce the engagement. "It is all a great pity because I loathe being undignified and also of joining the countless titles that roam around Europe meaning nothing," Wallis wrote Edward, who had to avoid seeing her until her divorce was final. When they married, on June 3, 1937, it was in the château of a slightly disreputable businessman, with no member of the royal family present. A renegade Anglican clergyman officiated, as Cosmo Lang steadfastly refused to allow any of his priests to marry divorced couples. On one of the rare occasions she had been in the same room as King George V—at a palace function Edward had insisted she attend and at which Queen Mary shook her hand before she realized who she was—Wallis perceived royalty for what it partly is, "the glittering tip of an iceberg that extended down into unseen depth I could never plumb, depth filled with icy menace for such as me."

She had—to change the metaphor—been, like Princess Diana, in some ways a latter-day Wallis Windsor, smashed against the rock that was royalty. But Wallis Windsor was tougher than Diana. When her bitter bargain was struck, Wallis Windsor kept her end of it. "You have no idea how hard it is to live out a great romance," she once said. But unlike Princess Diana, she was forced to live out the story long after it ceased to be a fairy tale. Sent into involuntary exile, never again to enjoy their romantic Fort, the duke and duchess lived in grand houses in Paris (though neither spoke fluent French), with escapes to New York, where they had an apartment in the Waldorf Towers and where—unlike in Europe, where their status was always suspect—society embraced them wholeheartedly.

No, of course she did not love him as he loved her—who could? She lived imprisoned by the love of a man about whom there were only two really interesting facts—that he was king of England and that he renounced his throne for the woman he loved. Beyond this and his harlequin charm, he wasn't really a very interesting man. Caroline Blackwood noted that one of the duke's favorite songs had the line "I want to be a bee in your bonnet"—perhaps a more refined age's version of Prince Charles's later desire to be Camilla Parker Bowles's tampon—and until he died he was a bee in the duchess's bonnet. His eyes always followed her around the room, and he was bereft if she stayed away from him for too long when she shopped or had her hair done. Perhaps for the duke, the fairly tale did not end.

She once said she'd rather be the mistress of a king than the wife of the governor of the Bahamas, where Edward was sent during World War II, the perfect job for an exile: remote, and since it was wartime, the governor of the Bahamas could not expect his wife to be received at court, as was the custom for His Majesty's governors. But she threw herself into being president of the Red Cross in the Bahamas and remodeling the governor's house. "Aren't I a busy bee," she said, adding wistfully, "but I wish it were somewhere else."

She bullied him and fussed over him and, most of all, tried to recreate his old life. No matter how she decorated or planned the menus, it would—could only—be a shadow of his life as king. Long after the ill will of the royal family had ceased to be raw, Prince Charles visited them in Paris. It was a depressing ménage:

"I drove up with no small degree of anticipation as to what I would find in the Bois de Boulogne," Charles confided to his diary, "and upon entering the house I found footmen and pages wearing identical scarlet and black uniforms to the ones ours wear at home. It was rather pathetic seeing that. . . . The Duchess appeared from among a host of the most dreadful American guests I have ever seen. The look of incredulity on their faces was a study and most of them were thoroughly tight. . . . The whole thing seemed so tragic—the existence, the people and the atmosphere—that I was relieved to escape it after 45 minutes and drive round Paris by night."

And yet if his first wife had had half the fortitude of Wallis Windsor, she might have been queen of England and a better helpmeet to Charles. In Wallis and Edward's thirty-five-year marriage, she strayed once, very publicly and very painfully for the duke. She had an affair in the 1950s with Jimmy Donahue, a Woolworth heir and flagrant homosexual. For a while they were a strange trio: the aging duke, his wife on the verge of sixty, and Donahue. A man of singular cruelty, Donahue played a practical joke on the duke and duchess that must have been the low point of their exile. On New Year's Eve 1952, with the coronation of Edward's niece looming, Donahue found two party hats and crowned Edward and Wallis at the nightclub El Morocco. "People laughed, but it was a tragic, awful moment," wrote Donahue's biographer, Christopher Wilson. Even her affair with Donohue did not break the Wallis spell over Edward, and, after it was over, both the duke and duchess, great pretenders that they were, acted as if it had never happened. They continued their travels between Paris and New York. England was still off-limits without permission.

The Duke of Windsor died on May 28, 1972, in their house in Paris. In life he had yearned for his family to recognize Wallis, and now, as his widow, she spent the night in Buckingham Palace. It was the first time she had been there since before the abdication. A photographer captured the grief-stricken and confused duchess looking out the window during the Trooping the Colour, a ritual which that year included a brief tribute to the former monarch. The onetime Edward VIII was buried with royal honors, with the Garter King of Arms proclaiming all his various titles in Frogmore, the royal cemetery at Windsor, a little way away from his parents, closer to minor royals, as befitted the man who had given it all up. "The Duchess of Windsor is now completely gaga," the photographer Cecil Beaton, a guest at the funeral, wrote in his diary.

The final phase of the duchess's life was not pretty. With no family except the royal family, who spurned her, she lived alone in the house in the Bois de Boulogne, sequestered by a strange and eccentric lawyer, Maître Suzanne Blum, who had gained complete control over the duchess and had a curious reverence, perhaps love, for her charge. Wallis lived in her bedroom, and there were rumors that she had shriveled and her skin had turned black, according to Caroline Blackwood's macabre book about the duchess's last years. Maître Blum stoutly insisted that the duchess was still beautiful, though she did not permit anyone to see her. Clearly demented, Maître Blum babbled on to Blackwood: "The Duchess is magnificent! *Elle parle, elle parle.* She never stops speaking! She is beautiful like you cannot imagine. She is covered with flowers!"

The Duchess of Windsor died on April 24, 1986, and her funeral was held in St. George's Chapel, Windsor, with Queen Elizabeth II, who but for Wallis Simpson would not have been queen, and other members of the royal family in attendance.

7

GOLD-PLATED GODMOTHERS:
Jackie O and Pamela Harriman

Although one had become a revered widow with a place in the history books assured at an age when the other was still an international playgirl with a more than slightly *risqué* reputation, Jacqueline Kennedy Onassis and Pamela Digby Churchill Hayward Harriman share the distinction of being the two junior members of the trinity of great twentieth-century fortune hunters (the first being the Duchess of Windsor).

Some may balk at the notion of Jacqueline Kennedy as a fortune hunter. She served the nation with dignity, leaving behind the indelible image of the young wife of an assassinated president walking in his funeral procession. Yet she was as much a fortune hunter as Pamela Harriman. Both came from privileged backgrounds, but in both cases there was something missing—and that missing element set them on the path of fortune hunting.

DAUGHTERS OF PRIVILEGE
The Honorable Pamela Beryl Digby was born on March 20, 1920. Her father was Edward Kenelm Digby, a major in the elite Coldstream Guards, the eleventh Baron Digby, who was tapped on the shoulders by Queen

Elizabeth II and made a member of the Order of the Garter, the most exclusive order of chivalry in the world. Like Sir Winston Churchill, Kenelm Digby, a World War I hero, received the honor because of service to his country. The child's mother, Lady Pamela—called Pansy because her face was said to resemble this delicate flower—was the daughter of the second Baron Aberdare, a coal-mining magnate.

The Digby family seat was Minterne Magna in Dorset, set in a sea of green and unspoiled villages. The house dated from the fourteenth century. Minterne Magna did not house one of Europe's great art collections, as Lady Diana Spencer's Althorp did. But it was a large, comfortable house with picturesque gables and portraits of Digbys past that sat on a 15,000-acre estate.

Lord and Lady Digby are inevitably described as caricatures of England's country aristocracy, which, of course, they were. Lord Digby, known as Carnation (he grew them and always wore one) was master of the hunt as befitted his rank as justice of the peace. Lady Digby was socially ambitious but dull. A friend of Pamela's told Sally Bedell Smith, author of *Reflected Glory*, an authorized biography of Harriman, that when Lady Digby left a room, "you heaved a sigh of relief." It was a solid, self-assured but provincial society, its ethos perhaps best summed up in King George V's famous remark, "I don't like abroad, [and] I've been there."

The Digbys, however, were forced by crippling estate taxes to live abroad for several years, in Australia, where Lord Digby was a military adviser to the governor-general. Lady Digby one day promised little Pamela a ride in her car. When the car stalled, Pamela said a man would come to help them. Lady Digby said that there was no man nearby; mother and daughter were arguing when, as if by magic, a policeman appeared and started the car. Pamela's biographers have made much of the incident as foreshadowing an older Pamela who always knew a man would be the solution to her problems.

After the Digbys returned to England, Pamela led the life of a child of her station, foxhunting with the adults and being taught at home by a governess. Lord Digby, fonder of Pamela's sister Sheila, was distant with Pamela, but Lady Digby doted on her. Pamela was a pretty little girl, outgoing and plump but hardly with the looks to set the world on fire. Lady Digby saw her eldest daughter as a great beauty, destined for great things in life.

Despite the bucolic tranquillity leavened by house parties and harvest dances, Pamela found county life lacking in excitement—it was stodgy and boring. A magazine profile of Pamela after she had become famous would tell how as a ten-year-old, walking her dog in the hills above Minterne Magna, she would look down on her ancestral house and vow, "When I am grown up, I will leave this place and live in a city." She had a taste of the city when Lady Digby rented a house in London's aristocratic Mayfair for Pamela's debutante season, in 1938. Chubby Pamela Digby's wardrobe was not as stylish as that of other debs—Lady Digby was very thrifty—and she seems to have attracted no serious suitors. But she was unhappy when the end of the season meant a return to the country.

In contrast, Jacqueline Bouvier, nine years younger than Pamela Digby, did not consider her upbringing provincial or dull. Jackie Bouvier divided her time between a duplex at 740 Park Avenue, one of New York City's ritziest addresses (her maternal grandfather owned the building), and East Hampton, a posh little town on Long Island. Jackie learned to ride, with her mother, Janet Lee Bouvier, a passionate and expert horse-woman who demanded perfection, as her instructor.

Whereas Lord and Lady Digby were well suited to each other, Janet Bouvier and John Vernou Bouvier were horribly mismatched. Jack Bouvier, who was known as "Black Jack," was a dandy who loved and attracted beautiful women. He took care to maintain a perfect tan in all seasons and worked out relentlessly at the Yale Club. A family legend has it that Black Jack gambled away all the couple's money and took up with Doris Duke, the tobacco heiress, on their honeymoon. Janet Lee Bouvier was a straight arrow, prim and proper. They were both Catholics, a rarity in high society then, which might have been a factor in their marriage. Janet's father, New York developer Jim Lee, also had something that Jack Bouvier liked very much and never seemed able to acquire: money.

Janet, who embellished her family tree, claiming kin to the Lees of Virginia, was determined that Jackie and younger daughter Lee succeed socially. She required them to speak French at the dinner table, would not drive them to horse shows because driving oneself was *déclassé*. When angry, she slapped her daughters. Jackie preferred her father, who adored his girls, Jackie more so than Lee, to the point of obsession. Once when Jackie called to say she'd changed her hairdo, he left the Yale Club early to see her and reassure himself about the haircut. "He was divine and dashing," a relative told Sarah Bradford, "and you could see where [Jackie] got some of her mischievous sense of humor."

When Black Jack would visit Jackie at Miss Porter's, the girls' school in Farmington, Connecticut—where she was known as one of the brainiest girls—they would play a game. Jackie would point to a classmate's mother, and Black Jack would tell his daughter whether he had "had" her or not. No doubt drawing on personal knowledge, Black Jack instilled in his daughters the notion that all men were "rats." He urged them to play hard to get. But Jackie also learned early on how to employ the Look. She knew to talk about the man, not herself, and to make him feel brilliant.

The Bouvier marriage continued to deteriorate. In 1936 Janet asked for a legal separation. The couple reconciled, but by 1940 it was all over, and Jackie got to read about her parents' divorce in the *New York Daily Mirror*: SOCIETY BROKER SUED FOR DIVORCE. The article included unsavory details about Black Jack's womanizing. Jackie put on a brave face, refusing to allow anybody to see her pain. When Black Jack contested the divorce, Janet went to Nevada for a quickie divorce.

While in Nevada, Janet made friends with another woman seeking a divorce, Esther Auchincloss Nash. She introduced Janet to her brother, Hugh Dudley Auchincloss—Hughdie. He was a large, stuffy man who had been twice divorced. The writer Gore Vidal, Hughdie's stepson when he was married to Nina Vidal Auchincloss, described Hughdie as "a magnum of chloroform." But he had the right WASP social credentials—and he was very rich. Janet and Hughdie were married in 1942, when Jackie was a seventh-grader. Janet finally had money—real money. "She loved money because it made perfection possible," Edward Klein wrote. "She was interested in the surface of things—the hem stitching on her Porthault sheets, the punctuality of the service at her meals, the drape of her ball gowns."

The Auchincloss marriage moved Janet and her Bouvier daughters, Jackie and Lee, several notches up in society. Jackie was fond of Uncle Hughdie—or Unk, as she called him—and not unaware of the advantage of the connection. Like Pamela, Jackie was a debutante—but a successful one. She had a tea dance at Hamersmith Farm, the Auchincloss estate in Newport, Rhode Island. The socially powerful Cholly Knickerbocker column, written by Igor Cassini, proclaimed Jackie "Queen Debutante of the Year 1947." Cassini glowingly described her as "a regal brunette who has classic features and the daintiness of Dresden porcelain. She has poise, is soft-spoken and intelligent, everything the leading debutante should be."

The debutante of the year was a bit of an outsider, however: a Catholic in a Protestant social world, for starters. But something else was missing, and that something was paramount in Jackie's worldview. The missing element was money. Jackie Bouvier might be growing up as an Auchincloss, living at Merrywood, an Auchincloss estate on the Potomac, but she was a poor relation—a brilliant, spectacular girl, but almost penniless. Even if Janet had not been obsessed with what she referred to as "real money," Jackie would have grown up deeply aware of the importance of money. "She grew up terrified of not having money—probably induced by Janet," the historian Arthur Schlesinger Jr. told Sarah Bradford.

RANDOLPH AND JACK

Although Pamela Digby was no poor relation, the Digbys were not nearly as rich as many of the great families of England. Pamela would need money—and plenty of it—to lead the life to which she aspired, a life of excitement, good talk, power, and, as she vowed on a hill in Dorset, a life lived in the city, far away from the boredom of Minterne Magna.

Through one of her debutante friends, Pamala was introduced to the Leeds Castle set, where the half-American Lady Baillie entertained the most fascinating people. Her guest list ranged from King Edward VIII to American movie stars such as Clark Gable and Jimmy Stewart to politicians. Pamela loved the gossip and high-level talk. She also enjoyed flirting with the men. "She was very plump and so bosomy we all called her 'the dairy maid,'" another debutante who frequented Leeds told Christopher Ogden, author of *Life of the Party*, a biography in which Pamela initially agreed to participate and then abruptly withdrew. "She wore high heels and tossed her bottom around. We thought she was quite outrageous. She was known as hot stuff, a very sexy young thing."

When Britain declared war on Germany on September 3, 1939, Pamela made a decision: She would find a job in London. One of the politicians she'd met at Leeds Castle helped her get a job in the Foreign Office, translating French (which she had studied with a Swiss governess and as a teenager in France). She rented an apartment from Lady Mary Dunn, daughter of the Earl of Rosslyn. Lady Mary Dunn was a friend of

Randolph Churchill, the dissolute son of Sir Winston, England's wartime prime minister. Lady Mary told a friend that she knew a "red-headed tart" who would be perfect for Randolph.

When Randolph subsequently asked Lady Mary to dinner, she suggested Pam Digby. On the phone he asked Pam what she looked like. "Red-headed and rather fat, but Mummy says puppy fat disappears," she replied, according to Randolph's cousin and biographer, Anita Leslie in *Cousin Randolph*. She joined him at Quaglino's, the restaurant near Piccadilly where Prince Edward threw a birthday party for Wallis Simpson.

Although Randolph entertained Pam as part of a group and paid almost no attention to her, he asked her to dinner the next night. She accepted. Randolph wanted to ensure that the Churchill name continued if he was killed, and he had a habit of asking girls he hardly knew to marry him. He asked Pam, and she accepted on the spot. Randolph was no prize, but his name would be Pamela's greatest asset for the rest of her life.

Pamela's friends (and some of Randolph's) mobilized to talk her out of marrying him. Pamela was told that he was obnoxious, a drunk, a gambler, and a spoiled brat. She confided to one friend that if the marriage proved untenable, she could always get a divorce. Whatever happened, she would be a Churchill.

Pamela and Randolph Churchill were married on October 4, 1939, at St. John's Church in London's Smith Square. The guests carried gas masks in case of an air raid. Randolph was in uniform and Pamela wore a blue dress with a matching fur-trimmed coat. The bride and groom left the church under the raised swords of members of the Fourth Hussars, to which Randolph belonged. On their honeymoon, four days at the estate of Lord Brownlow, the man who had escorted Wallis Simpson to France during the abdication crisis, Randolph read from Gibbon's *Decline and Fall of the Roman Empire* when they were in bed, as reported in *Reflected Glory*.

Randolph was soon away on his military duties. Pamela lived at the prime minister's residence at 10 Downing Street or at Chequers, the country residence. She and Winston Churchill hit it off immediately, and it was Sir Winston, not Randolph, who would further her career as an insider in wartime London. She was eager to have a tie to the Churchills that would continue if she and Randolph were unable to stick it out, and pregnancy soon gave her what would be an enduring connection to Sir Winston. When the Churchills repaired to a bomb shelter with bunk beds, the prime minister slept on the bunk above Pamela's—Pamela joked that she had a Churchill inside of her and another above her.

Both Sir Winston and Clementine Churchill adored Pamela, who played cards with the prime minister and tried to comfort him during the darkest days. Pamela was impressed when Clementine told her that she had dedicated her life totally to her husband. Pamela would bear this in mind for later, when she was married to somebody more worthy than Randolph. For now, Pamela was near the center of power. She was aware of who was who. "You didn't see any corporals or sergeants around Pam," CBS correspondent Larry LeSueur told Christopher Ogden.

As Randolph's gambling debts mounted, Pamela realized that the marriage could not last. But, of course, Randolph was not as important to Pamela as her father-in-law. Pamela by now knew that her warm relationship with Sir Winston, bolstered by the birth of baby Winston, could withstand divorce.

Without giving much thought to Randolph or their doomed marriage, Pamela was ready to make the most of wartime and London. Pamela soon began an affair with Averell Harriman, the American diplomat, serving as his guide to the ins and outs of politics in England. Pamela found the humorless and pompous American, son of E. H. Harriman, who had built a great fortune in railroads, the handsomest man she'd ever seen. Lord Beaverbrook, the newspaper owner and Winston Churchill intimate, regarded the plugged-in Pamela as a "catalyst on a hot tin roof" and was only too happy to promote the affair. It was felt that Harriman was essential to getting the United States into the war. Pam took a place in the country with Harriman's daughter by a previous marriage, Kathleen, the perfect beard.

When Harriman became sick from drinking contaminated water, Pamela helped nurse him back to health, foreshadowing what was to come decades later. The affair, which may actually have helped Anglo-U.S. relations, ended painlessly when Harriman left London in 1943—indeed, many assumed that Pam was already involved with John Hay Whitney, another American millionaire. According to Sally Bedell Smith, both men gave Pamela stipends. Harriman's would continue for three decades—a knowledgeable banker told the *Tatler* magazine that it was around $20,000 a year.

After Harriman, Pamela fell in love with Edward R. Murrow, whose

"This is London" broadcasts for CBS made him one of the most sought-after Americans in London. Christopher Ogden believes when one affair played out, Pamela was able to move to the next without undue turmoil. The Murrow affair would prove an exception. Ed, who was married, was handsome and women fell in love with him. A socialist, Murrow was still drawn by Pamela's glittering connections, most especially to the prime minister. Pamela was in love and wanted Ed's wife, Janet, to know about the affair—she was always leaving something, a glove or a book, where Janet would find it. Pamela's relationship with Murrow was unresolved when the war ended. She followed him to America, but he chose his wife and baby son instead. Pamela was brokenhearted.

Like Pamela Digby, Jacqueline Bouvier would marry the son of a political family. Unlike Pamela, with her allowance from the Digbys, Jackie could not afford to make a mistake. Pamela had the luxury of being able to make a spur-of-the-moment decision to marry Randolph Churchill. Jackie Bouvier had to choose more carefully.

Janet Auchincloss was worried about whom Jackie would marry upon her graduation from George Washington University (to which she had transferred from Vassar). Jackie had fallen in love with Jack Marquand, son of the author of *The Late George Apley,* during her junior year abroad in Paris (where she hung out at the Eléphant Blanc, the favorite pickup spot of the Marquis de Portago). Marquand wasn't rich enough for Janet, and she slapped Jackie for refusing to stop seeing him.

Jackie was briefly engaged to a Yale graduate named John Husted. He had impeccable WASP credentials but wasn't rich enough for Janet. Jackie also had doubts, which she conveyed to the novelist Louis Auchincloss, a nephew of her stepfather. They met by chance at a Georgetown cocktail party. Auchincloss's novel *Sybil,* about a woman married to a rich bore, had just been published. "My fate is to become Sybil Bouvier Husted, the dreary little girl in your novel," Jackie told him. "And it suddenly came over me," Auchincloss later told an interviewer, "that she would never marry Husted. What no one seemed to have known about Jackie at the time was that she wasn't this soft little passive, girlish person. She was tough. Very tough. The major motivation in Jackie's life was money. She loved money. And I had the curious conviction that this whole evening wasn't real, that her whole destiny would be different. A very different destiny."

Charles Bartlett, the well-connected bureau chief for the *Chattanooga Times,* and his wife, Martha, wanted to get Jackie and Jack Kennedy, the handsome young senator from Massachusetts, together. The dinner party took place at the Bartlett house in Georgetown. At the time, Jack Kennedy was aware that he had to settle down and have a family if he wanted to take a serious run at the White House. It was fine to be an eligible bachelor in the Senate, but that would not do for a presidential candidate. Joseph Kennedy, his father, was growing increasingly eager for his son to find the right Catholic girl to further his political career. Jack asked Jackie out for a drink after the Bartlett dinner, but she had a date for later in the evening. When Kennedy escorted Jackie to her car, the date was already ensconced there. He had been walking in Georgetown and, spotting Jackie's car, decided to wait for her inside her convertible.

Although Jack, who'd been impressed with Jackie's brains when they played charades the night before, called her the next day, he didn't ask her out immediately. Jackie went to New York to work for *Vogue* magazine. Upset that there were few men working for *Vogue,* Janet prevailed upon Hughdie to ask Frank Waldrop, editor of the *Washington Times-Herald,* to give Jackie a job. Jackie was hired as the newspaper's inquiring photographer—she would ask people on the street questions and snap their pictures. Jack Kennedy engaged in a spasmodic courtship, but Jackie seemed unable to close the deal. When Jackie was asked to go to England to cover the coronation of Queen Elizabeth, she didn't want to go. This time it was Janet who told her to play hard to get. "If you're so much in love with Jack Kennedy that you don't want to leave him, I should think he would be much more likely to find out how he felt about you if you were seeing other people and doing exciting things instead of sitting here waiting for the phone to ring." As the son of Ambassador Joseph P. Kennedy, reckoned to be the twelfth-richest man in the United States by one magazine, Jack was acceptable to Janet.

While Jackie was on the way home from London, Janet's phone rang, and it was Jack asking which flight Jackie was on. He was going to meet the plane, when it landed in Boston. Janet took it as a sign that Jack was finally serious about the relationship and would ask Jackie to marry him. She was right. Jack took Jackie to Hyannis Port to meet the Kennedy family.

Jackie was flabbergasted by Jack's rowdy siblings, but she got on well with the ambassador. He told her in great detail about his affair with the actress Gloria Swanson. The debutante of the year was not shocked. Despite her breathy little-girl voice and patrician manner, Jackie always adored men who were rough but dynamic—if they had money. Joe Kennedy admired Jackie as a woman who could bring a certain aristocratic polish to the marriage. Jack Marquand, however, was shocked when Jackie said she planned to marry Kennedy. In his book *Palimpsest,* Gore Vidal described the scene:

> He was appalled and said, "You can't marry that . . . that *mick!*" She was coolly to the point: "He has money and you don't." When he asked her how she would like to be married to a *politician* (she had grown up in Washington and had no illusions about the breed) she said, "Of course, I don't like politics and he's a lot older than I am, but life will always be interesting with him, and then there's the money."
>
> "What on earth is going to become of you in that awful world?"
>
> "Read," she said, "the newspapers."

The wedding took place on September 12, 1953, in a Catholic church in Newport, with the reception at Hammersmith Farm. It was a Kennedy extravaganza, with hordes of people and press, to Janet's chagrin. But the one thing that went seriously wrong was Janet's doing, not the Kennedy family's. Janet set up circumstances in which Black Jack Bouvier was almost certain to get drunk before the wedding. At the last minute Janet banished the stumbling Black Jack and substituted Hughdie, who gave the bride away. Jackie never forgave her mother for this treachery.

A DIVORCEE IN PARIS, A WIFE IN WASHINGTON

At an age when Jacqueline Kennedy was getting her bearings as a senator's wife, Pamela Harriman was not leading quite as respectable a life. She had a fling with Aly Khan, the incredibly wealthy descendant of the prophet Muhammad and the most notorious playboy in the world. She also met young John Kennedy in Ireland. Pamela accompanied him on a search for his Irish relatives, whom Pamela pronounced "just like *Tobacco Road*." Kennedy never forgave her.

Pamela moved to Paris in 1948, partly to escape England but also to be near Gianni Agnelli, the Italian Fiat heir, with whom she had begun an affair. He was as gorgeous as Apollo and as rich as Croesus. Paris, close enough to his factory in Turin, seemed the ideal place for them to see each other. It was felt that a Churchill could not live in Italy, which had been England's enemy. Rich as Agnelli was, he was awed by the Churchill connection and impressed when Pam introduced him to the Duke of Marlborough, a Churchill, at Blenheim Palace. Agnelli bought her a magnificent apartment with a view of the Seine and the Eiffel Tower. An organized housekeeper, Pamela created an atmosphere designed to make Gianni happy and comfortable. A famously attentive hostess, both in Paris and in his house at Cap d'Antibes, Pamela always made sure that there were extra bathing suits and suntan lotions; the meals were perfect. In this she resembled the Duchess of Windsor.

Randolph had been an opportunity for Pamela, but she was very much in love with Agnelli. She was hurt by his playing around with other women, which he made no attempt to hide. One night, when Agnelli and Pamela were staying at La Leopolda, his villa, Pamela walked in on Agnelli and much younger woman. Pamela threw a tantrum and ordered them to leave.

Agnelli was always a horrible driver, but that night he was even worse—he had been drinking heavily and using cocaine. He smashed his car into a truck carrying four butchers. Nobody was seriously hurt, except for Agnelli, whose jaw was broken, and his right leg was crushed. Pamela arrived at the hospital and got busy—a fortune hunter is a nonpareil nurse. Pamela had Gianni loaded into an ambulance and took him to a more sophisticated hospital in Cannes. Surgery was necessary to save Agnelli's damaged leg, but because he had been taking cocaine, the hospital refused to administer anesthesia. Pamela went into the operating room and covered his eyes during the operation.

During Agnelli's painful recuperation, Pamela was a dedicated nurse—but she made one big mistake. She asked Agnelli's sister Susanna to come help her. Susanna was as determined to prevent Pam from marrying her brother as Pam was to marry him. When Susanna told Pamela that Agnelli would never marry a Protestant, Pamela took instruction and was received into the Catholic Church. Pamela and Agnelli continued their affair for several years. When the annulment of her marriage to Randolph was granted, she knew that it would be a turning point—Agnelli would marry her, or it would be the end of the affair. Agnelli liked Pam, but he had decided that he was not going to marry her. Pamela was brokenhearted, but she had to find someone to replace Agnelli. "Love, fascination with, and focus on, a single man became secondary considerations behind taking care of her own needs," wrote one biographer. "There was nothing happenstance about the selection process. She targeted and chose carefully."

She next chose the banker Elie de Rothschild, scion of Europe's most famous financial family, Europe's premier Jewish family, and owner of the Château Lafite-Rothschild winery. A member of the horse cavalry in World War II, he had been captured by the Germans. Imprisoned in Colditz, he had married Liliane Fould-Springer, a childhood friend and a member of another leading financial family, by proxy. Elie demanded perfection. A story in the *International Herald Tribune* quoted him on how he liked to be treated in a hotel: "I want my bath to run hot in two minutes flat. I don't want to hear the plumbing noises. I want a good bed and pillows. I want my breakfast right away. I want good croissants. I want people to be polite to me, and I don't want to hear their side of the story."

Pamela was the perfect concierge to make his life run smoothly. Pamela had turned her attention to Elie while Liliane was pregnant. She cosseted Elie, who loved being waited on hand and foot, especially by a Churchill. She began learning more about furniture and art to keep up with Elie. She learned that preservationists who worked at Versailles could be hired to help her with restoring the fine pieces she bought. Pamela's interests always echoed those of her man of the moment. Sally Bedell Smith recounts that people in Paris knew that Pamela had a new man when instead of answering the phone, "*Pronto,* Pam," she took to saying, "*Ici,* Pam." Soon it was common knowledge that Pam was involved with Elie. The Duke of Windsor, seated next to Liliane at dinner one night, asked which Rothschild was having an affair with Pam Churchill. "My husband," she answered.

It would be a mistake to think of Pamela's time in Paris as carefree. She became more sophisticated and she had the best of everything, but she worked hard for her privileged life. Jacqueline Kennedy led a very different kind of life in Washington. She was finding out what kinds of sacrifices were required to be married to Jack Kennedy.

On their wedding trip to Acapulco, Jackie wrote a poem about Jack. Sarah Bradford regards it as evidence that Jackie was romantically in love with Jack. "He thought with his feet most firm on the ground / But his heart and his dreams were not earth bound," the young bride wrote. She would allude to his (and to some extent her) essential difference from many of the young men she had dated before Jack Kennedy, pillars of the Protestant ascendancy: "He would call New England his place and his creed / But part he was an alien breed / Of a breed that had laughed on the Irish hills. . . ." But it was on the honeymoon that Jackie got a preview of what was to come. The last leg of their wedding trip was to California, where Jack left his bride alone to go visit old friends—guys, not gals, but still a strange thing to do on a honeymoon.

Evelyn Lincoln, Jack's secretary on Capitol Hill, gave Jackie high marks for learning to cope with crowds and taking pains to learn about political shoptalk, though nothing in her background had prepared her for either. The Kennedys eventually bought a Federal house on 3307 N Street in Georgetown. Jackie hired Sister Parish, the society decorator, to help her. Wildly extravagant, Jackie redid the living room three times in the first four months they lived there. Jack found Jackie's spending maddening, causing him to remark that she had grown up with "too much status and not enough quo." Still, she was improving Jack's wardrobe and finding nice historical analogies to touch up his speeches.

Unlike Pamela, Jackie did not become a mother quickly. She had a miscarriage, a stillborn baby, and two children born prematurely who lived only briefly. She felt her loss all the more intensely as the other Kennedy women were famously prolific. She was seven months pregnant when Jack persuaded her to go with him to the Democratic National Convention in Chicago. It was 1956, and he was trying to get the second spot on the ticket. After the convention Kennedy set off on a recuperative Mediterranean cruise with his brother Teddy and Florida senator George Smathers. Jackie was expecting the baby in September, and it appeared that Jack would be back for the birth. On August 23 Jackie was rushed to the hospital, and a stillborn baby girl was delivered by cesarean section. Bobby Kennedy broke the news to his sister-in-law. It took three days to find Jack. SENATOR KENNEDY, ON SAILING TRIP, UNAWARE OF WIFE'S MIS-

CARRIAGE, a headline in *The Washington Post* noted. Jack reluctantly cut short his trip when Joe Kennedy told him he'd better get home quickly if he ever expected another woman to vote for him. Jackie retaliated by going on an extended European tour, visiting her sister in England. For the time being, she was too angry to swallow her feelings and behave like a forgiving fortune hunter willing to let her man get away with anything.

Jack had been sexually promiscuous as a bachelor and he did not stop just because he was married. He had taken his cue from his father, who cheated on Rose Kennedy throughout their marriage. Jack did not wait long to begin cheating on his own wife. In one particularly shocking incident, Jack Kennedy enlisted his father-in-law to help him. Acting almost as Jack's procurer, Black Jack asked a woman to wait around after a dinner to meet Jack.

Joe Kennedy didn't want the marriage to fail, because it would have meant the end of Jack's political career. But the story that Joe Kennedy gave Jackie a million dollars to stay in the marriage is just a myth, according to Jan Pottker, biographer of Jackie and Janet. In fact, Janet worried incessantly about what would happen to Jackie if the marriage broke up. "She has no children and no estate! What will she do?" Janet said again and again. But that was about to change. On November 27, 1957, Caroline Bouvier Kennedy was born at the Cornell University Medical Center in New York. Jack was present, and he was the one who brought the new baby to her mother. "I'll always remember the sweet expression on his face and sort of a smile," recalled Janet Auchincloss. Jackie was ecstatic.

A month after Caroline was born, a profile of Jack in *Time* magazine acknowledged what most people in Washington already knew—that he was running for the presidential nomination in 1960. Jackie had never learned to love politics, but she wanted to make Jack happy. She gave teas for the ladies of the press corps, a group that she was not especially fond of, and posed for pictures in numerous magazines. In one, her secretary was cropped out of the picture, giving the impression that Mrs. Kennedy undertook the daunting task of answering her mail unassisted. She was pregnant with John F. Kennedy Jr., who would be born shortly before his father was sworn in as president of the United States.

When John Kennedy was inaugurated on a cold, snowy day in 1961, the nation had never seen such a dashing couple move into the White House. A contrast to the Eisenhowers, the Kennedys personified youth, vigor, and style. It was a talent that abounds in fortune hunters that helped Jackie leave her mark on the White House—a skill for creating a beautiful environment. In this instance it was the nation's house she beautified. The White House Jacqueline Kennedy found was in sad shape. She determined that she would make it a grand house once again. She called upon Sister Parish, Jayne Wrightsman, and Henry Francis du Pont, whose home Winterthur contained perhaps the largest collection of American antiques in the world, to help her. Jackie also enlisted a man she had to hide from the public—Stéphane Boudin, the French decorator who had been in charge of restoring the Grand Trianon at Versailles and the Empress Joséphine's Malmaison (and who, by the way, had also helped Pamela Harriman with her apartment in Paris). But it would be inappropriate to have a Frenchman involved in restoring the president's house. "Jackie wanted to do Versailles in America," Oleg Cassini, the dress designer, said. As lady of the most important house in the world, Jackie had begun to see herself as a historical figure. She admired Madame de Maintenon, Louis XIV's mistress, and Madame de Récamier, who presided over a sparkling salon.

Jacqueline Kennedy still had to put up with her husband's sexual adventures, which, if anything, increased in White House. It's unclear how much she knew, but she knew quite a bit. She once said to a male admirer of hers that she didn't care how many women Jack slept with as long as he knew it was wrong, "and I think he does now."

Still, despite the pressures of living in the White House, JFK's brief tenure there may have been the high point of their marriage. Kennedy came to appreciate even more what an asset his wife was. During their celebrated trip to Paris, Jackie stirred mass adulation and captivated President Charles de Gaulle with her fluency in French and her knowledge of things French. De Gaulle wasn't the only president impressed with Mrs. Kennedy. "I do not think it at all inappropriate to introduce myself to this audience," JFK said at a press conference. "I am the man who accompanied Jacqueline Kennedy to Paris, and I have enjoyed it."

Kennedy was also more attentive during Jackie's last pregnancy. When Jackie was rushed to Otis Air Force Base several weeks before she was scheduled to have the baby, Jack was frantic to get there to be with his wife. The child, who was given the name Patrick Bouvier Kennedy, weighed only four pounds, one ounce, and it was obvious that he would struggle to live. When Patrick was flown to Children's Hospital in Boston, his father went with him, and the president of the United States sat by his tiny son's crib in a surgical gown. He was holding the baby's hand when he died. This time the death of their baby brought the Kennedys together. Like many fortune hunters, Jackie Kennedy ended up with a marriage that seemed—at last—to be filled with love. "Jack and Jackie were very close after Patrick's death," William Walton, an artist and friend of the Kennedys, told author Ralph G. Martin. "She hung onto him and he held her in his arms—something nobody ever saw at any other time because they were very private people."

After Patrick's death, Jackie was more willing to campaign with Jack, who was facing reelection the next year. On November 21, the morning they were going to Dallas, little John wanted to go to the airport to see his parents off. When his nanny hesitated, the president of the United States dressed his small son. The next day the president and the First Lady were riding in an open limousine in Dallas. The motorcade was about to go into a tunnel and the president was about to wave when the first shot hit him. It was not fatal. The next shot went through the lower part of Kennedy's brain. "My God, what are they doing? My God, they've killed Jack, they've killed my husband, Jack, Jack!" Jackie cried.

Jacqueline Kennedy was thirty-four years old when her husband was assassinated. She returned to Washington with his body and a horrific memory. She refused to change from the pink suit with his blood splattered on the front. She could not stop repeating over and over the grotesque details of his death as her family and friends gathered. Yet she was able to draw on something inside herself and pull herself together to plan and put on a flawless funeral. She knew instinctively that the model for her husband's funeral would be Lincoln's. Jacqueline Kennedy, heavily veiled and holding the hands of her two children, was grace itself. She had given her husband and her nation something that would never be forgotten.

Although Jacqueline Kennedy is arguably the most famous First Lady in history, she did the job on her own terms. She once bragged that she'd been given a list of ninety-nine things she'd have to do as First Lady and she hadn't done any of them. She was absent from the White House so much that one newscaster took to closing his broadcast with the words, "Good night, Mrs. Kennedy, wherever you are." She was different from her fellow fortune hunters in this one respect. Pamela Harriman would have done the job on her husband's terms, and she would have been faithfully at the White House to receive minor foreign or domestic leaders whom Jackie coldly put in the PBO (polite brush-off) category. Pamela, with her preference for generals over foot soldiers, wouldn't have cared any more than Jackie about minor visitors, but she would have been unwilling to risk offending the president. But Jackie had had Black Jack Bouvier as a father. His relative impecuniousness coupled with an appreciation for the finer things of life helped make Jackie Bouvier a fortune hunter, but his sense that she was the most wonderful girl in the world made her more independent-minded than most fortune hunters. She and Jack had a far from perfect marriage, but now she had one overriding goal besides her children—to guard the legacy of her husband.

LELAND AND ARI

If Jacqueline Kennedy's life with JFK ended in the most dramatic way possible, the end of Pamela Harriman's affair with Elie de Rothschild was a fade-out. Though Elie thought about marrying Pam, and even discussed the possibility with friends, he ultimately did not want to marry his mistress, even if she happened to be a Churchill. As Pamela neared forty, it became clear that Elie was not going to leave Liliane. "Pamela is not a sulker," noted Christopher Ogden. "She cries when she is hurt, but she does not wallow in self pity. . . . When discouraged, she picks herself up, turns aggressive and seizes the next available opportunity."

When the affair with Elie ended, Pamela, who had always loved Americans, wanted to visit the United States. Pamela's speed in finding her next man provides yet another warning, if one is needed, that you should keep an eye on your husband if he's rich and there is a fortune hunter nearby. It was actually legendary New York socialite Babe Paley who asked Slim Hayward, another renowned socialite, if her husband, Leland Hayward, the Hollywood agent and Broadway producer, might take Pamela to a Broadway play. Paley wanted to distract Pamela from her own husband, CBS founder Bill Paley. With insufficient thought, Slim, who was going to Europe, said yes.

It is not recorded if Pam and Leland, a Princeton dropout whose hits included *South Pacific* and *Mister Roberts,* enjoyed the play, but they ended up in bed that first night. They telephoned Bill Paley to tell him. Still living in Paris, Pamela invited Slim and Lauren Bacall, who was traveling with her, to her apartment. When Pamela casually asked about the state of her marriage, Slim replied that "no marriage is perfect."

Slim's lukewarm reply tipped Pamela that Leland was a prospect. Their courtship moved forward when Leland was in Europe negotiating with the Baroness von Trapp for the rights to *The Sound of Music,* the story of her marriage and her family's escape from Nazi Germany. Leland promised Pam he would marry her. She could wait in Paris, trusting in Leland's promise, or she could move to New York and pursue her goal. She chose the latter. A friend was astounded that both Elie and Gianni showed up to watch Pam pack up her apartment and were very friendly to each other. Most of what she was crating had come from them. Pamela would sell the apartment, a gift from Gianni, for half a million dollars.

While plans to divorce the still-unsuspecting Slim were already afoot, Hayward invited his daughter Brooke to dinner at his favorite New York restaurant, Le Pavillon, to tell her about Pamela. It was Brooke's twenty-second birthday. Brooke wanted to know what Pamela was like. He told her that Pamela was "the greatest courtesan of the twentieth century," a remark that became "the greatest charmer of the twentieth century" in Brooke's book, *Haywire.* Lawyers forced her to make the change. "Father loved the idea that he and all these very rich, powerful and talented men were all sharing her. It energized him. He was part of a club. The Pamela Club," Brooke told biographer Christopher Ogden.

Pamela had followed a crucial rule of fortune hunting: Location matters. She had realized that America was where the boys were, at least the boys who would be willing to marry her. Pamela busied herself placing stickers on the pieces of furniture she wanted from the Hayward household.

Leland had to establish residence in Nevada to get a quick divorce. They were married in Carson City, Nevada, on May 4, 1960. It was his fourth marriage. Like Marylou Whitney, who had also become a fourth wife in Carson City, Pamela set out to make a cozy nest for her man.

On the road with Leland, who traveled to out-of-town theater openings, Pamela cooked chicken hash, a favorite dish of the producer's, on a hot plate in their room. The protean Pamela had reinvented herself again—the chubby debutante, the confidante of the prime minister, the mistress of rich Europeans, was suddenly deeply interested in the theater.

"An opening night is like an election," Pamela told *The New York Times* in 1965. "The tensions, rewards, and disappointments are very much the same." Leland's career, which had been so meteoric, fell into decline after he married Pamela. *The Sound of Music* would be his last big hit.

At home in New York, Pamela devoted herself to taking care of Leland, who loved being cosseted and fussed over and having his favorite meals prepared. Pamela also threw herself into decorating the couple's apartment on the Upper East Side and a country estate called Haywire, which they bought in Yorktown Heights, eighteen minutes away from New York by helicopter. Pamela had helped buy the New York apartment with money earned by selling her apartment in Paris. It was at 1020 Fifth Avenue and had been owned by a Vanderbilt. Stéphane Boudin did some of the plans for the interior redecoration. Leland appreciated the finished product, though he was shocked by the bills.

The only obvious blot in the marriage was Pamela's cool relationship with Hayward's children, Bill and Bridget, who were by no means fond of her. When Margaret Sullavan, their mother, committed suicide, Leland tactlessly sent Pamela, to whom he was not yet married, to inform Brooke. "The last thing I'd asked for was the insinuation of an outsider," Brooke recorded in *Haywire*, "particularly a lady who was working too hard to become my next stepmother." When Bridget subsequently committed suicide and left her trust fund to her father, Pamela (as recalled in Brooke's book) remarked to Brooke that the inheritance "certainly will come in handy at this particular time." When Bill had a girlfriend in Germany, Pamela verbally attacked him for traveling with a woman to whom he was not married. Bill noted the irony, according to Sally Bedell Smith, who also reported that Pamela pointedly suggested to Leland that they leave their Pollock to the Metropolitan Museum of Art after Dennis Hopper, who would marry Brooke, said he liked it. Still, Hayward and Pamela were happy.

If Pamela's moving on after de Rothschild was ready to end the affair was a testament to her innate optimism, Jacqueline Kennedy's survival after having her husband murdered before her eyes was a sign of inner strength. Shortly after Kennedy's funeral, Jackie and her children moved to a temporary refuge, Averell Harriman's Georgetown residence at 3036 N Street (the very house where Pamela would one day reign). Jackie was inconsolable for a while, and not quite as rich as people thought. Jack's estate was estimated at nearly $2 million, which might have sounded like a princely inheritance for many widows but was a pittance for a woman with Jackie's taste. She had an allocation of $50,000 a year from the government, $150,000 a year from a trust in her name, and an additional $50,000 that Bobby Kennedy, to whom she turned for companionship in her grief, had made available from Kennedy funds. She worried about money and was stingy with her staff. She sometimes thought they were pilfering food and was upset when asked to pay overtime. Jackie tried to provide a stable environment for her children, but she was deeply depressed. The papers of a Jesuit priest, the Reverend Richard McSorley, to whom Jackie confided, indicated that she entertained the notion of suicide, though she knew she could not let her children grow up without her. After buying another house in Georgetown, she realized that she didn't want to stay in Washington. After a year of intense grief, she was beginning to think of moving to New York.

New York had always been Jackie's home. She bought a fifteen-room apartment at 1040 Fifth Avenue and eventually started going out with men again. She dated John Warnecke, a handsome ex–football star and prominent architect, and was frequently squired around by the men from her husband's administration, not always with the approbation of the wives of Camelot. Still, Jackie worried about money and yearned for the kind of privacy for herself and her children that only "real money" could buy. The fortune hunter was ready to awaken.

Aristotle Onassis, the Greek shipping magnate, was not unknown to Jackie. Her sister, Lee, had had an affair with Onassis, and he had hosted a cruise on his yacht, the *Christina,* after the death of Patrick Bouvier Kennedy. The president had begged Jackie not to go; he regarded Onassis as "an international pirate." The wild parties that supposedly took place on his yacht would make for bad press with an election looming. But Jackie had gone and been impressed by Onassis's extravagance. Onassis gave her a ruby-and-diamond necklace estimated to be worth $50,000 as a memento of the cruise. When Kennedy was killed, Onassis showed up for the funeral and slept on a sofa in the White House. His devoted mistress of many years was Maria Callas, the opera singer.

Squat and ugly, Aristotle Onassis was the billionaire's version of what has infelicitously been dubbed a star-fucker. He was inordinately proud of rumors that he had bedded Eva Perón, Greta Garbo, and Gloria Swanson.

When Onassis was in New York with Callas in 1964, he decided to give Jackie a call. She invited him to her house for Sunday brunch. Callas insisted that he make sure she was included in the invitation. "Regrettably, there is only one place still available and the invitation is limited to Mr. Onassis," they were told, according to the writer Nicholas Gage's biography of Onassis and Callas. It turned out that all the guests were men. Jackie was acting like a fortune hunter; Callas was not—she should never have asked Ari to make sure she was on the list. Ari began sending Jackie large bunches of roses. "The way Jackie snared him was classic," a friend of Callas's told Gage. "She set a trap for Onassis and caught him. She had very little money after JFK died and debts piled to the ceiling. When she was invited on the cruise by Ari, she saw how he lived and spent money and how he treated her sister Lee. A smart woman can get any man if she makes it her life's goal."

Onassis was back in the United States for Easter, and he graciously flew Jackie and her children to Palm Beach in his private plane. He hid when photographers were present. Jackie made a second cruise on the *Christina* shortly afterward, a leisurely cruise around the Virgin Islands. Maria had been on the yacht, but Ari asked her to leave. Foolishly, she did. Joan Thring, a personal assistant to Rudolf Nureyev, was on the cruise and was ordered to stand next to Jackie whenever they encountered paparazzi so that it wouldn't appear that she was with Ari. Nobody knows when the subject of marriage was broached, but it is not unlikely that it happened on this cruise. "Jackie wanted to marry Onassis more than Onassis wanted to marry Jackie," Dorothy Schiff, former publisher of the *New York Post*, is quoted saying in Jeffrey Potter's *Men, Money & Magic*.

Bobby Kennedy was aghast. He was running for president, and asked Jackie to hold off on any announcement about a marriage until after the election. When Bobby Kennedy was assassinated in Los Angeles's Ambassador Hotel after winning the California primary, she had no reason to maintain secrecy. She also had more reason than ever to marry Onassis— with Bobby's death, she feared for the safety of her children. She was also bitterly angry at America because two people she loved had been killed. Onassis had the money to provide security such as few could.

The notion of the slain president's widow marrying Onassis was shocking to the public. When Doris Lilly, the ladylike gossip columnist, broke the story on *The Merv Griffin Show,* she was booed and hissed at by the audience. She was hit by several viewers, and one woman dug her nails into Lilly's arm as she was leaving the set. "The Queen had abdicated. The Princess was marrying a toad," Sarah Bradford wrote. Back in Virginia, Janet Auchincloss, who had worshipped "real money" so faithfully, had to admit that she was physically repulsed by Ari. Real money or not, she begged her daughter not to marry Onassis.

A fortune hunter must be shameless, and Jackie proved that she was by marrying Onassis in the face of world outrage. The wedding took place on Onassis's private island, Skorpios, on October 20, 1968. With a small band of reporters who'd managed to run the gauntlet of Onassis's security watching, they were married in a small chapel of the Virgin on the island. A bearded Greek Orthodox archimandrite officiated as the bride and groom—Jackie towering above the froglike Ari—wore tiny crowns of flowers, looking absurd. A reporter for the London *Times* noted that Jackie looked drawn and concerned. "Their hands never touched," *The Times* reported. "One observer said, 'It was like a business transaction.'"

One of the myths about Jackie and Ari is that they flew off on their honeymoon on an Olympic airplane that had been specially fitted out for amorous activity. Ari owned the airline—so it would have been possible—but in all probability it wasn't true. Jackie seems to have stayed on Skorpios while her bridegroom flew to Athens to negotiate a deal with George Papadopoulos, one of the colonels who had seized power. But just as Jackie had done what she pleased as First Lady, she would do as Jackie O. She was a fortune hunter in her orientation toward a goal, determination, and shamelessness. But she did not intend to hover around Ari the way Pamela hovered around Leland. She flew to New York after about a month on Skorpios, and for the rest of her marriage to Onassis she would spend much more time in New York than in Greece. Perhaps she figured that allowing Ari to marry her was enough. Her status, after all, was utterly without parallel.

For the first year or so, the couple appeared to be pleased with their marriage, at least in public. Ari frequently traveled to New York, taking her to Elaine's, the celebrated literary hangout, where they were flirtatious with each other. But all was not well. If Leland Hayward's children had conceived a strong dislike for Pamela, it was nothing compared with the violent hatred Onassis's two children, Christina and Alexander, felt for Jackie. They saw her as a gold digger who cared nothing for their father beyond his vast wealth. They could barely stand to mention her name.

Onassis had seen his marriage to the most famous woman in the world as a public relations coup. It went to his head, and he became a megalomaniac, negotiating business deals in an entirely different way, an executive told writer Nicholas Gage. When his business took a turn for the worse, Ari's associates began to talk about a "Jackie jinx."

Ari himself came to embrace the notion of the "Jackie jinx" and to feel that his marital coup had ended up making him the laughingstock of the world. Jackie was always in New York, not with him, and even married to one of the richest men in the world, she spent enough money to shock her husband. In Ari's view, the marriage had become nothing more than "a monthly presentation of bills." He felt that Jackie had duped him. Ari talked to lawyer Roy Cohn about a divorce. There was one thing he didn't want to do: spare Jackie's feelings.

A tragedy intervened. Alexander Onassis, to whom Aristotle hoped to leave his empire, was killed in a plane crash in 1973. Alexander had been a passenger on a test flight for a new Olympic plane, a task for which he had volunteered. As Alexander lay in a hospital, the right temporal lobe of his brain crushed, Ari was distraught. Jackie joined the family at the hospital. In an incredible show of callousness, she asked Fiona Thyssen, to whom Alexander confided everything, if she knew what financial plans Ari had made for her if they divorced. Alexander Onassis was dead shortly after this conversation, and Ari never recovered from the loss.

Jackie must have been quite desperate to make such a faux pas. If Ari divorced Jackie, she would need to get the best deal possible. She had lavish gifts from Onassis and he had given her $2 million when they married. But he was her main source of income. He was a sick man, devastated by loss, and had a series of wills drawn up that would prevent Jackie from becoming a rich woman because of his death. His last will would have given her $100,000 a year for the rest of her life, with $25,000 for each of her children until they reached the age of twenty-one. She would also get a one-fourth share of Skorpis and the *Christina*. At Onassis's behest, the Greek colonels got a law, "Lex Onassis," passed that would have validated a waiver he had forced Jackie to sign in 1972. Before Lex Onassis, waivers signed abroad by Greek nationals were not valid. Everything he did showed the intensity of his hatred for Jackie. But Ari's well-laid plans to hurt her were interrupted by a health crisis.

Ari collapsed in Athens and was flown to Paris, where Jackie joined him. Ari had been suffering from myasthenia gravis, which caused his eyelids to droop (he taped them with Band-Aids), and his general health was deteriorating rapidly. His gallbladder was removed, and Jackie flew back to New York. Ari's friends felt she spent just enough time in Paris to avoid looking cold. She was in New York when she received the call that Aristotle Onassis was dead. It is safe to say that Maria Callas, who had been prohibited from entering the hospital room but talked to the dying Ari on the phone, was far more devastated than was his wife. Onassis was buried on Skorpios, and his funeral offered another opportunity for breathtaking callousness. As the funeral cortege approached the chapel, Ted Kennedy reportedly looked at Christina Onassis and said he wanted to discuss financial arrangements for Jackie.

Christina Onassis was determined to prevent the detested stepmother from benefiting from the marriage. She was cheered on by a large cadre of people who thought Jackie had married Onassis purely for money and hadn't been a good wife. After negotiations, Jackie received $20 million. It was at that point that Onassis's last will surfaced, allowing Jackie's lawyers to go back to the bargaining process and add the $100,000 annual income. She issued a statement shortly after Onassis's death: "Aristotle Onassis rescued me at a moment when my life was engulfed with shadows. He meant a lot to me. He brought me into a world where one could find both happiness and love. We lived through many beautiful experiences together which cannot be forgotten, and for which I will be eternally grateful."

He meant a lot to me. . . . It was not exactly the love affair of the century. But Jackie was about to enter into perhaps the most rewarding period of her life. She was richer for having married Onassis, and probably quite relieved that he was gone.

AVERELL AND MAURICE

Pamela's second marriage had been far happier than Jackie's. She had made Leland Hayward happy, even though his career had been in free fall throughout their marriage, and she seemed to have been happy, too. When Hayward's health began to fail, she was attentive to him. He died on March 18, 1971. However, when her brother, now Lord Digby, read Leland's will Pamela was shocked. He had not changed it since 1948, when he was married to Margaret Sullavan. But it wouldn't have mattered if he

The Duke and Duchess of Windsor on their wedding day. As Edward VIII, he renounced his throne for her. She was devastated that not a single member of the royal family attended their wedding. "You have no idea," she remarked many years later, "how hard it is to live out a great romance." *(Bettmann/Corbis)*

Georgette Mosbacher amid copies of her book *The Feminine Force*. Georgette relied on her feminine force for the courage to get out of her abusive second marriage, to George Barry, president of Fabergé. Next came Texas oilman Robert Mosbacher. Divorced for the third time, Georgette is an entrepreneur, hostess, and fund-raiser in New York. *(Lynn Goldsmith/Corbis)*

Marylou and Cornelius Vanderbilt Whitney. On marrying the famously ill-tempered scion of two grand American families, Marylou vowed, "I am the fourth Mrs. Cornelius Vanderbilt Whitney, and I'll be the last Mrs. Cornelius Vanderbilt Whitney." To the surprise of many, she did it, and, after Whitney's death, married John Hendrickson, thirty-nine years her junior. *(Bettmann/Corbis)*

Carroll Petrie at a garden party hosted by the Museum of Modern Art in 2006. Her first marriage, to the Marquis de Portago, gave the daughter of South Carolina one of the oldest titles in Spain, and her fourth, to ready-to-wear magnate Milton Petrie, made her an enormously rich New York widow. Her daughter calls her Scarlett—as in O'Hara. *(Getty Images)*

Gayfryd Steinberg and Ann Bass share a moment at the American Ballet Theater gala in 1988. Gayfryd married Saul Steinberg so soon—that would be the next day—after her divorce from scandal-ridden New Orleans oilman Norman Johnson that Johnson publicly accused her of bigamy. Ann and Sid Bass were Fort Worth's golden couple before Ann lost Sid Bass to the then Mercedes Kellogg after a roll toss at Blenheim Palace. *(Photo by Marina Garnier)*

Birthday girl Mercedes Bass exits a New York restaurant with social doyennes Annette de la Renta, far left, and Mica Ertegun, and the late Atlantic Records tycoon Ahmet Ertegun. She reportedly broke the news that she was moving on to billionaire Sid Bass to the late diplomat Francis Kellogg, her first husband, with the words, "Good-bye, darling, I'm marrying Sid." *(Photo by Marina Garnier)*

Princess Diana caused the greatest risk for the monarchy since the Duchess of Windsor. She had cold feet the night before her royal wedding and felt "calm, deathly calm. I felt I was the lamb led to the slaughter." Her sisters insisted it was too late to back out because her face was already on the souvenir tea towels.
(© *Graham Tim/Corbis Sygma*)

Jacqueline Kennedy Onassis, wife of the slain president, and Aristotle Onassis appeared happy the first year of their marriage. He provided money and security and she gave him status, but then it turned sour. Onassis died before he could divorce her. *(Bettmann/Corbis)*

Pamela Harriman's starter marriage was to Randolph Churchill, the son of Sir Winston. She subsequently went from being the mistress of rich men in London and Paris to marrying wealthy diplomat Averell Harriman. She became a citizen of the U.S. and served as ambassador to Paris. She made a mess of managing the Harriman estate. *(Catherine Karnow/Corbis)*

Fashion designer Tory Burch has been married to two rich men. Christopher Burch, her second husband, was helpful in launching her line of apparel. She was considered New York's "uptown darling" before that marriage hit trouble, and now the world of high society is waiting to see if there will be a third rich husband. *(Scott McDermott/Corbis)*

Slovenian-born Melania Knauss was that rarity: a stay-at-home model. One night Melania was persuaded to go to a party at New York's Kit Kat Club, where she met Donald Trump. She initially didn't want to give him her phone number because he was with another woman. She eventually became the third Mrs. Trump. *(Stephane Cardinale / People Avenue / Corbis)*

Former flight attendant Susan Gutfreund and husband John. She came to New York after a rocky marriage to a much-married Fort Worth oil heir and asked a friend to introduce her to the owlish Gutfreund, the managing partner of Salomon Brothers. She stuck with him after his troubles and won plaudits from New York society. *(Photo by Marina Garnier)*

had updated it carefully—there was no money. Hayward had always lived beyond his means and nobody had guessed that he was not a rich man. Brooke later told a journalist that she wondered if Hayward had concealed the truth about his finances because he felt that Pamela wouldn't have stayed with him if she'd known. Brooke immortalized Pamela's acquisitiveness in her 1977 book, *Haywire*. She recalled that Pamela had insisted on keeping pearls that had belonged to Maggie Sullavan, which were Brooke's, in a safe-deposit box. When Leland died, Brooke asked for her pearls. The pearls were nowhere to be found.

Pamela was in her early fifties and was desperate about her financial future. As luck would have it, Leland's death came not long after that of Marie Harriman. Her husband, Averell, Pamela's wartime love, was lonely and miserable. Pamela called Peter and Cheray Duchin—Peter had been brought up by Marie, whom he regarded as a surrogate mother, and was close to Averell—and asked them to let Averell know about Leland. (Peter Duchin would later marry Brooke Hayward.)

Pamela's chance came when both were guests at a luncheon given by *Washington Post* publisher Katharine Graham in Washington. Pamela had been asked belatedly to fill in for Graham's daughter, Lally Weymouth, who couldn't be there. Averell and Pamela were seated back-to-back at nearby tables. Pamela has denied that she arranged the seating. But talk they did. Pamela felt it was as if nothing had happened since the war years. A romance was reborn. Shortly afterward Harriman asked Peter and Cheray to include Pamela in a weekend house party. Duchin was amused that the elder statesman knocked over a lamp climbing through the window of Pam's bedroom. The Graham party had been in early spring, and in September Averell publicly announced that they were going to wed. They were married a few days later in a quiet ceremony in New York at St. Thomas More Roman Catholic Church (where Jackie Onassis frequently attended Mass), greeting friends at a small party afterward at Harriman's New York brownstone. Leland Hayward had been dead six months. Harriman would turn eighty in November. Pamela Digby Churchill Hayward Harriman, fifty-one, was entering the prime of her life.

As the wife of a very rich man at last, Pamela began decorating Averell's town house in Georgetown (the one where Jackie had been so unhappy). She had to conceal some of the expenses from Averell, who was notoriously tight-fisted, but she created an elegant place to throw parties for the Democratic Party, which, as Mrs. Averell Harriman, she made her pet cause. Not only was Pamela finally the wife of a rich man, she was now able to be taken seriously—something she wanted badly. Pamela had reinvented herself as a policy wonk. (As biographer Sally Bedell Smith pointed out, her wonkery required a phalanx of advisers such as perennial insider Richard Holbrooke and future Kerry campaign strategist Bob Shrum to write her lines—Shrum came up with "I am an American by choice and a Democrat by conviction.")

Pamela started her own PAC (political action committee—a fund-raising entity), informally called PamPAC, raising enormous amounts of money by inviting people to her Georgetown house. Going to the Harrimans and hearing Pamela talk about Sir Winston—her speech would take on his cadences, according to Sally Bedell Smith—was an evening that carried great cachet. Pamela's fund-raising earned her the nickname Duchess of the Democrats. Henry Kissinger was not the only person to observe that had Pamela not married Averell, she would have been a Republican.

She no doubt remembered how all those years ago Clementine Churchill had confided to her that she had dedicated her life totally to Winston. Pamela was busy having a ball as a political power, but she followed in Clementine's footsteps, too, in that she devoted herself utterly to making her husband happy. Averell considered his time with Pam the happiest of his life, and his eyes always sparkled when she entered the room. Harriman died on July 26, 1986, at the age of ninety-four, leaving the bulk of his estate to Pamela. She had probably kept him alive far longer than he would have lasted without her. Pamela now owned all four of the Harriman residences, interest on a trust fund, and the rest of Harriman's estate, which was estimated to be around $145 million.

As a rich widow, Pamela continued to work for the Democratic Party, supporting Bill Clinton early. In gratitude for what she did for him, Clinton appointed her U.S. ambassador to France, allowing her to return in triumph to the city where she had been the mistress of two rich men. She had triumphed over her own reputation and she had always had the optimism to go on. In her seventies, she was more beautiful than she had been in her fifties, thanks to the gentle art of Dr. Sherrell Aston, a New York plastic surgeon. Life had turned out well for Pamela—there was just one minor cloud on the horizon. She was being hauled into court by Harriman heirs who claimed that through bad investments she had frittered away their trust money. She was not being accused of dishonesty but of gross negligence. Still, it was serious and the investments made by Harriman and the advice given her by Clark Clifford, the ultimate Washington insider, were being dissected in the press.

Pamela was forced to cut her living expenses to try to raise money for the Harriman heirs. She bounced back after the initial shock and enjoyed being Madame Ambassador. The settlement with the Harriman heirs was confidential, but it was obvious that Pamela had lost a lot of money. Sally Bedell Smith has suggested that Pamela had spent too lavishly because, once she was rich in her own right, she became grandiose. She died on February 5, 1997, in her embassy in Paris and was buried from Washington's National Cathedral, with the president of the United States, Bill Clinton, among the mourners. It was a far cry from being Elie Rothschild's mistress.

Thanks to her successful fortune hunting, Jackie Kennedy enjoyed the best decades of her life after her mid-forties. She seemed to find at last that she wanted a career of her own, independent from the men who had always defined her. She became an editor at Viking and later at Doubleday, and was able to attract writers through the allure of her name. Louis Auchincloss, who had spotted her as a young woman obsessed with money at that Georgetown cocktail party, came to see her as an excellent editor.

For all of the invasions of her privacy, the press remained remarkably discreet about her relationship with Maurice Tempelsman. A diamond dealer with business interests in South Africa, Tempelsman brought stability to Jackie's life. Although he never divorced his wife, he moved in with Jackie. They enjoyed talking about books and speaking French to each other. Maurice did a brilliant job of parlaying Jackie's fortune into an even larger one through wise investments.

Jacqueline Kennedy Onassis had been a great fortune hunter, but when she died in 1994 the nation mourned her as an admired First Lady. Her funeral Mass was held at the Church of St. Ignatius Loyola on Park Avenue, where Jacqueline Lee Bouvier had been christened, and she was buried next to John Kennedy in Arlington National Cemetery. The trashy interlude with Aristotle Onassis was all but forgotten.

8

TRUMPING EACH OTHER

One of the greatest tabloid stories of the late eighties and early nineties was the War of the Trumps, as it was known. The actors were the developer Donald Trump and the two women who wanted him: the first Mrs. Trump, Ivana, and the second Mrs. Trump, Marla Maples. The two Mrs. Trumps engaged in a relentlessly chronicled war over the larger-than-life real estate mogul with the most distinctive comb-over in America, and later over the spoils of marriage. They learned about the uses of publicity, the limits of love, and the ins and outs of the prenuptial agreement. Would they have fared better if they'd never been contestants for Mr. Trump's affections?

ACCIDENTAL FORTUNE HUNTER

She became the emblematic "Mrs. Got Rocks" of the eighties, but Ivana Trump was an accidental fortune finder. Left to her own devices, she (like Diana, Princess of Wales) would not have made it into this book. Ivana was not on the lookout for a rich husband when Donald Trump spotted her in Maxwell's Plum, a New York restaurant. And, irony of ironies, it would become clear as the story unfolded that Ivana Trump lacked several essential ingredients in the template of the successful fortune hunter's personality.

She had certainly encountered no millionaires growing up in Zlín, a small industrialized town 135 miles from Prague, where Ivana was born. The economic mainstay of Zlín was the Bata shoe factory. Ivana's father, Miloš, worked there as an electrical engineer. His wife, Maria, was the operator at the telephone collective. Ivana Maria Zelníčková, born prematurely, spent the first months of her life in the hospital. Miloš, a skiing champion, felt that sports would make his frail child strong. Ivana was winning ski competitions by the age of six. "Ivana was her daddy's girl," a family friend told Harry Hurt III, who wrote about her in *Lost Tycoon*, a biography of Trump. "She was very emotionally dependent on her father."

Achievement, not marrying a rich man, was emphasized in Ivana's family. When Ivana brought home grades that Miloš thought below her abilities, he sent her to work on the assembly line at the shoe factory for the summer. "I promised myself that I was never—ever—going to do that kind of work again," she said in an interview many years later. Ivana, a pretty girl with long brown hair, improved her grades.

She was a highly competitive athlete when she entered Prague's Charles University in 1967, where she studied physical education and was on the ski team. Her boyfriend was George Syrovátka, another athlete from Zlín. Syrovátka was the son of an architect who had close ties with Alexander Dubček, who tried to liberalize the regime. Once, upon returning from a competition abroad, Ivana was questioned by the authorities. According to Hurt's report, she claimed she "played dumb," but Hurt noted: "As subsequent events attested, she was wiley as a fox."

Ivana was out of the country (travel abroad was permitted because her father was affiliated with a sports club), working as a mother's helper, when the Soviet Union ended the Prague Spring. Ivana faced a terrible decision: She could defect and leave her family behind or she could remain in a drab, communist country. Miloš packed her belongings and met her at the Austrian border. However, she was unable to bear the thought of not seeing her parents for years, perhaps forever. When George Syrovátka decided to get out of Czechoslovakia a few years later, Ivana still could not face leaving her family forever. George and Ivana resorted to a common trick: a Cold War marriage that would give her a dual passport. Ivana entered a skiing competition in Austria, where she married Alfred Winklmayr, a friend of Syrovátka's—a marriage that, according to Hurt's sources, was never sexually consummated. She could leave Czechoslovakia without defecting.

Assured the right to come and go, Ivana decided to stay. She had fallen in love with Jiří Štaidl. He was at the center of artistic life in Prague and made money writing songs. They lived together in an artist's colony near Prague. "I met Ivana when she was seventeen or eighteen," a boyfriend who preceded Štaidl told *Vanity Fair*. "She was very natural and more intelligent than girls her age. They didn't have the ambition to show their brains, but Ivana had this. It's not easy to make a career in Prague as she did. Even when you see her choice of partner, Jiří Štaidl—he was not the most handsome man in Prague, but he was certainly one of the most intelligent men in Prague. It shows she was not silly." Štaidl's family was not as sold on Ivana. "She was the type who loved parties, drinking, and meeting high society people," Jiří's brother told Harry Hurt. She was in love, however, and obtained a divorce to marry Štaidl.

But Štaidl was killed in a car wreck late in 1973. Ivana would always commemorate the anniversary with a wreath sent to his grave. Ivana resumed her relationship with Syrovátka, now living in Canada. Her divorce did not deprive her of her dual citizenship, and she joined him there. Syrovátka was operating a ski shop, and the couple lived in a three-room apartment in Montreal. She had studied "the English at the Berlitz." Although not at heart a fortune hunter, Ivana does have the fortune hunter's talent for self-reinvention: She became a blonde and signed on with the Audrey Morris modeling agency. Well-disciplined and ambitious, she was an immediate success. She drove an Austin-Healey and spent Christmas in Aspen. She was able to send her parents money every month.

According to Trump biographer Harry Hurt III, Ivana desperately wanted Syrovátka to marry her. She made a wistful remark about "my husband" in an interview with the *Montreal Gazette* in 1975. "If modeling becomes a career," she said, "there's no time to go to the theatre, read books, and go on vacation. Modeling is a job to me, not a career. I have my social life, my husband, and my home."

She was about to meet Donald Trump, an up-and-coming New York developer with roots in Queens. Trump has said that he met Ivana when he attended the Olympics and she was on the Czech ski team. Ivana was an excellent skier, but she was never on an Olympic team. When Donald met Ivana, she was standing in line for a table at Maxwell's Plum, a New York restaurant and singles bar.

Maxwell's Plum, which had stained-glass ceilings and blended the clubby feel of "21" with the casual ambience of P. J. Clarke's, was one of the regular stops for Trump. It was always knee-deep in models, airline stewardesses, and other good-looking women. Ivana, in New York on a modeling assignment, was waiting impatiently with three other models from Canada when a stranger said, "Hello, my name is Donald Trump." He wanted to know if they'd like him to use his influence with the owner to get them a table. Ivana was concerned that the stranger would want to sit with them, but she was overruled by her friends, who wanted to sit down. Ivana was right, of course—Trump not only sat with them but insisted on driving them back to their hotel. He sent Ivana a dozen red roses the next day.

If Ivana, twenty-seven, had been a genuine fortune hunter, she would have immediately done everything to cultivate her new admirer. At thirty, Donald Trump was already quite a catch. Shortly after the meeting in Maxwell's Plum, *The New York Times* lionized Trump as DONALD TRUMP, REAL ESTATE PROMOTER, BUILDS IMAGE AS HE BUYS BUILDINGS.

"He is tall, lean, and blond, with dazzling white teeth," wrote the late Judy Klemesrud. Trump claimed to be worth more than $200 million.

Trump had grown up in Queens, the son of Fred C. Trump, a dapper, mustachioed developer who had made a fortune there. "He didn't like wimps. He thought competition made you stronger," a relative would say in Fred Trump's *New York Times* obituary. Fred repeatedly told his sons, "You're a killer!" Donald was Fred's favorite of his three sons. Perhaps trying to trump his father, Donald moved into the high-powered world of Manhattan real estate. The Trump boys adored their mother, Mary, in part because she put up with the difficult Fred.

Donald took to bombarding Ivana with phone calls; she didn't play hard to get—she was genuinely eager to marry her poorer boyfriend. But Trump proposed marriage in a letter to "Sweetie Pie" only two months after the Maxwell's Plum meeting. "Have you ever seen anybody that's so beautiful and so smart?" he would ask friends. "My God, why does he do these things?" Ivana asked in her heavily accented English after he flew to Canada just to spend a few hours with her.

When Ivana went to Aspen for her usual Christmas vacation, Donald followed her. There she surprised him by saying yes. She was giving up on George, who didn't seem to want marriage and a family. When Donald returned to New York, he bought Ivana a three-carat diamond ring from Tiffany's. But Ivana dithered. Over Donald's protests, she went to Tahiti to think things through. Donald sent her a telegram urging her to return at once. She waited a few weeks, but then she told Donald that she was ready. Donald—or "the Donald," as Ivana, who had not mastered the use of the article in English, called him—was thrilled. But he insisted on a prenuptial agreement. "It was a very exciting time in my life, but not so exciting that I rushed into marriage without a prenuptial agreement," Trump wrote. Prenuptial agreements weren't as common then. Today they are almost automatic. A prenup does not have the "till death do us part" ring of marriage vows about it, so the question is: To sign or not to sign? Actually, the choices may be more limited than one might like. Trump has said that he would not marry a woman who refused to sign. The best thing one can do is get good legal advice—a prenup is hard to break.

Trump sprang the prenup on Ivana a month before the day set for the wedding. Not surprisingly, Ivana was horrified. Trump explained that it was essential: In the event of a protracted divorce, his property could be put in limbo, curtailing his capacity for wheeling and dealing—or "scheming and beaming," as Ivana, with her propensity for original usages of the English language, put it. Donald's lawyer was the controversial Roy Cohn, and on Cohn's recommendation, Ivana hired as her lawyer Lawrence Levner, a friend of Cohn's. Negotiations broke down repeatedly. Cohn had put a "give-back" clause in the agreement—stipulating that if the Trumps divorced, Ivana would return gifts from her husband, including jewelry—which angered Ivana. To counter, Ivana demanded a "rainy day" fund of $100,000. Donald balked, and Ivana got up and ran outside. The give-back clause was eventually eliminated, but as Hurt noted, Ivana got her rainy day fund.

The couple signed an agreement less than three weeks before their wedding. The amounts do not look generous in light of the holdings Trump claimed—Ivana would get only $20,000 after a year of marriage, but that would increase to $90,000 after thirty years—but the agreement would be renegotiated three times during the course of the Trump marriage. Ivana would improve her lot each time, with the final agreement stipulating that Ivana would receive significantly more—around $25 million, with $10 million in cash—if the Trumps divorced, though that's not much for the wife of a man reputed to be a latter-day Medici. With the prenuptial agreement signed, Donald was ready to get married.

A Trump gala with all sorts of family friends—Mayor Abe Beam, Queens borough president Donald Manes, and an assortment of developers—the wedding took place at the Marble Collegiate Church on Fifth Avenue, where Fred and Mary Trump went to services. Presiding was the Reverend Norman Vincent Peale, of *The Power of Positive Thinking* fame, another close friend of the groom's family. Wearing a white chiffon mid-calf-length dress, Ivana walked down the aisle to become Mrs. Trump. The wedding was followed by a seated dinner at "21," the dark-paneled, masculine steak house favored by Fred and Donald, with comedian Joey Adams as master of ceremonies. His wife, gossip columnist Cindy Adams, destined to play a big role in the lives of the couple, was also there.

When they returned from their honeymoon in Acapulco, Ivana was already pregnant, and the young Trumps gave every impression of being a happy young couple in love.

THE "WIFE-TWIN"

As if to compensate for the drabness of Zlín, Ivana became active in the social life of New York, indulging in $25,000 outfits by such designers as Scaasi, Dior, Givenchy, and Chanel. She was asked to serve on charity committees and became friendly with Estée Lauder, the cosmetics magnate, and C. Z. Guest, the Old Guard stalwart who spoke with the lockjaw accent favored by New York blue bloods, but liked partying with more exciting types. Jerry Zipkin, the tart-tongued social moth and Nancy Reagan intimate, and Kenneth Jay Lane, the brilliantly well-connected designer of jewelry, squired her around town. The irrepressible Ivana was fun to be with, and people liked her. She threw ladies lunches at which writer and man about town Christopher Mason was hired to make up songs about the guests. "Ivana was great," Mason told Gwenda Blair. "Every time I'd sing, she'd open her eyes wide and look totally surprised and say, 'Vot! I pay heem money and den he insults me!'"

Still, Ivana's taste—which found its purest expression in the garish Trump Tower, Donald's signature building at 725 Fifth Avenue—did provoke a degree of mirth. In the case of the Trump Tower, the mirth was laced with anger over Donald's surreptitious destruction of the antique nickel-grille entrance and irreplaceable art deco sculptures of the old Bonwit Teller building, to make way for his masterpiece. Crews worked through the night to get the job done. Trump wanted this location: It was next door to Tiffany's—literally, the Tiffany location. Ivana designed doormen's uniforms that included Beefeater hats like the ones worn by guards at the Tower of London. She bought the most expensive marble, pinkish breccia, for the public spaces. She was irritated to find her taste under assault. "What do they prefer—the cheap white travertine [marble] that is used in banks? It is too cold, too common. Donald and I are more daring than that."

Her sense of aesthetics flowered in their eight-bedroom apartment inside Trump Tower. Its style has been compared to that of the casinos Donald was acquiring. Because the ceilings are so low, one visitor wrote that being inside felt like being the filling of a sandwich—that is how I felt when I went to a party there. Framed by more gilt than I'd ever seen, with the gentle tinkle of a fountain and beneath an incredibly ornate chandelier, Fabio, the guest of honor, a hunk who posed for covers of romance novels, somehow look just right. I almost expected him to point to the canapés and say, "I can't believe it's not butter," his trademark line in his ads for Brummel & Brown's low-fat spread. But the two-story windows in the dining room looking out over Manhattan—such a feeling of power!

When Ivana married Trump, he already was rich and powerful; as the aureate eighties progressed, he was becoming even richer, more powerful, and more full of himself. He reached new heights of grandiosity after he renovated and reopened Wollman Rink in Central Park, which had been closed for years. According to an anecdote in Hurt's book, "After that Donald started referring to himself in the third person. He'd call [a friend] and say, 'What did you think about that story about Trump in the newspaper today? What did you think about the story about Trump on TV?' [The friend would] say to him, 'Hey, Donald, you are Trump.'"

Something strange was happening to Ivana, too—she was turning into the Donald. Fortune hunters always adopt the causes of their husbands. If he aspires to political power, they join his party and raise funds. If he sees himself as an artist, the fortune hunter rushes out to buy paints and an easel for herself, but she makes sure that whatever she puts on canvas is vastly inferior to his work. The fortune hunter does not try to become her husband—and certainly, under no circumstances, does she compete with him. She is his geisha, not his alter ego. Fatally, Ivana began to emulate and compete with the Donald. The Ivana even began to talk like the Donald—in her own inimitable East European way, of course. "The first time we met," Chicago socialite and writer Sugar Rautbord told a reporter, "she was saying things like, 'It's so incredible fucking party,' and, 'Look at it, it is fucking wonderful.' She was so beautiful and glossy, and she spoke in such a soft, silky voice, and then out came these words that she had obviously borrowed from her husband's business vocabulary. It was clear that this was not just a husband with an arm-piece wife—they were very coupled."

Although Ivana prided herself on being a good mother to the couple's three children (Donny, Ivanka, and Eric), she was determined to work. Donald gave her a job in the Trump organization, and Ivana became so much a female version of Donald that she called herself his "wife-twin." "If Donald were married to a lady who didn't work and make certain contributions, he would be gone," she told *Time* magazine. A smart fortune hunter might have opened an antiques shop.

She was next put in charge of running Trump's Castle, a casino in Atlantic City. Ivana was at the casino daily, flying in by chartered helicopter and leaving about five to be home for dinner with the children. Taught competitiveness on the ski slopes of Czechoslovakia, Ivana now struggled to be her husband's equal in the business world, something no real fortune hunter would dream of doing.

In 1988 Donald bought the Plaza Hotel on Fifth Avenue, a New York landmark. The hotel was such a symbol of the luxury and style of the past that Ernest Hemingway once advised F. Scott Fitzgerald to leave his liver to Princeton and his heart to the Plaza. Eloise, the little girl made famous through Hilary Knight's drawings, was the hotel's most famous imaginary guest. Trump put his wife in charge of the hotel, bragging that he paid her "one dollar a year and all the dresses she can buy." The remark offended Ivana's sense of dignity, and she was determined to show him. She acquired a reputation as the boss from hell. Ivana personally demonstrated the correct way to scrub a bathroom floor. A cover story in *Spy* magazine described Ivana as a "wicked witch," a "Bengal tiger," and "a madwoman."

After confiding to columnist Liz Smith that she never intended to look a day over twenty-eight, no matter how much her eternal youth cost the Donald, Ivana went to Dr. Steven Hoefflin, the L.A. plastic surgeon credited with making Ivana look like Brigitte Bardot. The makeover included breast augmentation, to which Donald reportedly reacted badly, a charge he denied. "I remember one horrible article in *Vanity Fair,* of course totally untrue, that claimed that I was repulsed by Ivana after she supposedly had plastic surgery on a certain part of her body," he fumed in print. " 'I wouldn't touch those things,' I was quoted as having said. Just for the record, all parts of her body are beautiful."

Trump loved the limelight, but he didn't care for Ivana's style of entertaining. He often went to his room before Ivana's splendid dinner parties ended. "Ivana is what I'd call a traditionalist," he wrote. "She aspires to the aristocracy. She believes people in our position should lead a certain kind of life—a life involving night after night of society people and gala society events, tuxedos and expensive ball gowns." At Mar-a-Lago, the Palm Beach property that had belonged to Marjorie Merriweather Post, Ivana asked guests to sign a leather-bound guest book and handed out printed schedules of the day's activities. For Trump, according to one biographer, the opulence of Mar-a-Lago, the private planes, and Trump Tower were marketing tools. Ivana did not grasp this. For the Donald, her formal parties were a bore. They might be right for members of the Lucky Sperm Club (as he called those born to privilege) but not for a hard-charging developer.

More than her social aspirations, it was the "wife-twin's" obsession with business that irritated him. "The problem was, work was all she wanted to talk about," Donald wrote. "When I got home at night, rather than talking about the softer subjects of life, she wanted to tell me how well the Plaza was doing, or what a great day the casino had. I really appreciated her efforts, but it was just too much. I work from six o'clock in the morning until seven at night; to come home and hear more was just not tolerable. And Ivana just wouldn't stop."

Both Trumps had been schooled in childhood to compete by ambitious fathers. A genuine fortune hunter would have masked her competitiveness, but Ivana could not do that. She wanted to be Donald's "wife-twin," not his geisha. "For Donald Trump," wrote Gwenda Blair, "[the trouble] was that he had married the wrong parent. Instead of choosing a mate like his mother, eager to play quiet backup to a towering success, he had selected someone more like his father, someone who was a born contender, who could not hold back and go second even if she tried."

THE WAR OF THE TRUMPS

As Trump was realizing just how unhappy he was with his competitive wife who wanted to talk business while he wanted to relax with a tasty treat from his beloved Cakemasters, he happened to meet Marla Maples, the effervescent, Bible-thumping beauty queen from Georgia. Trump was walking down Fifth Avenue when he spotted Marla, bosomy and blond, in front of the Pierre Hotel. She looked familiar, but Trump wasn't sure if they'd met before. She realized he was looking at her. "Hello, I'm Marla Maples," she said, extending her hand and reminding Trump that they had seen each other at a party in Atlantic City a year before.

When Marla called Tom Fitzsimmons, an old boyfriend and ex-policeman who was a bit actor and friendly with Trump, to get the low-down later that day, he reminded her that Trump was married. When Trump called Fitzsimmons to ask him to bring the stunning model to a party for his new book, *Trump: The Art of the Deal,* the soon-to-be intermediary—who happened to have Marla on hold on the other line—reminded Trump of the same thing. Fitzsimmons was hesitant—he felt protective toward Marla, with whom he had lived when she first came to New York—but he didn't want to refuse Donald, either. Fitzsimmons agreed to escort Marla to Trump's book party.

The party was held at Trump Tower, with all six floors of the atrium decked in lights and poinsettias. The black-tie crowd included model Cheryl Tiegs, movie star Michael Douglas, and socialite Anne Bass. It was clear to an astute observer that Donald and Marla were deeply attracted to each other. When Trump—who'd been winking at Marla all night, even though he was standing next to Ivana—finally managed to talk to her, he was bashful, unusual for Trump. Donald did get Marla's telephone number.

Marla Ann Maples, a model and aspiring actress, had grown up in Dalton, Georgia, a town *The Washington Post* would hail as the home of the "Killer Blondes," a reference to Dalton's two most famous exports, TV personality Deborah Norville and Marla. Dalton was also known as the "Carpet Capital of the World" because of the several hundred carpet manufacturers and factory outlets. Marla was the only child of Stan Maples, a real estate developer who sang in the Baptist choir and longed to get on *Ted Mack's Original Amateur Hour,* and Ann Locklear Maples, a distant cousin of actress Heather Locklear. Ann also had performing aspirations—she had wanted to be a professional dancer. Marla grew up in a split-level ranch-style house. Her adoring grandparents, Ding Daddy and Meemaw, like her parents, spoiled Marla. Looks ran in the family. A scout for *Playboy* magazine asked Marla and Ann to pose for a mother-daughter picture when Marla was a teenager. They turned down the offer—Marla wasn't old enough to pose for *Playboy,* anyway.

Somebody once wrote that "getting to know Marla is akin to pressing your thumb on an aerosol can and watching mountains of Reddi-wip flow out." Marla's fizzy personality was the product of nature and nurture—the nurture being her training as a contestant in beauty pageants. She began appearing in local fashion shows at an early age. If Ivana learned competitiveness on the slopes of Czechoslovakia, Marla learned how to charm men on the beauty pageant circuit. Along with beauty tips, her coach, Margaret Culberson, told the girls how important it was to remain a virgin until marriage.

Stan, troubled by financial reversals, and Ann, a frustrated woman obsessed with keeping the house clean, divorced when Marla was sixteen, destroying Marla's sense of security. She began a hot and heavy relationship with Jeff Sandlin, a high school athlete who would sell his story to *The National Enquirer.* According to Sandlin, Marla had had an abortion. "I held her gently in my arms and told her I was willing to marry her—but I really didn't want to," Sandlin said. "It was against Marla's religious beliefs to think about an abortion. But she wanted to be a movie star—not pregnant in some backwater Georgia town. We decided on an abortion."

When Sandlin got an apartment in Atlanta—partly to escape Marla—she found him and persuaded him to let her move in. They fought constantly. Sandlin felt that Marla was ambitious to know the rich and famous, which wasn't the world he aspired to. Sandlin left after six months. About the time of the breakup, Marla, who'd been doing some modeling, started thinking about going to New York, where she would have a better chance of becoming an actress. In 1985 Marla moved to New York and met Tom Fitzsimmons. She moved into his two-bedroom apartment on Ninety-first Street and Third Avenue.

"There was nothing distinguishing about her except her genuineness," an otherwise blasé New Yorker who dated Marla told *Vanity Fair's* Maureen Orth. "She was a sweet girl from Georgia, all Southern charm, the antithesis of high-society, megabucks-type people. She probably can't act, but who cares? She's pretty and sexy. She invited me to her church."

She was not an accidental fortune finder; as a beauty pageant veteran, Marla was trained to attract men. She would go on to prove that she could not be embarrassed by anything. Ultimately, however, she would make a mistake no astute fortune hunter would make, behaving in a manner that was more suited to reeling in a high school football star than a high roller in New York real estate.

After the book party at Trump Tower, Donald asked Marla to lunch. Donald had squired around other pretty young things in the course of his troubled marriage to Ivana, but people who know him believe that most of his extracurricular activities before Marla had been platonic—Donald is obsessed with germs to the point that he doesn't like to shake hands, and this obsession might have been a factor. Marla was different from the other girls, though, and Trump found himself hopelessly attracted. She thought Trump was sweet. Marla moved into a room at the Trump-owned St. Moritz Hotel on the Upper East Side, a stone's throw from Trump Tower, and became a frequent guest at the Trump Plaza in Atlantic City, where she went by the name of Fitzsimmons. She was much more popular in Atlantic City than the boss's martinet wife.

While keeping Marla out of sight, Trump approached Ivana and asked her if she would be willing to try an "open marriage." Ivana was scandalized, and Trump dropped it. But Ivana was one of the few top people in the Trump organization who wasn't aware of Marla. Marla, for her part, was sick of being Donald's secret mistress. Reportedly, she took solace from *Emmanuel's Book,* a popular New Age classic that was purportedly "channeled" by a spirit named Seth. It was becoming increasingly difficult to keep Marla hidden. She nearly came face-to-face with Ivana at the funeral of a Trump executive killed in a helicopter crash. In the summer of 1988 "Page Six," the *New York Post's* gossip column, ran a blind item about a "shapely blonde" who was "involved with one of New York's biggest tycoons, a married man," and who "supposedly goes around to all the stores in Trump Tower saying, 'Charge it to Donald.'"

Donald prepared for his winter skiing holiday in Aspen in 1989. Both his ladies loved Aspen. Donald and Ivana stayed at the Little Nell, a fancy hotel owned by the late Marvin Davis, and Trump rented a condominium for Marla and her girlfriend, Kim Knapp. When Donald and Ivana stopped in for lunch at Bonnie's Beach Club, a popular Aspen eatery, Marla and Kim were also having lunch there. Somehow Ivana, who was hearing rumors, realized that the other woman was in the restaurant.

The Trumps began arguing publicly and went outside. Marla followed and stood in front to Ivana. "Are you Moolah?" Ivana demanded. "Why don't you leave my husband alone?" Marla was undaunted. "Are you happy?" she asked Ivana as the crowd looked on in horrified fascination. "I love him and if you don't, why don't you let him go?" Marla said. Strangely, the scene wasn't reported in the press for more than a month, when it appeared in Liz Smith's syndicated column, but paparazzi did snap pictures of the trio—Donald, Ivana, and Marla—huddling in their ski suits during the confrontation.

Although the Trumps continued to be seen together, Ivana quietly began making plans, talking to a lawyer and urging her husband to see a psychiatrist. It was while she was undecided about her future with the Donald that his *Playboy* interview appeared. Asked in the interview if his marriage was monogamous, he replied, "I don't have to answer that." For Ivana, this was important information. When Donald left for a trip to Japan to promote a Mike Tyson fight, Ivana took the initiative—she called Liz Smith of the *New York Daily News* and told her that she and Donald were divorcing. It was a crucial move, ensuring that the powerful Smith would be in her corner during the ordeal that would follow. Ivana spoke on background—Smith could use the information but could not say it came from Ivana. Still hoping to save her marriage, Ivana most likely hoped that this leak would bring Donald to his senses. He was flying back from Japan when he received a call on his private plane that Liz Smith had the story. LOVE ON THE ROCKS was the headline for a front-page story revealing, "Mrs. Trump is reportedly devastated that Donald was betraying her . . . Intimates say Ivana had every chance to continue being Mrs. Trump by allowing her husband to live in an open marriage so he could see other women. But the bottom line is that she won't give up her self-respect to do it." Ivana was portrayed as having been so busy with her job and raising the couple's three children that she had not realized her husband was cheating. Trump was furious that his wife had beaten him to the punch.

The War of the Trumps would from then on be fought both in the courtroom, where Ivana tried to up her settlement from the agreed-upon $25 million, and in the press, with *Time* and *Newsweek* doing stories on it. Trump made an effort to recruit Smith, who became part of the story. Smith reminded him that she'd been trying to get the story for some time and that he hadn't helped her. "You gotta dance with the one who brought you," Smith told Trump. Trump was left with Cindy Adams of the *New York Post* as the recipient of his leaks and as his media champion. The Trump divorce, wrote Liz Smith, was "the biggest story I ever saw happen that wasn't important—next to Elizabeth Taylor and Richard Burton."

All super rich people risk a certain amount of coverage in the tabloids—it is the price of being super rich. But the Trumps fed the beast, reaping unprecedented publicity, in part because, as Smith observed, they created themselves through publicity. In this, they were like Princess Diana, another media manipulator, who searched for her identity by reading her press clippings. Trump had been planting stories and flattering reporters by returning their calls for years, so it was ironic that Ivana turned out to be better at the game. One of Ivana's greatest triumphs was a Valentine's Day lunch at La Grenouille, the fancy French restaurant on East Fifty-second Street. It turned into the St. Valentine's Day Massacre of the Donald—but oh so nicely. The guests included Carroll Petrie, Liz Smith, Anne Bass, Barbara Walters, Georgette Mosbacher, and Shirley Lord, the novelist and *Vogue* editor, and the Donald's mother and sisters and then sister-in-law, Blaine.

As Ivana, wearing a bright red Chanel suit and flanked by two enormous bodyguards, stepped from the limousine to enter the restaurant, the crowd demonstrated that they were Ivana people. "Get the money!" a bystander called out. "Get the Plaza!" yelled another. "Twenty-five million is not enough!" shouted somebody who had clearly been reading the newspapers. Over champagne and lamb chops and a birthday cake sent by Saudi entrepreneur Adnan Khashoggi, the women rallied around the tearful Ivana. Somebody had thought to send a pretend telegram from Nelson Mandela, recently freed after years of imprisonment, begging Ivana, "Give me a break, and get off the front pages." Blaine, whose refined demeanor had always contrasted with Ivana's flamboyance, offered a cryptic toast— "We are always going to be as close as we are now." Everybody was impressed with the way Ivana was bucking up in the face of Donald's betrayal. When it was time to go, Liz Smith and Barbara Walters escorted Ivana out of Le Grenouille, past the press and supportive crowd and into the waiting limousine. Ivana, once the tyrant of the Plaza Hotel, was now so popular that somebody coined the term Ivanamania. The debonair jeweler Kenneth Jay Lane sided with Ivana, making her cause popular with the ladies who lunch.

About the time of the St. Valentine's Day Luncheon Massacre, the *New York Post* outed Marla as the Other Woman in a story that quoted the Georgia peach summing up the Donald's prowess as "the best sex I ever had." Donald must have been pleased that she thought so. But Marla was about to do some more hiding. Chuck Jones, Marla's public relations man, somehow hit upon the idea that it would be better if she ran from the press, thereby creating a delicious story line: the hunt for Marla. She holed up in the Southampton home of a friend of Trump's, escaping— with the press at her heels—to the house of Resorts International president Jack Davis and his wife, Caroline. Marla then flew to Guatemala, where she had a friend in the Peace Corps. The Peace Corps volunteers humored her by pretending not to recognize her. Upon her return to the United States, Marla granted an extensive interview to Diane Sawyer of *Primetime Live* in which she claimed that Trump was not supporting her financially. As for Ivana, "I think she's an absolutely beautiful woman," Marla said, adding, as catty Southern girls know how, that Ivana was beautiful "before her surgery. I . . . and . . . I mean, now, she's . . . she's very, very gorgeous."

Strange as it may seem, Ivana Trump still seemed crazy about the Donald and devastated over the breakup of her marriage. In addition to the private pain, there was the public spectacle. She was the target of ugly stories in the press and nasty comments from Trump. The *New York Post* broke the story of Ivana's "dark past," dredging up her heretofore secret Cold War marriage to Alfred Winklmayr and erroneously reporting that she had grown up in a "filth-ridden" flat in Zlín. From Australia, Winklmayr commented to the *Star,* a supermarket tabloid, "I can't help but think she's finally getting what's coming to her." When Ivana showed up for work at the Plaza Hotel one day, she found that the locks had been changed. Donald started comparing his wife with Leona Helmsley, the hotelier who had gone to prison and who was known as the Queen of Mean, while his ally, Cindy Adams, portrayed Ivana as a "smart . . . savvy . . . well-educated" woman who was holding out for the "big bucks."

In the midst of the publicity circus, Ivana managed to ditch her old image and become a sympathetic figure. Like Gayfryd Steinberg and Susan Gutfreund, confronted by different kinds of scandals, she had held her head high. She had shown herself to be, as previous generations might have put it, a lady—and thanks to her own insistence on having her prenuptial agreement renegotiated over the course of her marriage, not a shabby genteel one. Ivana walked away from the marriage with $25 million, $10 million in a certified check. No, it was not a grandiose take for somebody who had been married for thirteen years to a difficult man who either was or wasn't, depending on the speaker, a billionaire. Ivana and her lawyers had fought hard to abrogate the agreement and failed. However, when the marriage was dissolved in the fall of 1990, less than a year after the confrontation on the slopes and after a tabloid mudslinging contest, Ivana had a lot of money and her dignity.

Could it be argued that the prenuptial agreement, albeit renegotiated, far from being a disaster for Ivana, was actually her best friend? Trump was going through a slump at the time of his divorce—some cynics said he faked it to avoid paying Ivana more—and his attitude toward women, based on his own words, seems to be one of both attraction and fear:

> The smart ones act very feminine and needy, but inside they are real killers. The person who came up with the expression "the weaker sex" was either very naïve or had to be kidding. I have seen women manipulate men with just a twitch of their eye—or perhaps another body part. I have seen some of the roughest, toughest guys on earth, guys who rant and rave at other tough guys and make them cry, and yet they're afraid of their 120-pound girlfriends or wives. I know a man who makes mincemeat out of almost

any guy he looks at. . . . But when his five-foot-two wife calls him and screams at him that he's always late for dinner and it better not happen again, he rushes out of the office without a moment's hesitation, shouting, "Donny, I have to go, she's going to kill me. I swear she's going to kill me."

Most women could not have survived the public humiliation to which Marla was subjected. A Trump employee calling himself John Miller told *People* magazine that the romance was over and that both Madonna and Kim Basinger were pursuing Trump, who already had another girlfriend. Miller added that the new girlfriend, Carla Bruni Tedeschi, had dropped Mick Jagger for Donald. When the reporter, Sue Carswell, played the tape for her colleagues, they told her that John Miller was Donald Trump. Carswell asked Marla to confirm that Miller was Trump. She was brokenhearted. But she did not retire from the fray. Cindy Adams called her "the future Miss Maples."

Instead of hiding, Marla used her notoriety to get a guest gig on the then top-rated show *Designing Women*, where she made a sly joke about Donald's "big ego." She also landed a role on Broadway in *The Will Rogers Follies* and was so awful that a critic from *Newsday* said, "She doesn't easily embarrass." That is a good epitaph for any fortune hunter.

Whereas Ivana had been pursued by Trump, Marla pursued. She pursued by occasionally leaving him to make him jealous. At one point she accepted Donald's proposal and then found that he was reluctant to announce it publicly. She took up with musician Michael Bolton in September of 1991, which seemed to make Donald interested again. Throughout the minutely chronicled romance, the Georgia peach proved she was no softie. She once threw a shoe at Donald and screamed that she would never marry him, but she knew she would. Some people who knew Trump suggested that he liked to fight with Marla. Early in 1993 Marla became pregnant with Trump's child.

Eventually, Marla's fortitude and shamelessness combined with an unrelated event. The notorious slaying of passengers on the Long Island Rail Road in 1993 by a deranged shooter reminded Trump of the brevity of life and turned his attention toward matrimony. But there had to be a prenup—and in having a child, Marla had made herself vulnerable. The only negotiating tool for the poorer party in prenuptial talks is the threat of walking away. Lawyers are well aware that this is less likely if there is a child involved.

Marla failed where Ivana (to a greater degree) succeeded. Marla's prenuptial agreement, signed a mere two days before the wedding, stipulated that she would receive between $1 million and $5 million if the couple lasted only a few years. The agreement would go out of effect after five years, and Marla would be eligible for a larger portion of Trump's fortune. (Marla told *Vanity Fair* that "I feel that we have what he needs right now for his business. And then, in five years, I have what *I* need for a true marriage.")

The Trump wedding, held in the Plaza Hotel to which Ivana had devoted so much of herself, surpassed standards for lavishness, if not good taste. With nearly two hundred ladies and gentlemen of the press credentialed to cover the wedding, twenty-five TV crews, eighty news photographers, and thirteen hundred guests, it did not go unrecorded. Julie Baumgold of *Esquire* magazine noted the schmaltzy music—"There's a Place for Us," "Make of Our Hearts One Heart," and "Stranger in Paradise"—and the candlelight bouncing off sequins, as many guests, a sizable portion of whom hardly knew the couple, asked themselves, *Why am I here?* Baumgold memorably quipped that there "wasn't a wet eye in the house." It was five years after the encounter in Aspen; Tiffany Arianna Trump, daughter of Donald and Marla, was two months old; and the couple was at long last married.

A few wags suggested that Ivana was still competing with the Donald when only a few weeks later she announced that she, too, was getting married. Her fiancé was a suave Italian businessman named Riccardo Mazzucchelli. Ivana admitted that she was feeling, as Cindy Adams had put it, "very much the bounced Czech" when she met Mazzucchelli. This time it was Ivana, in the process of launching her own home-shopping business, who demanded the prenuptial agreement. "Riccardo always walked about eight steps behind Ivana," Palm Beach socialite Jackie Cowell told a reporter. "Ivana was always the center of attention. Riccardo was like a prince consort to her."

Unlike Ivana, Marla sat quietly and looked on adoringly as Donald talked. Nevertheless, after three years Trump wanted out—some have suggested the looming five-year mark stipulated in the prenup was a factor. The couple issued a statement saying that the marriage was over. *The New York Times* noted that neither Donald nor Marla was speaking to the press, "a veritable news article in itself." After a three-and-a-half-year marriage, Marla ended up with around $2 million and expenses for their daughter.

Ivana's marriage to Mazzucchelli was briefer—a mere twenty months. Donald, of course, claimed that Ivana was still in love with him—and he may have been onto something. She may also have learned from Donald a great deal about protecting her money—a supermarket tabloid claimed that she was dumping Mazzucchelli because he was not as good a businessman as he claimed. She reportedly didn't want to risk having him gain a part of her by now $50 million House of Ivana clothing line or other Ivana ventures. "My prenup says what's mine is mine and what's his is his. It's ironclad," said Ivana. She refused to go into detail, saying, "I don't wash the dirty laundry in front of nobody."

One of the sobering truths about fortune hunting is that, as in other lines of work, even talented people sometimes fail. Marla was far more of a natural fortune hunter than Ivana. But she failed as a fortune hunter. She is past forty now and has yet to marry another rich man. Marla was engaged briefly to Michael Mailer, the film producer (his credits include the Kevin Bacon movie *Loverboy*) and son of Norman Mailer. While Ivana functions as a high-powered entrepreneur, Marla lives in Southern California with ten-year-old Tiffany. She has made a fitness video, put in a much-derided appearance on *The Nanny,* and in 2000 released a video called *Intimate Portrait: Marla Maples Trump,* her life story. Marla is active in Beverly Hills's celebrity and semi-celebrity Kabbalah Centre. She accompanied Madonna on a trip to Israel to explore kabbalah and reportedly tithes to the center. She has also posed scantily clad and wrapped in a red string—the red string in important in kabbalah—for a center billboard. As for her acting career, Marla recently told a magazine she is "thinking of comedy" as her next move.

It appears that Ivana, the reluctant bride and competitive wife, trumped all parties: her two husbands and a beauty queen from Georgia. But she can't stop competing: When ratings for Donald's *The Apprentice* soared, she negotiated for her own TV show. Fox announced that the show—*Ivana Man,* with Ivana as a matchmaker on an unscripted two-hour show—was in preparation. But so far, it hasn't aired.

9

UNIVERSALLY ACKNOWLEDGING:
The Uptown Darling
and the Lady from Ljubljana

Somehow it seems wrong to write an entire book about fortune hunters without once invoking the English language's most famous insight on marriage and money: "It is a truth universally acknowledged, that a single man in possession of a good fortune, must be in want of a wife." That memorable first sentence of *Pride and Prejudice* is just as true in 2006 as it was when Jane Austen penned it in Regency England.

Never mind that one of the swains in this chapter was a lad of fifty-eight with two headline-grabbing divorces to his credit when he made his third trip to the altar. In wedding thirty-four-year-old Slovenia-born model Melania Knauss—a woman described in *Vogue* magazine as "so beautiful it's otherworldly"—in Palm Beach in 2005, New York developer Donald J. Trump, most recently the star of the hit NBC show *The Apprentice,* in a way launched the ultimate reality show: Will the third Mrs. Trump trump the previous two Mrs. Trumps by having the staying power to be the final Mrs. Trump?

The Trumps inhabit a world of flashbulbs and flashy money; one of the other reigning social figures of New York, Tory Burch, seemed to have stepped from a charity ball on Philadelphia's Main Line, where she grew up, or perhaps an updated version of a Jane Austen novel until she stunned society by parting company with her venture capitalist husband, Christopher Burch. She had preferred the honorific *Mrs.* to *Ms.* Burch had made his first fortune with a preppy line of clothing called Eagle's Eye, which he reportedly started with $2,000 while still an undergraduate at Ithaca College and sold for $60,000. A more recent venture is the Faena Hotel in Buenos Aires—the Burches took a bevy of young New York socialites with such blue-chip surnames as Tisch and Mortimer to Argentina for the hotel's opening. *Divine* is the word most often employed in describing the couple (a word that has rarely been applied to Donald Trump, though it is certainly applicable to Melania).

But then the Burches separated and lost some of their divinity. Unlike the Austen character of yesteryear (*and* the fortune hunter of yesteryear), Burch had always worked outside the house. "Have money, will sew," is how one newspaper characterized her venture into the business world with a new line of predominantly mid-priced clothing, Tory by TRB. Christopher Burch backed his wife's venture. The article likened the "uptown darling" to Gloria Vanderbilt, Diane von Furstenberg, and Carolina Herrera, three other hardworking socialite designers. Perhaps Tory is her generation's answer to Blaine Trump, patrician wife of Robert Trump, Donald's brother, before the marriage broke up. The society darling of her day, Blaine was dubbed "Her Blondness" by William Norwich, a leading society scribe of the eighties; the authoritative *W* magazine's Robert Haskell has called Tory Burch "New York's reigning blonde."

If Jane Austen had fled her father's parsonage, where she wrote her novels, and entered a time warp that dropped her in New York in the early twenty-first century, Miss Austen (like Mrs. Burch, she would undoubtedly eschew Ms.) would recognize that these two women, Tory Burch and Melania Knauss (pronounced Kuh-naus), couldn't be more outwardly different but that both have been catapulted to the top through beauty, natural talent, application—and marriage to a single middle-aged man in possession of very good fortunes. What is their secret?

Like the first Mrs. Trump, Melania was a model who grew up in Europe and speaks heavily accented English. Unlike Ivana, Melania grew up in affluent circumstances. She is the daughter of a fashion designer mother and a father who ran a chain of automobile and motorcycle dealerships in Ljubljana, a city with baroque architecture that has been the capital of Slovenia since the fall of the Austro-Hungarian Empire. The Knauss family took ski trips to the mountains and went to the beach for holidays. Melania began modeling at the age of five, and she completed her course of studies at the Academy of Design and Architecture in Ljubljana. She went on to modeling jobs in Milan and Paris, and in the mid-1990s went to New York as a protégé of modeling guru Paolo Zampolli of ID Models. The five-foot-ten-and-a-half Melania posed in catalogs for Lord & Taylor and Bergdorf Goodman, the same department store that helped launch Carroll Petrie's high-flying career as an international beauty.

Not a party girl, Melania, perhaps unexpected for a model, lived quietly in an apartment near Union Square. She loved staying home, reading, designing clothes (she once made a coat for a friend), and watching old movies on TV. "It was unusual for her to go out; she never went to clubs or bars," Zampolli recalled for a newspaper reporter. "This is a woman who modeled for Camel cigarettes on a huge billboard in Times Square, but stayed home all the time." A friend remembered the stay-at-home model as reminiscent of "strawberry ice cream, sweet and smells nice."

One night Melania was persuaded to go to a party hosted by Zampolli. It was held at New York's Kit Kat Club, and Donald Trump arrived with Celina Mildefart, a wealthy Norwegian woman, on his arm. When Zampolli "briefly introduced" Trump to Knauss, "Mr. Trump was fascinated," he told me. Trump asked Melania for her telephone number on the spot but was rebuffed. Melania was more appalled than fascinated (though she would later claim that she had also been attracted at their first meeting). Edit Molnár, a model and friend of Melania's, told a reporter that Melania felt Trump was "absolutely out of the question." Molnár recalled, "Melania said, 'He's here with a woman. I am absolutely not giving him my number.' . . . She wouldn't even consider it."

Though hardly a stay-at-home girl, Tory Robinson had an even more deeply ingrained sense of reserve than Melania Knauss—and a far more privileged background. She was, however, a bit of a tomboy growing up with three brothers on her family's Spring Meadow Farm on Philadelphia's aristocratic Main Line, though some snobs carped to *Vanity Fair* magazine that the undeniably stylish and well-heeled Robinsons in fact live in Valley Forge, which is not generally considered on the Main Line; they also cattily pointed to the irony (as they saw it) of Burch's clothing line epitomizing the WASP look when she is Jewish by heritage. "The Old Line is just a railroad. We were at the end of it," a "slightly annoyed" Burch was quoted replying. She also noted that she grew up celebrating Christmas and Easter. The farm was a congenial place—Tory's mother, Reva, who owned an events-planning company, helped raise the housekeeper's son, who was almost another brother to the Robinson children. Tory's father, I. E. Robinson, was a prominent investor. Tory graduated from the exclusive all-girls Agnes Irwin School, also on the Main Line, and went on to the University of Pennsylvania, from which she graduated in 1988, with a degree in art history.

After Penn, Tory went to New York, where she got a job as an assistant to Zoran, the designer, a friend of her mother's. She also worked in an editorial job at *Harper's Bazaar* and went on to do public relations for Vera Wang, Ralph Lauren, and Loewe. "She was a great public relations person," recalled a New York fashion editor. "She knew what her assets were. She knows she's attractive and smiley with a pretty-girl look. She had a very accessible manner. She had that WASPy prettiness that fit in at Ralph Lauren."

"She's shy and she's not charismatic," explained somebody else who has worked with Tory. Unlike Melania (and most women in this book), "Tory doesn't light up a room when she walks in, and she can come across as prim," the colleague added. "That said, people who spend time with her always say she's nice." A friend described her as "nice, warm, and calm," adding, "I think she wants her life to be fun and interesting, and she's driven by an idea of making it happen."

Something interesting did happen to Tory in 1993—she married William Macklowe, scion of one of New York's richest real estate families. The marriage lasted a little over a year. It was something neither discussed, the one hint that Tory might partake of human imperfection. "People who know her now don't know about this marriage," said an acquaintance. People have reported that Tory has said that she and Macklowe found out they didn't have the same ambitions—including her desire to be a mother—which is why the marriage quickly failed. The mystery is why somebody as careful as Tory Robinson didn't know that until after the marriage.

During her brief marriage to Macklowe, Tory's brother introduced her to handsome forty-year-old venture capitalist Chris Burch at a Christmas party in 1993 in Philadelphia. At the time, Burch was married to a Main Liner named Susan Burch, another alumna of the posh Agnes Irwin School; his first encounter with Tory seems not to have made an indelible impression.

A few years later Tory was working at Vera Wang in New York, and Burch's office was in the same building. Both divorced, they struck up a friendship and began dating. Burch had no recollection that she was Tory Robinson from Philadelphia.

For Trump, on the other hand, it was love at first sight. "There were a lot of very beautiful people there, some of the top supermodels. She stood out by a mile," he later told a reporter. His first encounter with Melania, in 1999, the same year his divorce from Marla became final, was almost a replay of his initial meeting with a reluctant Ivana waiting in line at New York's Maxwell's Plum. Once again, Trump was willing to pursue. "He liked her a lot," Zampolli recalled. The initial stages of their courtship were conducted quietly. "My girlfriend and I had no clue they were seeing each other," Zampolli told me. "Donald did all the work," Melania's friend Edit Molnár told a reporter.

Although Donald may have done the original courting, Melania soon succumbed to his charms and under Trump's tutelage was quickly transformed from a stay-at-home girl to a party girl. "She's changed her style," Molnár told a reporter. "She was more laid-back. Now she shops at the best stores in the world and she's always got her Manolos on." When Trump made a brief foray into national politics with a feint at running for president in 1999, the newly outgoing Melania, who was still working as a model and keeping her downtown apartment (but often staying in Trump's more luxurious digs), was at his side. As First Lady, she told *The New York Times,* "I would be very traditional. Like Betty Ford or Jackie Kennedy. I would support him." Still, it is hard to imagine Betty Ford or Jackie Kennedy ever granting a joint interview with Gerald or JFK of the sort Trump and Melania had recently given to radio shock jock Howard Stern. The couple dropped broad hints that they might be clad in nothing more than what the Great Couturier in the sky had given them. Stern wanted to know if Melania's beauty was marred by cellulite. Sounding eerily like Ivana, Melania pronounced it "shallalite." Donald told Stern that Melania didn't know what cellulite was because Trump didn't "deal with cellulite."

The *New York Post* responded to the Stern interview with a cartoon depicting Melania and Trump in bed—she had a dollar sign over her head. "The press could be sometimes very mean," Melania confided to *New York Times* writer Joyce Wadler. "They love to make a joke, that's how they're selling the newspapers." Melania insisted that she was not after Trump's money. "I think you can't be with the person if it's not love, if they don't satisfy you. You can't hug a beautiful apartment, you can't hug an airplane, you can't talk to them."

Did she mind Trump's discussion of their sex life on Stern's show? "It's the man thing, that's how the man talks," she told Wadler. The reporter noted, "Mr. Trump's public ways, which might seem to some women to suggest the objectification of women—'Where's my supermodel?' Mr. Trump yelled from the stage at a 'town hall' meeting at the University of Pennsylvania—do not trouble her."

As a helpmeet on the campaign trial, Melania was, in the eyes of many, a definite asset for Trump. When they broke up at one point, *USA Today* founder Al Neuharth wrote that it was Melania who had "gotten most of the 'oohs and aahs' at Trump campaign stops. Without her at his side, fewer lenses will click." Trump insisted that he had broken up with Melania, but her friends claimed she had ended the romance. The *New York Post* reported that Trump had had a sneaky encounter with a Victoria's Secret model at his apartment and been caught by Melania, who reportedly found traces of the other model's makeup on a towel. *National Enquirer's Uncovered*, the tabloid's TV show, had Trump and pugnacious gossip writer A.J. Benza, who had also been involved with the model, airing "dirty laundry. The filthy rich tycoon and greasy gossip got into a name-calling contest. Benza accused Trump of stealing his girlfriend." The breakup occurred about the time that British *GQ* came out with a cover featuring Melania—who gave every impression of being in a state of nakedness—on a fur in Trump's private jet.

Far removed from such trashy doings, Tory Robinson and Chris Burch had a quieter courtship, eventually falling in love. "It just happened," Tory, who as a rule abhors personal questions, told Roxanne Patel of *Philadelphia* magazine in what, by Burch's standards, was a wildly revealing remark. (Her publicist was aggrieved that I had left a voice mail for Mrs. Burch at her residence, and her friends were suspicious that I had called.) "We were really good friends for a long time first." Tory and Chris Burch were married in 1997 at Spring Meadow Farm. On being asked what brought them together, Tory's popular mother, Reva, who decorated the farm for the wedding, chuckled, "I would *hope* they married because they're in love."

After marrying two very rich men, Tory Burch is definitely a fortune finder, even if she is so discreet about her private life that her fortune hunting, if any—was it all just good luck?—is a state secret. Patel's article suggested that "in Chris, Tory had found her balance: Where she's reticent and even-keeled, he's outgoing and irreverent." The piece compared Tory with the Main Line's other "iconic blond princess," the late Princess Grace of Monaco.

As newlyweds the Burches divided their time between a residence on the Main Line and a pied-à-terre in a New York hotel where they enjoyed "a cozy three years" before Tory became pregnant with twins. The Burches acquired a two-bedroom in the same Fifth Avenue hotel to accommodate the twins and then moved into a 9,000-square-foot apartment at the same posh address. Laughingly describing their original digs as no bigger than her kitchen, she showed journalist Hamish Bowles around the new residence. Bowles wrote that the apartment had been bought "at a giddy price" and included "a length of corridor from the hotel itself—a gesture so extravagant that it became gossip-column fodder." "It's a large space," Burch admitted to her visitor, "but I didn't want it too grand. I wanted a real family apartment. I didn't want any rooms that the children couldn't go into." Indeed, the children have found that the "bowling-alley-long entrance gallery is an irresistible arena for skateboard and bicycle practice, and its princely Regency giltwood console table has become an object to be scaled for their youngest boy." Friends noted that Tory ran their apartment and her business with precision.

On happier times, a writer once described Tory Burch as having three houses, three sons, and three stepchildren. She also was known for a surprising close friend: Susan, her husband's first wife. Many women who marry big fortunes try to erect a barrier between the husband and his previous family, a course that leads to enormous suffering (even if it can ensure that the second Mrs. Rich ends up with all the riches). Tory did not adopt this painful policy. "When she and Chris got married, she inherited three stepchildren," recalled Ann Hamilton, another Agnes Irwin girl, who is close to both Susan and Tory. "Most thirty-year-old girls would not be able to get married, let alone raise stepchildren. But these children worship Tory. Tory and Susan have a mutual interest in making sure these girls are raised well." When Tory was invited to show her collection on *The Oprah Winfrey Show*, Susan went to New York to watch the show on television with the Burch daughters. When Tory took some of her "chic pals" to Buenos Aires to celebrate the opening of her husband's new hotel, a delighted Pookie Burch, clad in Tory by TRB, and now in her early twenties, exclaimed to *W*, "It's so weird to say that I'm wearing Tory. It's like saying I'm wearing Stepmom."

Burch was almost at pains to show that she too took motherhood very seriously. She also enjoys it. She has said that her favorite pastime is lounging on the bed with her children. "It makes you want to vomit, but I think it's sincere," said a catty observer. "She can be a royal pain in the ass. She's very self-protective, but ultimately very gracious," said a journalist who worked with her. She is active in New York's more established charities (Society of Memorial Sloan-Kettering Cancer Center and American Ballet Theater), and in 2004 she launched her line of clothing, with Christopher Burch as chairman and CEO of Tory by TRB, which makes sophisticated fashions available at less-than-astronomical prices. Bergdorf Goodman was an early wholesale customer, and she has outlets in downtown New York and Los Angeles. Oprah has dubbed her "the next big thing in fashion." "We mean business," she told Josh Patner of *The New York Times*, "in a baked alaska tone" that Patner found "both icy and hot."

She came across as part Princess Grace and part aspiring Carolina Herrera, and many people insisted that she was living proof that good marital karma could just happen to a very nice person. There was nothing, her society scribe friend Rob Haskell claimed, behind the Miss Nice image. "With someone who's so clearly the total package—glamorous, a mother of six, a successful businesswoman—people tend to look for the ugly stuff roiling under the surface. In this case I'm not sure there is any."

But clearly, in retrospect, there must have been something roiling under the surface of what seemed high society's perfect marriage. "In social situations, Chris's trademark bluster now seemed to embarrass Tory, especially when her girlfriends rolled their eyes," *Vanity Fair* reported after news of the separation broke. And there seems to have been competition between the two business partners. When her clothing line succeeded, the couple "wrangled over credit." "At least half of the success—at least—is due to my brother's efforts," Robert Burch told the writer Michael Shnayerson, seeming to downplay some of Tory's stated claims about going to Asia to do preparatory work. These differences highlight two perils: The successful fortune hunter's tacit bargain always to be second fiddle and her ability to put up with anything Mr. Rich does are difficult for a woman today. Can you imagine Marylou Whitney caring if her girlfriends rolled their eyes at Sonny Whitney? Tory Burch is thirty-nine, and she has already been married to two very rich men. Society scribes are no doubt dying to know if there will be a third, or if Tory will take the path of Georgette Mosbacher, in the next chapter. But Georgette became a single entrepreneur after three marriages, not a paltry two. Tory already has been linked with billionaire Ron Perelman. But it is her romance with Tour de France cyclist Lance Armstrong that has garnered the most ink. He reportedly called her after the *Vanity Fair* article on her divorce (though, according to the *Houston Chronicle,* he promised her that this was his first such action with a woman).

Behind the facade, the X-rated chatter on the Howard Stern show, or the photograph on the cover of British *GQ,* Melania Knauss is said to be just as nice (she's been described as "too nice for New York")—but she had to call upon the fortune hunter's gifts, and she had to do so with the world looking on. Trump had made the initial overture, but Melania had to practice the art of closing the deal. It took grit. She had to be shamelessly undeterred by Trump's alleged infidelity or his tabloid antics, she had to stick to him no matter what, and she always had to put him first. As Tina Brown once wrote, "For Melania it's never, Ask what the Donald can do for you. It's ask what you can do for the Donald."

After a six-year relationship, doing for the Donald finally paid off. She heard the magic words, which one hopes were "Will you marry me?" rather than "You're hired," his signature line on *The Apprentice.* She, of course, accepted and Trump got a good deal on a wedding ring—a 13-karat ring that diamond dealer Graff reportedly let him have at a bargain price in exchange for a second appearance on *The Apprentice.* Paolo Zampolli thinks that her fidelity to Donald—she's "not a player," he said—finally tipped the balance. "I think it is very important in this century, when marriages don't last forever, it is very important for a man to trust his woman. Mr. Trump wants complete trust," he told me. "She's been loyal to him six years, and it was the right move for Mr. Trump [to marry her]. It is in the nature of a woman to want to get married. I'm sure they'll have a baby—Mr. Trump really likes kids." (Zampolli made this prediction to me a few months before the Trumps announced in October 2005 that Melania was pregnant.) Needless to say, there was a prenup— "And the beautiful thing is that she agrees with it. She knows I have to have that," Trump bragged to columnist Liz Smith over lunch at Le Cirque—before the bride walked down the aisle in an Episcopal church in Palm Beach in April of 2005. Throngs of well-wishers crowded around the outside of the church as jet-setters observed from pews. She had had expert help choosing her Dior wedding gown—*Vogue*'s arbiter of fashion André Leon Talley and a fleet of photographers had accompanied Melania to Paris to shop. When one fashion adviser "repeatedly told Melania to do something about her fiancé's hair, she answered with a smile, 'I like him the way he is,'" the magazine noted.

But will it last? "If the Trumps celebrate their tenth wedding anniversary," a columnist in Scotland tactlessly observed, "I'll do a half-time flash during a Scotland game at Hampden." Tina Brown, the former magazine editor who knows all the boldfaced names, thinks it might. "Underneath all her fabulousness and gloss," Brown gushed in a piece celebrating the nuptials, "Melania Knauss's staying power in his life is based on a shrewd understanding of her quasi-commercial role. One feels she will not make [Ivana's] mistake of competing with the Trump brand. But she also knows, as second wife Marla Maples did not, the difference between being mere arm candy and high definition product enhancement."

If she is to be the last Mrs. Trump, Melania will need to take note of Donald's one-sided view of what makes a marriage work. "A marriage has to be easy . . . if you have to work at it, it's not going to work. It sort of has to be a natural thing," he breezily told Liz Smith. Melania has her work cut out for her.

Oddly enough, it is Melania, the model, not Tory, who in the end is the old-fashioned wife, devoting herself to her man. Jane Austen would recognize her choice. Will she be able to pull off a Marylou and be the last Mrs. Trump?

10

AFTERWARD . . .
UNSTOPPABLE REDHEADS

When Mr. Rich walks out, Mrs. Successful Fortune Hunter Rich may seek solace by locking herself in the bedroom of her Fifth Avenue apartment and weeping copious tears. However, she soon dries her eyes and sheds the extra pounds as she prepares to scale new heights. This, of course, is assuming that she made shrewd financial decisions while married to Mr. Rich. The wise fortune hunter does not make the fatal mistake of thinking that because she married money, she *has* money.

Georgette Mosbacher and Arianna Huffington have done considerably better than merely surviving high-profile divorces. In a way, the two redheads outdid the greatest fortune hunter of them all, the Duchess of Windsor. Whereas the duchess bravely lived out the disappointing aftermath of a great love story, Georgette and Arianna lived happily ever after—alone. It is not surprising that Arianna has been called "the most upwardly mobile Greek since Icarus" or that Georgette, having initially failed to take Washington by storm, has gone on to become a powerhouse in Republican politics.

Georgette and Arianna aren't close. Could it be, however, that when one looks in the mirror, the other peers back? Yes, there are many differences, but under the red manes, they both are women who are in control of their own destiny, women at the center of an exciting drama that will always have a happy ending, thanks to their own exertions.

GEORGETTE

When her father, George Paulsin, a Highland, Indiana, pipe fitter who resembled Clark Gable, was around, Georgette felt that nothing could go wrong. Walking home from school one cold day, savoring the prospect of her snug house, Georgette turned the corner and saw that her house was surrounded by cars. George Paulsin had been killed by a drunk driver. In the crowded living room seven-year-old Georgette heard a snatch of conversation that alarmed her: "Hope they don't have to split up the kids. *Hope they don't have to split up the kids.* It took a painful moment for that to sink in, but as soon as it did an urgent voice inside me said, *I have to keep us together.*" Georgette, the eldest child, gathered her four siblings together. "I looked at the stricken, frightened faces around me," Georgette wrote, "and took a deep breath. 'We're staying together,' I started slowly. 'We don't have a father anymore, but we're still a family. Mother isn't feeling very well, but don't worry—*I'll* take care of you. I'll protect us.'"

While mother Dorothy Paulsin, a widow at twenty-seven, went to work—demonstrating products in grocery stores, checking into hotels to evaluate services for the travel industry—Georgette was in charge at home. "Personally, I had no time for toys," she would recall. "I was too busy taking care of the other kids, budgeting, shopping and doing the laundry. I always had my eye on the big picture. . . . You can't climb a tree while you're figuring out how to run a household."

Some might be inclined to look back with bitterness at a childhood in such straitened circumstances. Not Georgette. She particularly loved going to work with her Grandma Mary Bell, a night switcher for the Baltimore Ohio Railroad and possibly the most influential person in Georgette's life. Grandma Bell had divorced her husband, "Red" Bell, a charming Irishman with a gambling problem—a daring act in that era. She took the railroad job because it allowed her to spend the day at home with her children. On the way to the switching shanty, Mrs. Bell would stop at a bar to buy Georgette snacks. "Here," Georgette would later note, "was an attractive woman entering a working-class bar with only a child in tow, and I never once remember a remark or a whistle or any kind of unseemly suggestion made to me or her. She had a presence and a dignity that quelled any horseplay. She simply overpowered them."

Culture was not neglected in the Paulsin household. An opera buff, Dorothy Paulsin drove her children to Chicago to hear live opera—from the most inexpensive seats, but it was exciting nonetheless. The family finances improved somewhat when George, seven, began working as a child actor in commercials. Dorothy was his manager. The family was able to move into a Dutch Colonial house. Dorothy claimed to have visualized the house before she actually saw it. "Making fantasy reality was much more satisfying than losing yourself in the safe sanctuary of endless daydreams" was the lesson Georgette learned.

While other girls dated and hung out at the country club, Georgette was also at the club—but she was ironing linens. Far from being envious, Georgettte appreciated anything that helped her save money for college. She was so good at ironing, she wondered what other ordinary talents she could use to make money. She loved glamour magazines, and though she was not yet the striking woman she would become—she was a bit mousy, to tell the truth—she loved experimenting with hairstyles. That gave her the idea that she could make money by doing hair. Georgette was too busy to be a great student or go to dances, but since she was a big-picture gal, this hardly mattered.

She managed to save enough money to enroll at Indiana University. While there, she worked as a store clerk, carhop, and switchboard operator. She also sold shampoo—Dorothy bought large bottles wholesale, and Georgette sold it in smaller quantities. "My goal was to graduate, period, and to do that I did whatever it took, including visualizing that outcome daily," she recalled. Georgette graduated with a B.S. in communications in 1969, the first woman in her family to get a college degree.

She would later say that she was "just a girl with good role models and one immediate goal"—escaping Highland. Georgette landed a job with Grey Advertising in Detroit. There Georgette made a life-altering decision: She became a redhead. "I had a strong sense of who I was on the inside, but what I saw on the outside didn't reflect me," she would recall. As she thought about it, wasn't it significant that Grandma Mary was a "*powerful* redhead"? "I decided to take the first step in reinventing myself," she would write. "I walked out of that salon a flaming redhead. I looked in the mirror and thought, I wasn't born a redhead, but I was born to be a redhead."

ARIANNA

While Georgette Mosbacher was cooking and budgeting for her single-parent family, Arianna Stassinopoulos, two years younger, was growing up in more prosperous circumstances in Athens. Her father was a journalist and later a management consultant who had been in the Greek under-ground. Her mother, Elli, wore caftans and sandals and was devoted to child-psychology texts. After Constantine and Elli divorced—with preco-cious Arianna's approval—Arianna and her sister, Agapi, spent holidays with their father, who took them on glamorous trips. A bookish child, Ar-ianna once dismissed the other children at her birthday party because she wanted to read.

At an early age Arianna conceived the ambition of going to England to study at Cambridge, one of the world's great universities. "I don't re-member ever wanting anything in my life as much as I wanted to get into Cambridge," she told Jesse Kornbluth. "It wasn't just studying. Cambridge was a way of life that would open new dimensions beyond getting a de-gree." Arianna was so dedicated to getting into Cambridge that, during a period of political unrest, she defied her mother to go to her entrance-exam tutor, only to be turned back by an armed member of the military. But her determination paid off, and Arianna was accepted at Cambridge.

Newly arrived at the university, Arianna overheard somebody remark that the Cambridge Union, the debating society, was the route to fame. Despite her almost incomprehensible accent, Arianna signed up. She was a disaster. Arianna was so awful that she quickly became notorious. "Some-times I was called to speak after midnight because I was so bad," she cheerfully told Kornbluth. "I spoke at every debate, preparing for each one as if I were a featured speaker." Her speaking style has been compared to Zsa Zsa Gabor channeling Lenny Bruce.

When the British foreign secretary, headed the next day for a Council of Europe meeting, attended a debate, Arianna seized the moment. Dis-carding her prepared remarks, she addressed him directly, offering her own insights on Greece and the international situation. It was her break-through moment. She became an overnight sensation. She went on to become the second female president of the Cambridge Union. Her fame spread beyond the university.

While Arianna was still an undergraduate, the London *Times* profiled "the delightful Miss Arianna Stassinopoulos." Noting that Arianna was not the typical "push bike and long scarf type of student," the *Times* enthused, "she is glamorous with lots of charm. . . . [A]nd the long hair and her looks make people think, 'Yes, she reminds me of Jackie Kennedy.'" She was not without detractors. "Perhaps because of her affluent style and considerable social and political success in Cambridge," the article admitted, "there is quite a bit of antagonism and jealousy towards her. She was likened to the wooden horse of Troy by last term's retiring [Union] president who said he saw himself as King Priam and her supporters as Greek warriors. Someone else came up with Virgil's 'timeo Danaos et dona ferentes' [I fear Greeks, even when bearing gifts].'"

With the feminist movement riding high, Arianna chose to define herself in opposition, a smart move. After a publisher heard Arianna criticizing Germaine Greer, the celebrated feminist, in an interview, he awarded Arianna a book contract to refute Greer. As outgoing president of the Cambridge Union, Arianna selected the topic for the year's last debate: "This House would explode the myth of Women's Liberation." She invited the right people: acerbic Auberon Waugh, son of the novelist Evelyn Waugh and a leading figure in English journalism, for her side; *Penthouse* editor Bob Guccione, accompanied by two lovelies, argued for the other. Not bad for an undergraduate.

The Female Woman came out a year after she left Cambridge. Embracing equal pay, it nevertheless begged feminists "not to throw the baby out with the bathwater." A bestseller in England, it made Arianna known in the United States. She was at every A-list party in London, appearing regularly on TV. The ultimate accolade: having *Private Eye,* the satire magazine, poke fun at her as "the Greek pudding." Arianna was "careful to present herself not as right-wing but as different, unpredictable, which allowed her a sort of silken deniability," *Vanity Fair* writer Christopher Hitchens, who knew Arianna in England, explained to journalist Margaret Talbot.

A fortune hunter gravitates toward the men with the money. But the first important man in Arianna's career gave her something else: additional entrée, emotional support, and literary advice. He was the diminutive

Bernard Levin, a columnist for the *The Times* and one of the most influential journalists in England. Arianna attended a lecture given by him. Although Levin was gleefully described as twice Arianna's age and half her size, they hit it off. "He used to say that going to bed with him was a liberal education," Arianna told *The Washington Post*. Levin helped her write the after-dinner toasts that contributed to the success of her social evenings.

Like Levin, a follower of the Indian guru Bhagwan Shree Rajneesh, Arianna was a spiritual seeker. At the London apartment of a friend, she was introduced to John-Roger Hinkins—known simply as John-Roger—leader of the New Age Church of the Movement of Spiritual Inner Awareness. Deeply impressed by "the Mystical Traveler," as John-Roger was called inside the church, Arianna went to Los Angeles to study his Insight course; reportedly she was baptized, while chanting John-Roger mantras, in the Jordan River. It is the most curious aspect of her life. Everything else displays unflagging ambition.

The London period of Arianna Stassinopoulos was about to end. Lord Weidenfeld, the publisher, gave her useful advice before she left to seek her fortune in the New World: "Don't bother with the men. You'll only make the wives jealous. Concentrate on the key women, and, if you play your cards right, you'll be a success."

GEORGETTE

Georgette's brother George was living in Los Angeles, and his letters convinced Georgette, emboldened by her new status as a redhead, that Los Angeles was a "land of dreams, a place where people went to create and reinvent their lives." Georgette, ready to reinvent more than the color of her head, bought a ticket to L.A. and moved in with George. By watching for celebrity yard sales, she furnished George's humdrum apartment with antiques. Like many socially ambitious people of modest means, the Paulsins learned the art of going to posh places and nursing an inexpensive soda all night.

A Sotheby's auction of movie props from 20th Century-Fox, a nice way to spend an afternoon—and perhaps meet some rich movie buffs—was to transform Georgette's life. She was fascinated when one man bought an entire lot of replicas of ships made for the movie *Tora! Tora!*

Tora! Georgette and George were heading home when she ordered her brother to turn around. When an official refused to give her the name of the big spender, Georgette blurted out, "Well, I'm from *Time* magazine, and we're doing a story on Sotheby's." Georgette got the name and number of Robert Muir. Most women would stop there—they might follow Muir's doings in the society pages or at most try to run into him. But a fortune hunter is not most women.

Still pretending to be a reporter, Georgette called Muir's office on Monday. She extracted the essential information from his secretary: He was a Mormon real estate mogul in his forties. Best of all, he was divorced. The secretary told Georgette that she could come right over to interview Muir. As Georgette pulled up, she couldn't help but be impressed that the Muir Medical Center loomed before her. Muir took Georgette to a fancy restaurant, where Georgette wasn't too rattled to notice how the waiters fluttered around Mr. Muir. "Well, okay, shall we start the interview?" he asked. Georgette took a deep breath and confessed that she had no affiliation with *Time*. To Georgette's immense relief, Muir threw back his head and laughed.

Georgette met Muir less than two weeks after arriving in Los Angeles. After a year of dating, they married, in August 1972. Georgette quickly set about improving Muir's social life by throwing big parties. They moved into a large house in Beverly Hills. Muir was very generous with his young wife—generosity is one of Georgette's main qualifications for a husband, as she later stipulated in her autobiography. As the couple drove past a Rolls-Royce dealership on Wilshire Boulevard, Georgette confided that as a child she'd imagined herself riding around in a Rolls. Muir went back and bought Georgette a royal blue Corniche convertible. Once home, Georgette sat in the car parked in the drive, listening to the stereo.

And then Georgette made a wrong turn. Muir had already made his fortune and he led a staid life full of gin rummy and golf. Marylou Whitney would have embraced gin rummy and golf, but Georgette took up instead with George Barrie, the dynamic CEO of Fabergé, the giant cosmetics firm and owner of Brut, a film production company. He pioneered the use of celebrity endorsements and knew everybody. Not just a businessman, G.B., as he was called, had composed the music for the movie *A Touch of Class.* Impressed by Barrie's power and a manner of living that included a private jet, Georgette felt that she could attach herself to G.B. "and watch my career soar."

Georgette went to work as a production administrator at Fabergé's Brut Productions, where people quietly—very quietly because G.B. was powerful—urged her to escape the abusive magnate. "G.B. had the clout to make you a corporate mogul or a star," Georgette observed. "I wanted glamour, and I wanted power. Her divorce from Muir was quick and amicable, though she would claim she walked away with nothing beyond the Corniche and personal property. Barrie's divorce took two frustrating years.

Georgette's wedding to Barrie took place in Las Vegas at Caesars Palace, with Roy Cohn, the controversial lawyer and Joe McCarthy associate, as best man. Cohn wanted Ann-Margaret, who was doing the dinner show, to announce the wedding from the stage. "I said she never does that, but Roy can be very persuasive," recalled Jack Martin, the New York gossip columnist, a member of the wedding party. Ann-Margaret obliged. The next day the foursome—Georgette was carrying a microwave oven—boarded the Fabergé jet. The plane landed in L.A. "I got off with the bride, and Roy and the groom went on to Acapulco," Martin said. "She had things to do in L.A. She was going to put the house in working order and go to Acapulco."

When Georgette wrote her autobiography/self-help book in 1993, it opened with a drunken Barrie berating her. The couple was living in New York at the time. "I almost forget how stupid you truly are," G.B. says. G.B. was on his sixth or seventh vodka, and Georgette was numb with fear. This was standard behavior for Barrie; this time he punched her in the nose. Georgette was relieved to find out in the emergency room that it wasn't broken.

Leaving the hospital, Georgette ducked into a phone booth. "But as I raised the quarter to the slot, I froze. Who on earth could I call?" Georgette realized that all her friends were really Barrie's friends. If recognizing as a seven-year-old that she had to be the one to keep her family together was an empowering moment, now the knowledge that she had to leave Barrie was another. A *Texas Monthly* writer once wrote that Georgette "takes refuge in platitudes." She does—and they're always empowering platitudes. For example, her plight in the phone booth made her realize that she was "going to have to be my own best friend to get myself out of this."

Although Barrie owned the apartment, she forced him to leave the next day. She began dating. Georgette was beginning to sense once again her ability to control her destiny—or as her book, *Feminine Force,* might put it, she was learning to "release the power within to create the life you deserve." "You can bet to lose or you can bet to win . . . it's your choice," Georgette says. With her decision to divorce G.B. "the era of living life by Feminine Force had begun."

Georgette had felt helpless because she worked for Barrie. Leaving him could cost her her job. Now she refused to cave when Cohn told her she'd be fired and end up on the streets if she divorced Barrie. "With my Feminine Force back on my side," she wrote, "I could be scared [by Cohn's threats], but I could not be stopped." Barrie did eventually fire her, but she began to dream about owning her own cosmetics company. She considered the business education she'd received from Barrie the "one great legacy" of the marriage.

Georgette unabashedly asked friends—*badgered* might be a better word—for help in lining up eligible men. She went through her address book and made an A-, B-, and C-list of friends who might know single men. "I was going to use the same strategy for dating that I did for reaching my business goals," she wrote. She went out with her share of duds, but she continued to press forward. "A cold call is a cold call whether you're looking for the love of your life or a steady paycheck," she reasoned. "Was I embarrassed? No. Never let embarrassment get in the way of achieving your personal goals, either."

ARIANNA

Arianna arrived in America with something more concrete than Lord Weidenfeld's advice—his introductions to some key women: then Chief of Protocol Lucky Roosevelt, ABC's powerful on-air personality Barbara Walters, Kitty Carlisle Hart, and socialite Marietta Tree. With friends like these, she felt she should throw herself a housewarming party. She decorated her rented apartment on New York's fashionable East Sixty-first Street with flowers and candles. "I said, 'My word, who *is* this girl who's written this book and done all these divine things,'" a wowed Barbara Walters confided to *New York.* Arianna and Walters soon shared exercise class for two, as other invitations poured in.

In no time, Arianna was at all the best parties in New York. She would recall for a reporter that she was "this new young thing on the New York scene." She moved to a new apartment on East Sixty-fourth Street—it had formerly been Cornelia Otis Skinner's digs—where she entertained such luminaries as Oscar de la Renta, Placido Domingo, Carolina and Reinaldo Herrera, Dan Rather, and Bill Paley. Lucky Roosevelt invited her to lunch with First Lady Nancy Reagan. The woman who would be dubbed the "Sir Edmund Hillary of social climbing" had advanced far beyond the foothills.

In addition to her Rolodex, charm, striking good looks, and moderate fame as an author, Arianna employed the most deadly weapon in the fortune hunter's arsenal—what Georgette calls the Look. Cultivating the Look is number one in Georgette's "Ten Proven Techniques for Turning a Moment into a Lifetime." "If you do any research on the great femmes fatales throughout history—and I mean from the French court favorites through modern heroines like Jacqueline Kennedy Onassis and behind-the-scenes political hostess Pamela Harriman," notes Georgette, "you'll find they all have one characteristic in common. And that is the ability to silently and wholly lock on a man with their attention." Georgette counseled that one's eyes must not roam even if a flying saucer with little green men landed.

Arianna raised the art of listening to such a level that when she targeted a male dinner partner (or a socially prominent woman, for that matter) with the Look, the rest of the room melted into nothingness. "At a certain point in the evening," one man who had experienced the Look told Jesse Kornbluth, "she focused on me as if I was somewhere between Jesus Christ and Belmondo. I thought, 'This woman is playing the role of a great conversationalist, and I know it—but it's still working!' Hers is the sort of intimacy that always supports your values no matter how hideous they may be."

Arianna was dating an eclectic collection of beaux—billionaire David Murdock, est founder Werner Erhard, real estate and media mogul Mortimer Zuckerman, and the elusive Jerry Brown, fellow spiritual seeker and former governor of California. Gossip columnist Liz Smith reported that Arianna was engaged to marry Brown, an item that turned out to be manifestly untrue. There was a theory in some quarters that the "news" had been leaked to Smith by none other than Arianna. According to this theory, Arianna realized that Brown wasn't going to marry her but thought she might get some publicity mileage out of the romance. Everyone assumed that she wanted to marry Zuckerman, but the romance fizzled after a few months.

As at Cambridge, there were critics. "Her mother, Elli, was there cooking and everything was warm and friendly," an associate told Jonathan Van Meter. "She had a good mix of people, but eventually I realized that everything she did was calculated. The wheels were always clicking. She's only interested in power and money."

A magazine profile raised an intriguing question that many high-profile New Yorkers were also asking: How did Arianna support her fabulous life of nonstop entertaining for people who only knew the best? She had made money from her writing, but not enough to live as she did. During a plane trip across the country with San Francisco socialite Ann Getty, wife of George Getty, a son of eccentric billionaire J. Paul Getty (and one of the people Arianna had met through Weidenfeld), the two women decided it was time for Arianna to settle down and have children. Not long afterward, Ann Getty called Arianna from Tokyo to announce, "I've met the man you're going to marry."

GEORGETTE

One evening on a business trip to Houston, Georgette was down in the dumps, expecting that her blind date for the evening would be yet another dud. When the elevator door opened, there stood handsome Texas oilman Robert Mosbacher. Georgette knew that this man was too dazzling to be her blind date. She was looking around to spot the geek who would be taking her out that night when Mosbacher spoke. Over dinner in a restaurant in the Galleria, she decided that Mosbacher was "gorgeous and courteous" and "radiated integrity." Research was in order. Upon returning to her hotel, Georgette called an old friend, Susan Glesby, scion of an old Texas family, to get the lowdown. "You had a date with Robert Mosbacher?" Glesby shouted. "I mean, he's only the second most eligible bachelor in the world." (Prince Rainier was the first.) Georgette learned that Mosbacher was the son of East Coast wealth who as a young man had gone to Texas to make his own fortune. His worth was put at around $150 million in 1983, before the oil slump. A prominent Republican fund-raiser, he was close to George H. W. Bush. His first wife, with whom he had four children, had died of leukemia. A brief second marriage had ended in divorce. He was nearly twenty years older than Georgette.

On their second date, in New York, Georgette told Mosbacher that she planned to marry him. Mosbacher was flattered but said that twice was enough. Georgette ignored this on the theory that a man who has married two times will marry a third. And because "there's no part of 'no' that I understand."

In her pursuit—for it must be called that—of Mosbacher, Georgette did what all successful fortune hunters do: She pampered him and flattered him and dreamed up so many activities that "when I wasn't there, there was a hole in his life." Georgette insisted that the stay-at-home oil-man take a trip to Europe (when she got him to go to Monte Carlo a business associate wondered if they'd found oil there), introduced him to her Hollywood friends (he was skeptical at first), and took him to the theater. There was even a jaunt to the Bronx Zoo. She showed him that a trip to the zoo as an adult is even more interesting than it is as a child.

Mosbacher was enjoying himself thoroughly—but the program wasn't working. He refused to marry her. Georgette was so distraught that she even saw astrologers. But she didn't let Mosbacher's reluctance stop her. Having proposed to her two previous husbands, Georgette continued to raise the issue. She threatened to end the relationship twice and he promised to marry her both times, only to back out at the last minute.

Georgette's inner voice, her Feminine Force, dictated that this state of affairs could not continue. Georgette wanted to marry Mosbacher, but if she couldn't, it was time to move on and look for somebody else. She "deserved marriage" and knew that she "would have" marriage, even if it had to be with somebody else. In February 1985 she gave Mosbacher an ultimatum; when he didn't agree to marry her, she returned to New York. When she didn't hear from him, she decided that it was time to "try the oldest trick in the book, my last stab." She would start dating another man. She sought the richest, most high-profile candidate she could find. When Georgette called a friend to arrange the date, the friend said she'd make inquiries and call her back. That wasn't good enough. Georgette ordered her to put her on hold and make the call as Georgette waited on the other line. "I can't take any chances on this one," she said. "You might get back to me, and you might not." When the date was arranged and the man (who has never been identified) took her out, Georgette made sure everybody knew. After only three dates, the phone rang—it was Mosbacher. Although Georgette felt that he "sensed the new intensity of my Feminine Force," she wasn't sure she was going to win. But she agreed to lunch.

Over lunch at Adam's Rib, he asked her if she thought it would be a good idea to get married on Friday. They had reached this point before, only to have Mosbacher change his mind. When he insisted, she accepted, knowing that if it didn't come, this was really the end. On Friday she flew to Houston, still not convinced, and picked up Mosbacher at a business meeting. They drove to College Station, Texas (away from the media), where they were married, with Georgette weeping so hard that she could barely repeat her vows; Mosbacher was calm. The wedding took place on March 4, 1985, less than four years after the phone-booth decision to leave George Barrie.

As Georgette was to learn, however, Houston society was, as the *Texas Monthly* writer Mimi Swartz put it, harder to hook than Mosbacher had been for the "part Damon Runyon broad, part Cosmo girl" Georgette "They weren't impressed that she kept her social calendar on spreadsheets, or that she had her eyebrows permanently darkened by a Gary, Indiana, tattoo artist," wrote Swartz. Georgette's New York nickname—Jawsette—was revived in Houston. Houston giggled at the sight of Georgette zooming around town in her Maserati, barking orders to her employees into the car phone. They were even more vastly amused when they learned that she traveled with her makeup in a Ziploc bag. But does any of this matter? "Perhaps Georgette hasn't mastered the rules of etiquette, or perhaps she is just too economical in her use of them. Not that it matters—she's won, after all," Swartz concluded.

ARIANNA

The man Ann Getty had picked for Arianna was Michael Huffington, tall and blond, the shy heir to Huffco, a Texas oil company. His father, Roy M. Huffington, had built Huffco into a $600 million enterprise. Roy Huffington had appointed his son president of Huffco. Getty arranged to introduce them at the opening party of the San Francisco Opera. Some thought Michael was a nonentity—but not Arianna. "The funny thing is," Arianna told a reporter, "he made it all right the minute he walked into the living room where we were all gathered before the opera. He came straight up to me and took me aside. He asked me, what was the most important thing in my life. I said, 'God. My spiritual life.' He said, 'In mine, too.'"

Arianna, who was at work on her biography of Pablo Picasso, went to Europe for a month. When she returned, she met Huffington again at the house of media mogul John Kluge and his wife, Pat, near Charlottesville, Virginia. "That was the time we declared ourselves to each other," she recounted to a reporter. "I remember that long walk on the grounds when I said to him, 'You seem very mysterious.' There's a part of Michael that doesn't open up to everybody. He said to me, I'll only fully reveal myself to the woman I marry.'" It was becoming clear that Arianna was to be that woman. They were engaged a few months later.

Ann Getty may not have been the only person instrumental in bringing about the marriage. An ex-member of the John-Roger cult told *Vanity Fair*'s Maureen Orth that Arianna once stood up at a John-Roger retreat in 1987 and declared, "Dahlings, if you want to marry a rich man like I did, then tithe!" John-Roger reportedly advised Arianna on her prenuptial agreement.

Ann Getty gave the couple a very handsome present—one of the most talked-about weddings in the annals of New York society. "In a year of big weddings," a magazine noted, "including Caroline Kennedy's and Prince Andrew's, the one people are still talking about is that of Arianna Stassinopoulos, the popular Greek-born scribe, to Michael Huffington, a shy Houston oil heir."

Held in St. Bartholomew's Episcopal Church on Park Avenue, the candlelight extravaganza featured a bevy of mature bridesmaids whose presence was a tribute to Weidenfeld's sagacity—Lucky Roosevelt, Barbara Walters, and Ann Getty as matron of honor. Henry Kissinger, who was among the guests, famously remarked that the Huffington wedding had everything "except an Aztec sacrificial fire dance." It was also more than Ann Getty had bargained for; she reportedly intended to spend around $10,000 on the wedding, but the cost was more like $100,000. Getty and Arianna stopped speaking.

A fortune hunter must have something specific to offer the man she seeks to marry. She must bring something to the table—different fortune hunters have borne different gifts. Jacqueline Kennedy gave the rambunctious Irish Catholic Kennedys a patina of patrician old wealth. Marylou Whitney cooked for C. V. Whitney and pampered him in a way that none of his other wives had thought to do. Arianna gave Michael a very special gift—himself. She repackaged the dim heir as an engaged politician with big ideas—her ideas. In exchange for Michael's making her chatelaine of Villa Ruscello, a $4.3 million house in the tony Santa Barbara neighborhood of Montecito (Michael remained in Texas briefly and then followed Arianna to California), she made him an up-and-coming politician. Michael had held only one job in government, a minor appointment in the Reagan Pentagon. Everybody remembered him as a nice guy. But that was all. Arianna's book *The Fourth Instinct* argued that the instinct for spirituality—the fourth instinct—is just as powerful as the three other basic instincts (survival, power, and sex). If people acted on their spiritual nature, they would volunteer to help others, and welfare programs would not be needed. This idea became the basis for Michael's political career. In an astounding and well-financed first outing, Michael took on a veteran California congressman and, to everybody's amazement, won. The verdict in California politics: it was the wife who had the basic instinct for politics. Arianna was ready for her Washington period.

GEORGETTE

Georgette had been through two bad marriages, and though she was in love with Mosbacher, she set about building her own financial security. Unlike fortune hunters of the past, contemporary ones will almost always be asked to sign a prenuptial agreement. "I had an emotional conversation with each husband first," she wrote, "but it's a no-win situation. When you sign it, you give away any rights you might have to your husband's property. But if you refuse to sign it, he can say you don't have his best interest at heart. There's nothing to do but grin and bear it." (Georgette warns that it's a good idea not to get a lawyer from the Yellow Pages. Hire the best; he will.)

Georgette signed the prenup, but then she made sure that, whenever possible, assets created during her marriage went under her name. She insisted that the deed to the couple's Fifth Avenue apartment be in her name. She was listed as part owner of the house in Houston. "Men never give up money and control easily," she wrote, "no matter who they are and how much they have." In a candid confession, Georgette admitted, "I was careful to pick the most propitious times to talk to Robert when I wanted to make a change in the way we listed ownership of some important asset. I'd wait for a vulnerable moment—say, after a friend's husband had just died—so I could use that event as a fresh example of why I was so determined to protect myself. I'd dig down deep and explain what I was feeling and why the change was important to me in a way that I hoped would strike an emotional chord. When I wanted to switch ownership of the New York apartment from both of our names to my name only, for instance, I talked about how unprotected I'd felt as a child after my father died and, as a result, how important it was to my emotional well-being to have the security of a home of my own and to know that no one could ever take it away from me." And then, as if the shamelessness of it all were a bit much even for Georgette, she added, "This was not some coldly calculated ploy on my part; it was the emotional truth, pure and simple."

Georgette used the knowledge she had acquired at Fabergé to run her own cosmetics company. She pursued La Prairie, a European skin-care company built on the restorative power of sheep placentas, the same way she had pursued Mosbacher—single-mindedly and equipped with good research. She badgered Sanofi, the French concern that owned La Prairie, for more than a year before it was willing to sell. With the support of her husband and other backers, Georgette beat out Revlon, Estée Lauder, and Avon to acquire it. A *Vanity Fair* piece wryly noted, "If there were once women who married so that they wouldn't have to work, today the same women marry so they can work the way they want to." As CEO of La Prairie, Georgette not only did normal CEO sorts of things but also paid visits to cosmetics counters and personally gave makeovers to customers.

The flamboyant makeup entrepreneur was about to meet her match—the dowdy women of Washington, D.C. When George H. W. Bush was elected president, Texas went to Washington. Robert Mosbacher was tapped to be secretary of commerce. During the campaign, when I was a feature writer, I was one of the first reporters to call Georgette to ask about the couple's possible role in Washington. A reporter from *Texas Monthly* was there when I called, and she wrote that after hanging up, Georgette appeared "relieved and happy, wearing a satisfied look that says she could handle just about anything."

She had not yet met the social and political arbiters of Washington. When Mosbacher was preparing to go before the Senate for confirmation hearings, a prominent senator (she has not identified the culprit) suggested that Mosbacher not bring his wife. She watched on TV. Georgette was simply too flashy for Washington. A *Washington Post* profile nicknamed Georgette "Hurricane Georgette," and the long knives were out for her. "I hadn't even shown up yet," she recalled. "I was in New York, running La Prairie. Yet in a city where wives were rewarded for staying in the background, they saw me coming."

Robert Mosbacher was on his way to becoming the first cabinet member in history to be known as "husband of." Georgette spent most days in New York, flying down to Washington evenings to entertain in the couple's house in the exclusive Kalorama section. Washington thoroughly enjoyed Georgette—in a catty, malicious, frumpy way. Georgette felt that she had become the "official target of the Bush administration." She was said to have worn an inappropriately flashy outfit to a dinner party given by George-town's aristocratic hostess Susan Mary Alsop. She was spotted walking her dog Adam in formal evening attire. She was reported to have been seen at the Kennedy Center wearing her trademark leopard pin suggestively on her breast. (Georgette would insist that if you looked at the pictures from the event, you'd see that this simply wasn't true.) Georgette was hurt, but she didn't blame herself, she blamed others—the women of the press, in particular, whom she regarded as jealous of her success. She decided to make minor adjustments such as not wearing her shortest skirts in Washington, but refused to put away her bright lipsticks and nail polish. "Following their code would cut me off from my Feminine Force," she concluded. She almost succumbed to their code when invited to a party given by a socialite. She was going into the lion's den and considered dressing sedately. But her Feminine Force wouldn't let her betray herself: " 'Georgette,' I finally said, 'you are not going to play into their hands by wearing black. Don't let it get to you. Wear what you feel comfortable in.' " She felt comfortable in an orange and yellow metallic suit—and she was the hit of the party. In her autobiography, she ridiculed the city's sedateness by calling Washington "the only city in the world where you can go from a B cup to a C cup without surgery."

Georgette is said to be difficult to work for; a magazine profile of her once referred to "a perpetually cowed secretary named Louise." I ran into Georgette one day during the George H. W. Bush administration at a tap-

ing for a TV show about Washington mores—we were in the makeup
chairs at the same time, and I kept thinking that, while they were slather-
ing it on me, they must have had to *remove* some of Georgette's. But the
most amazing thing was the way Georgette's sister, Lyn Paulsin was flut-
tering around to find ways to make Georgette more comfortable, waiting
hand and foot on her big sister, including spraying Georgette with a new
scent La Prairie was promoting at $350 an ounce. We should all have sis-
ters like Lyn, but most of us simply don't know how to make the world
orbit around us. Georgette does.

Georgette was spending most of her time in New York. She had sold
La Prairie in 1991 to Beiersdorf, a German conglomerate, for $46
million—it was said that she got $8 million of that for herself—and was
now CEO of Exclusives by Georgette Mosbacher, a line of cosmetics sold
in more down-market outlets such as Sears. But Georgette was breaking
two of the canons of the care and feeding of Mr. Rich: seeing him as her
job and focusing entirely on his comfort and enjoyment of life, and never
letting him out of her sight for long. Remember Marylou Whitney, who
took up painting because that's what her rich husband enjoyed? She knew
that if she didn't keep him content, there were women who would. Georgette seemed to be regarding La Prairie, not Bob, as her job.

One day Georgette picked up the phone to hear Mosbacher say,
"Georgette, you're not going to like this, but I thought you should know
that I've just filed for divorce." Georgette was stunned at what she described as the "betrayal." When she asked Mosbacher what was wrong,
Georgette told reporter Lloyd Grove, "He said to me that 90 percent was
perfect. Like, okay, I guess 90 percent isn't enough."

ARIANNA

Like Georgette, Arianna instantly attracted attention in Washington. But
in a different way. Perhaps because she had written books, stodgy Wash-
ingtonians chose to regard her as a serious person. "Everybody is crazy
about her," socialite Jayne Ikard told *The Washington Post.* The Huffingtons bought a $4.25 million stone house off Foxhall Road and hired the
former servants of Pamela Harriman, who was U.S. ambassador to France.
This, unfortunately, did not turn out well. *The Washington Post* soon reported that erstwhile Harriman staff members had "fled" the Huffing-

tons, charging that they were treated "like slaves." Oh well. Arianna was busy gratifying Washington's basic instinct for dinner parties—but with something extra. She had written that only when a "critical mass of pioneers" chose to follow the fourth instinct will "values like responsibility, forgiveness, gratitude and compassion be practiced with the same frequency that they are preached." She called her dinners "critical mass" dinners (also the name of her TV show on a conservative network). She invited socialites, media VIPs, and intellectuals. The dinners quickly became the talk of the town. But not in a good way, as the initial embrace was replaced by cattiness. "Every time anyone goes to one of these things, the phone is always ringing off the hook the next day and everyone is laughing," a guest told *The Washington Post*. It didn't help when word got out that Arianna was secretly taping her dinners. Arianna went blithely on as a hostess, seemingly unaware of the mirth she was provoking in stuffy old Washington. There was even a certain amount of chatter about Arianna as her adopted country's First Lady, even though Michael, unaided by his wife, was hardly presidential timber.

On Capitol Hill, Congressman Huffington was known as pleasant—nice enough, to be sure—but not a powerhouse. Then *Vanity Fair's* Orth unearthed the congressman's unnerving tendency to bestow unsolicited hugs on his male staff members. He was also fond of calling home to consult Arianna when an opinion was needed. And he said odd things—he once remarked that he didn't want anybody working for him who needed the paycheck. Still, after scarcely a year and a half as a congressman, Michael and Arianna decided it was time for something bigger. Michael Huffington, neophyte congressman, in 1994 challenged Dianne Feinstein, one of the Senate's leading Democrats, in her bid for reelection. There was more talk about Arianna's measuring the curtains for the White House.

"In the Hillary Rodham Clinton era, it is nothing new for a politician's wife to be a major factor in a campaign, especially if she is opinionated and has had a successful career of her own," *The Washington Post* intoned in a story headlined HIS MONEY, HER BRAINS. "But Huffington must face more than just bad jokes about who wears the pants in the family. He must answer the charge that he is just a vehicle for Arianna Huffington's considerable ambitions."

The Huffington campaign would turn out to be one of the most expensive Senate races in history, consuming $28 million of his money. Ed Rollins, the veteran Washington insider, ran the campaign (with lots of interference from the wife). Some of the ideas Huffington advocated (such as the fourth instinct as a way to reduce welfare dependence) had grown out of Arianna's own writings and her involvement with mystical traveler John-Roger.

Michael may have been the merest cipher on Capitol Hill, but his well-financed campaign actually moved the polls in his direction at several points. This drove the media mad. Frank Rich of *The New York Times* pitched a fit in a column that dubbed Michael "the Manchurian Candidate" (after the movie that featured Angela Lansbury as a controlling force behind the scenes of a presidential campaign). "How could this pair—an empty suit and a crackpot—have risen so far?" Rich asked. SHOULD THE HUFFINGTONS BE STOPPED? Margaret Carlson of *Time* magazine asked. Frank Rich reflected further in a "Manchurian Candidate II" column.

In the end, the Huffingtons were stopped, and Republican strategists weren't a bit hesitant about heaping blame for Michael's loss on the wife. Had Arianna not meddled, they said, Michael could have won. Ed Rollins wrote a book portraying Arianna as the nemesis of Michael's campaign. In *Bare Knuckles and Back Rooms,* Rollins described the campaign as "bizarre and chaotic," asserting that Arianna had hired a private detective to investigate *Vanity Fair* reporter Maureen Orth when she was researching a story on Michael. "I soon realized that I was trying to manage two candidates," Rollins wrote, "and the truth of the matter is she truly was the better one. She's very bright, incredibly fast on her feet, a good people person, and a tremendous debater."

Arianna watchers might have been inclined to conclude that Michael's loss opened a Pandora's box for the couple. They divorced in 1997. The next year, in an interview with controversial journalist David Brock, Michael dropped a bombshell. He revealed a long-kept (but not unsuspected) secret—he was gay. Michael confessed to Brock, who is also gay, that he had been "guilt-ridden and depressed" about his sexual orientation in the 1970s and had made a vow to stop sleeping with men. He insisted that Arianna had known going into the marriage. At the time, she would only say, "I wish Michael well; all that matters to me is that he's a good father to our children."

She would insist to *W* magazine four years after the divorce, "I did not know my husband was bisexual when I married him." Michael—who seemed to have found his own voice at last—responded with an angry letter to the magazine. "Normally I don't write letters to the editor," he began, and went on to say, "I would never go into a marriage without telling someone I love about my sexual orientation. On December 23, 1985, Arianna and I were sitting on my sofa in the living room of my town house in Houston when I told her about my deepest secret, being bisexual. She fully accepted it and me. This was thirteen days before I asked her to marry me and more than three months before our marriage. Why she feels the need to rewrite history I do not know. But it is disappointing me and an injustice to our children." It may be that both Huffingtons were telling the truth. A close friend of Michael's suggested to me that perhaps he *thought* he had told Arianna but used so much roundabout language that Arianna had no idea what he was trying to tell her.

Whatever she did or didn't know about her husband's sexuality, Arianna Huffington's Washington period had come and gone without her having presided over a "critical mass" dinner in the White House. Perhaps Arianna, like the mythical Icarus, had fallen to earth.

GEORGETTE

That the Mosbacher marriage was on the rocks was big news. "Never, not since the Trump split, have I encountered such private interest as has been expressed in the breakup of Robert and Georgette Mosbacher," wrote New York gossip columnist Liz Smith. "At lunch last week in Manhattan I was 'rushed' by over a dozen women when I came in the restaurant door. The effect was almost like a football scrimmage. Every one of these best-dressed denizens wanted me to 'tell all,' give the inside hot skinny and clue them in to whatever it was they were sure I hadn't printed yet." Smith reported that Georgette had gone to Houston, "weeping and begging for a reconciliation."

Georgette volunteered to give up her life in New York and move to Houston. It was too late. "Love her? He doesn't even like her anymore!" a family friend told Liz Smith. One Texas socialite told a perhaps apocryphal story of an angry Mosbacher, so frustrated by the egotism of his wife, that he swept his arm across a table that held numerous pictures of her, breaking the picture frames.

Georgette subsequently surmised that the problem was one that inevitably besets the wife of a rich man who stints on the continuing-care program—the Other Woman. Before reaching this conclusion, Georgette decided to surprise Mosbacher by showing up for an after-Christmas cruise he had arranged with his grown children. But he wasn't there. Apparently getting wind of Georgette's presence, Mosbacher showed up the next day. "It really wasn't another woman," Robert Mosbacher told a reporter, "and it isn't another woman. It didn't have to do with anyone else. It is very different priorities. I've wanted to spend most of my life in Houston, where I've lived since I got out of school, and is the home of my children and grandchildren, and she wanted to live in New York." Robert rejected Georgette's belated offer to move back to Houston and was quoted saying, "[B]less her, she loves the fast lane."

Perhaps this is the peril of fortune hunting today, when Mrs. Rich regards it as her right to have her own self-fulfilling career. In April 1998, after thirteen years of marriage, the Mosbachers were divorced. She was forty-nine; he was sixty-nine. Georgette was devastated, but she was financially well-off. Not only did she have her own business and the property she had put in her name, but Robert also agreed to pay her nearly half a million a year in tax-free alimony. Mosbacher, the man who said he'd never marry a third time, is now married to his fourth wife, the much younger Mica Mosbacher. They live in Houston.

ARIANNA

After moving back to California, Arianna seemed to flounder. She did not lose touch with Washington and was briefly Newt Gingrich's new best friend, throwing fund-raisers for him and trying to interest him in the fourth instinct. Their parting was not amicable. Instinctively, Arianna knew it was time to reinvent herself.

Arianna soon had an entirely new set of friends—liberals. Her new new best friend was Bill Maher, the left-wing political talk-show host. Maher urged Arianna to use humor to survive attacks by her critics. When Maher spoke, the great listener listened and, as she had with Weidenfeld, heeded his advice. Playing off Ed Rollins's unflattering characterization of her, Arianna began appearing on Maher's popular show *Politically Incorrect* as "the evil Arianna." With Maher's help, the humorless Cambridge debater transformed herself into a comedian and became a star on Maher's show. She went on to a gig called "Strange Bedfellows" on Comedy Central that featured Arianna and Al Franken, the liberal commentator and author, in bed together debating the issues. (Arianna was still a conservative—just barely.)

Newt Gingrich's former soul mate was reincarnating herself as a liberal pundit, changing her political stripes and having fun doing it. She wrote a column that occasionally got her in hot water—she once accused President Clinton of having an affair with the wife of a big contributor. She also threw glittery parties, at one of which Arianna single-handedly hatched the notion that Warren Beatty, one of those present, should run for president. The proposal was briefly taken seriously, creating a ripple of publicity. In the same year, the former Republican wife penned a book urging the overthrow of the government. It was called *How to Overthrow the Government*. When it came out, *W* magazine proclaimed, "Arianna Huffington may have changed her political stripes, but her growl is just as loud." Reviewer Joe Conason dismissed the book as "less Tom Paine or Che Guevara than Helen Gurley Brown."

But Arianna's basic instinct hadn't changed—the liberal Arianna had just as much lust for the spotlight as the conservative Arianna. With maverick Republican senator John McCain, Arianna hosted her own "shadow conventions" during the 2000 presidential race, ostensibly held to provide a foil to both the Democratic and Republican conventions. It was also an Arianna platform. I attended and introduced myself to her as somebody who had covered her when working for "Page Six." Arianna brightened, graciously pretending to know "the famous Charlotte Hays." It was flattering, even if transparent. As Georgette had written, "Flattery will get you *almost* anywhere." She pulled back and became frosty when I asked for a later interview for this book. She simply couldn't grant it, because she wanted to spend more time with her children.

Arianna was able to tear herself away from her motherly duties long enough to launch an abortive run for governor during the California recall election. Michael angrily charged that the girls didn't want her to run, and they moved in with him while their mother was on the campaign trail. But even if she was never going to win, the campaign featured delicious moments of pure Ariannaness: knocking down a bank of microphones to squeeze next to fellow candidate Arnold Schwarzenegger for the photographers. "With Arnold as a foil for Arianna, I see no downside in her giving the race a whirl as an Independent candidate. Her whole career has been one of fantastic reinvention," wrote Tina Brown, who was initially miffed that Arianna had interrupted a holiday with Brown to rush to California to register as a candidate.

The candidacy turned up an embarrassment: Arianna—who called for closing tax loopholes for the rich—had paid less than a thousand dollars in income taxes over a two-year period. In the end, Arianna bowed out, not because she was chagrined over her taxes but because she wasn't going to win. Even so, the gubernatorial race had turned into another one of Arianna's excellent adventures. Arianna's latest is her much-ridiculed celebrity blog the *Huffington Post,* hailed by *LA Weekly* as "such a bomb that it's the movie equivalent of *Gigli, Ishtar* and *Heaven's Gate* rolled into one." Nevertheless, the *Huffington Post* went on to become a prominent liberal blog, frequently quoted and known for interesting theories on current events. Famous people such as actor Alec Baldwin, *Seinfeld* creator Larry David, and writer Nora Ephron contribute to it gratis. Not inappropriately, Arianna's eleventh book, published last year, was a self-help autobiography (in the Georgette mode, but far less candid) entitled *On Becoming Fearless . . . in Love, Work, and Life.*

A man who has known Arianna over the years was asked what would have happened if she hadn't married rich. After all, by the end of her New York period, people were beginning to wonder: How does she finance her parties and other accoutrements of the Arianna style? Would Arianna, without the spoils of a Midas marriage, have faded from the scene? No, he said, not Arianna. "Arianna would have done something to pull dollars out of the air," he said. "Even if she had had to scale down, she'd have written a book on voluntary simplicity. The point: Arianna doesn't lose, because she refuses to lose." During the New York period, *Town & Country* had hailed Arianna as Aphrodite, goddess of love; but her real model is Proteus, the god who could change shapes at will. It is Proteus, the god of self-reinvention, who inspires the fearless Arianna on her path through life. But if you look carefully, you will see that the more she changes, the more she remains the same. There will always be an Arianna.

GEORGETTE

After her divorce was final, a crushed Georgette found herself unable to sleep and uncharacteristically unwilling to go out. She gained twenty pounds, mostly from doughnuts and chocolate. One of Georgette's most important attributes, as described in her first book, is an ability to move past failure. "Success Is the Process of Not Accepting Failure" is the title of one of her chapters. Georgette is an optimist who will always bounce back stronger than before. After a period of grief, Georgette bounced back. She took off the weight and emerged as one of the most effective Republican fund-raisers in the country.

As her Feminine Force reasserted itself, Georgette came out with a second book, *It Takes Money, Honey*. As with the first book, it's part auto-biography and part self-help book. Some have detected a more somber tone in the post-divorce book, but when not dwelling on Robert Mos-bacher's "betrayal," it is upbeat. It is also realistic, with chapters titled "Don't Live in Denial" and "Put a Price Tag on Your Dreams," and such tips as having a "secret stash" that your husband doesn't know about (she doesn't tell you how to acquire the stash). One reviewer summed up the book's theme as "dollars are a girl's best friend."

Georgette has plenty of dollars, thanks to her own efforts. She began entertaining again, in her New York apartment with the twenty-foot ceilings, antiques, and enough gold leaf to put Fort Knox to shame. *Harper's Bazaar* proclaimed an invitation to Georgette's "a hot ticket," adding that "the most dazzling element at any Mosbacher get-together is the hostess herself. Vivacious, generous and down-to-earth, Mosbacher knows how to have a good time and bring everyone else along with her." Georgette's motto, echoing Sophie Tucker, is an oft-stated observation. "I've been rich and I've been poor," she is fond of saying. "And let me tell you, rich is better."

11

SACRIFICIAL LAMBS?
The Children of Fortune Hunters

A book about fortune hunters isn't complete without a look at the next generation, the children of these awe-inspiring creatures. Like the offspring of other parents with demanding jobs, the sons and daughters of women who marry rich are all too often the ones who pay the emotional price for their mothers' success.

Though most fortune hunters don't excel at motherhood, some break the mold. Jacqueline Kennedy—who believed that nothing else mattered if you blew it with raising your children—was one who did. It was risky. She neglected her second husband, Arisotle Onassis, to spend time with her children. But Jackie was a rare combination of fortune hunter and dedicated mother. "Two days after Kennedy was assassinated," Pierre Salinger recalled to the author Sarah Bradford, "she walked into my office and said something which I think was her complete future because she said, 'Listen, I have only one thing to do now—I have to take care of these kids. I have to make them grow up well, they have to get intelligent, they have to move forward to get good jobs, they have to have a whole very important life because if I don't do that for them, they'll spend all their time looking back at their father's death and that's what they shouldn't be doing.' "

Outside of the Bible or Greek mythology, Jacqueline Kennedy's standing with her two small children as their father's coffin passes is possibly the most famous image of motherhood ever. The entire world remembers that she leaned down and whispered something to John F. Kennedy Jr. and that then the little soldier gave his father a final salute, one of the most touching moments in the annals of the American presidency.

Although the death of a race car driver, even an aristocratic playboy, isn't as historically significant as that of a president, the death of Alfonso, was also the subject of enormous fascination. Like the Kennedy children, the two Portago children, Andrea and Anthony, were thrust into the spotlight.

An old newspaper photo of the Marquesa de Portago, the former Carroll McDaniel, who went on to become the very rich Mrs. Milton Petrie, at the time of her husband's death, with her children in tow—accompanied by a governess, of course—begs comparison with the Kennedy tableau of grief. Antonio (or Anthony) Portago, in short pants and an Eton collar, reminds one of John F. Kennedy Jr. He was three and his sister was six, the same age as the Kennedy children. (John F. Kennedy Jr. celebrated his third birthday the day after his father's funeral.) There were as many differences as similarities behind the pictures in the newspapers. The Kennedy children would have something the Portago children didn't: a mother who always put them first. Jacqueline Kennedy and Carroll Petrie provide two different styles of mothering; unfortunately, Jacqueline Kennedy's is the less common.

Whereas Jacqueline Kennedy had been growing closer to her husband when he was killed, Carroll Portago was estranged from hers, living in New York while he lived in Paris. But both women now had two children to bring up on their own, and they also had their own careers to pursue. Jackie had always spent a lot of time with her children in the White House, where she established a White House school for Caroline. J. B. West, the chief White House usher in the Kennedy years, sometimes watched the First Lady playing with her children. "I felt, strangely, that this was the real Jacqueline Kennedy," he once said to author Ed Klein. "She was so happy, so abandoned, so like a little girl who had never grown up. Many times, when she was performing with such grace and authority the role of First Lady, I felt she was just pretending. 'She really belongs in a child's world,' I thought, 'where she can run and jump and hide and ride horses.'"

After the deaths of their first husbands, both women lived on Fifth Avenue in New York and then both married men who lived in exotic places. Jackie married Aristotle Onassis in 1968, on his private island of Skorpios, partly because his money could buy privacy for herself and her children. A reporter noticed her glancing anxiously at Caroline from time to time during the ceremony, however. When Caroline was enrolled in Concord Academy, a boarding school in Massachusetts, Jackie took a house nearby for weekends with her daughter. A friend of Jackie's told Jan Pottker that Jackie and Caroline were "like one soul." Jackie talked about her daughter's brilliance constantly, and she worried about John's propensity to be easily distracted. Onassis was angered that his trophy wife spent so much time in the United States with her children.

Though Jackie took a house to be near Caroline's boarding school, Carroll installed Andrea in a suite in the Carlyle Hotel during her teen years while she herself lived in Hong Kong or went big-game hunting. For adult supervision, Andrea had a governess. Andrea was in New York to study ballet with George Balanchine, the choreographer, who had accepted her into a prestigious class for younger dancers. Carroll may not have been as close to Andrea as Jackie was to Caroline, but she did take an intense interest in Andrea's ballet. "I'd never say my mother was a distant mother," said Andrea, "She didn't understand how different I was from her in essential things. My mother and I were both so focused on my being a ballerina." When Carroll was in New York, "we didn't go shopping; we went to the theater and museums. I was in love with ballet. Mr. B. took me into his school twice. I was his type physically, but I never developed feet."

A charming boy, Tony was only seven years old when he flew alone from Hong Kong to England to attend the Ludgrove School, to which Princes William and Harry would one day be sent. With his mother half a world away, Anthony Portago was probably far more stranded than the princes. For a while, before she moved to New York to study ballet, Andrea was at another well-known English boarding school, Heathfield, on a Georgian campus twenty-eight miles from London. The children made only occasional visits to Hong Kong.

Throughout their childhood, the Portago children knew little about a normal family life. "They had pretty awful childhoods," said a friend. When asked if Carroll had neglected them to pursue her own career, a close friend of Anthony's replied, "Those were Anthony's words exactly." A titled European lady was more blunt: "Carroll was never a mother to her children." For affection, the children turned to others, most especially their adoring stepgrandfather, Isidro Martin-Montis, an aristocratic Spaniard who had married Olga, the dowager marquesa, and lived with her in the fabulous Villa Carlotta in Biarritz on the Côte Basque. Martin-Montis was a devout Catholic with a calming voice. "Isidro gave Antonio the only parental warmth he ever had," said a close friend of Anthony's. Andrea said, "He brought love into the family."

As fond as the two needy children were of Martin-Montis, Carroll eventually reportedly ruled that she did not want them to make frequent visits to Biarritz. The apparent reason: Portago's family had adopted the late marquis's other son, Kim. The boy, son of Dorian Leigh, a model, was about Anthony's age. He had been legitimized after his father's death because the marquis had written his sister shortly beforehand saying that he wanted Kim to have the same opportunities as his other children. Kim looked exactly like his father, and Olga and Sol, Portago's sister, the Marquesa de Moratalla, adored him. "When I was thirteen, my grandmother had somebody tell me about Kim," recalled Andrea. It appears that Carroll, who understandably had been stung by her husband's infidelity, did not put her own feelings aside. She limited the children's visits to Biarritz whenever she could.

Jacqueline Onassis had to deal with a complicated past, too. Whenever fresh reports of JFK's philandering surfaced, she tried to make it clear to John and Caroline that their father had loved his family. To give them a sense of their father's place in history, she frequently invited people who had worked in the Kennedy administration to talk to the children about their father. "My children never knew their father," she once said to former U.S. senator Abraham Ribicoff, a family friend, "and the person who knew Jack best was you. And I'd like you to come and talk to them, so that they can understand who their father was and what he was."

Nobody seems to have tried to make Anthony Portago proud of his father. Carroll had loved having Fon Portago's title, but apparently she didn't appreciate it enough to hand down stories of the man who had given it to her. When the photographer Francesco Scavullo asked Anthony if his mother had talked much about his father when he was growing up, Anthony admitted that she hadn't. "My grandmother had a lot of pictures of him," Anthony told Scavullo for a book of profiles of glamorous men, "but my mother didn't keep pictures of him. He was never a symbol of what we were meant to become. We never idolized my father which was fine because he wasn't there. He never meant anything to me. . . . I suppose I got a clear picture of him about a year ago, when I was twenty-one. I formed an idea of what my father was because every young male at some point has to have some kind of identity with a man. I had that in a way, since I was sent to boarding schools from the ages of seven to eighteen. But there were so many different kinds of men whom I didn't like that I didn't want to identify with them anyway."

Andrea, who was old enough when her father died to remember him, clearly idolizes him. To this day, she is angry with Enzo Ferrari, her father's employer. She becomes heated talking about the day her father died, claiming the car he drove was defective. "It might be a romantic story for some people," she said, referring to her father's playboy image and early death, "but it came at a great loss. A lot of people like to focus on the salacious gossip, but my father was a gifted athlete."

Although Caroline Kennedy, the brilliant child, attended the Kennedy alma mater, Harvard, John chose Brown, where his friends tried to shield him from paparazzi. John, who suffered from dyslexia, had repeated the eleventh grade at Phillips Academy in Andover and was less academically directed than his sister. But he was a gifted actor and wanted to enroll in the Yale School of Drama. In what is possibly an example of a mother who can't let go, Jackie would not allow John to do so, even though a director called him "the best young actor I've seen in twelve years' when he appeared in an off-Broadway show in 1985. Nevertheless, John took a job as an assistant district attorney in the office of New York DA Robert Morgenthau, a family friend. Jackie adored John, who delighted her and was always more of a free spirit than his sister. But Caroline, who also had a law degree and was working on a book, was Jackie's ideal. She was married to Ed Schlossberg, a designer of museums and theme parks. Caroline guarded her privacy, but her brother sought publicity. He loved being in the tabloids and dating everybody from Sarah Jessica Parker to Madonna. If Caroline was settled, John was not; and Jackie worried about her son, particularly his relationship with the actress Daryl Hannah. Jackie found her lacking in the dignity required to marry the president's son.

Whereas John had gone to work in the DA's office, Anthony Portago had not settled down at an early age. Unlike John, he did not graduate from college. In a way, Anthony had followed in his father's prep school footsteps—Alfonso had been sent to Lawrenceville, the respected boarding school in Lawrenceville, New Jersey, but lasted only a few months. Anthony enrolled in Groton, another prestigious school. Like his father, he did not graduate.

With their name and good looks and tantalizing aura of tragedy— "lost souls" is how they have been described more than once—the Portago siblings, a bit older than the Kennedy children, were welcomed as part of the glittering New York nightlife scene. Andy Warhol and Scavullo were their friends. If Caroline was living up to Jackie's intellectual goals and John, while not yet following in his father's political steps, was showing himself to be a swinging Kennedy, Andrea and Anthony were in a way reprising their parental pasts, too.

They became well-known figures at Studio 54, the reigning nightclub, at 254 West Fifty-fourth Street; it became for them what the old El Morocco had been for their mother. "What made Studio 54 seem like the center of the universe," wrote Jim Holt in *Slate,* "was that every world— art, royalty, Hollywood, fashion, rock, Euro, literary, gay, political, bohemian, blue-blood—brilliantly intersected there. It solved, for a brief shining moment, what in game theory is known as the 'coordination problem.' Yes, Elizabeth Taylor, Norman Mailer, Warren Beatty, David Rockefeller, and Mick Jagger will go to a nightclub, but only if they are reasonably certain that Diana Ross, William F. Buckley Jr., Salvador Dalí, Betty Ford, Frank Sinatra, Mikhail Baryshnikov, and the king of Cyprus will show up too—and vice versa."

Anthony was considered a great catch by the women and an all-round nice guy by the Studio set. "We were all there laughing and dancing and drinking," Scavullo said in an interview shortly before he died. "Tony was a very charming, wonderful guy. There was nothing you could dislike." "He was not somebody who took drugs. He was very reserved, kind of trying to keep in the shadows, but all the girls were throwing themselves at him," said a former girlfriend. Like John Kennedy, Anthony Portago was the sort of young man people instinctively love. But unlike John, he had a hidden side. There were rumors about Tony's sexual orientation. "Sure, I had heard all the rumors," the former girlfriend said, "and it started to make sense." "I don't think he was homosexual," said another ex-girlfriend. "He had bisexual affairs when we were together," she admitted. She attributed his confusion to "a terrible, terrible childhood."

A woman who was involved with him talked about Anthony's strange relationship with his family's past. "Anthony showed me pictures, a family album, and there's a picture like John Kennedy and Caroline Kennedy," she said, referring to a picture taken of the Portago children at the time of their father's death. "It was a bit of the same kind of picture. He said, 'See this picture? It looks like I'm crying, but I'm laughing.'"

Although Carroll and Jackie had little in common as mothers, they both worried about the girls their sons dated. Jackie was particularly concerned about Daryl, and Carroll about the girls Anthony met at places like Studio 54. Carroll was, in the words of one of Anthony's girlfriends, "controlling." But this woman felt that Carroll's own ambition was the root of her concern. Like Madame de Pompadour, who neglected her daughter, Alexandrine, but wanted a noble title for her, Carroll wanted her Anthony to marry well. Or at least not to embarrass her. "Carroll Petrie wanted to protect her own reputation to climb higher and higher," the former girlfriend claimed. When Anthony and this woman, also a well-known figure on the nightlife circuit, went a trip out West, Carroll read about it in a gossip column and immediately called her son. Anthony and his girlfriend had taken pictures of each other. "After his mother called, he had me rip up pictures we'd taken of ourselves," she recalled. "It must have been fear [of his mother]," she said, adding with a chuckle, "I guess I didn't have enough titles or money."

Another curious glimpse of Anthony, who did not work but obviously had access to money, in this period came from gossip columnist Jack Martin. Visiting in Hollywood with a girlfriend, Anthony showed up at Martin's with a box of cuff links he wanted to sell him for $500. "I don't know how he arrived at that figure, but he must have been very desperate," Martin said. "It was sad when he showed me those cuff links. One pair of them was worth more than five hundred dollars." Martin added, "He was a very good-looking boy, almost to the point of being charismatic."

Jackie exerted influence on John's life, and it is unlikely that he would have married anyone who didn't pass her muster. When he did marry, he was in his thirties. Although the marriage turned out to be filled with problems, he worked hard to save it. Anthony Portago, who had had a controlling mother instead of a steady one, would marry three times. At the age of eighteen, Anthony married for the first time, to the former Barbara Schlubach. A blond socialite described as "a tough cookie," she is the daughter of Florence Van der Kemp, whose husband was Gerald Van der Kemp, the curator of Versailles. She had grown up at Versailles. "Barbara tends to let people think she grew up in the palace itself," joked a detractor. The marriage lasted two and a half years and left Anthony disillusioned. "I was deeply in love and was as high as I could ever go in love, but it didn't get me anywhere," Anthony said in the Scavullo book "I mean I'm sick of love in that way. It just gave me a lot of shit in the end. It gave me a lot of pain." Barbara de Portago declined to be interviewed. For a while, she was a prime object of hate for Carroll and Andrea, who, in an infrequent moment of unity, once considered suing her to prevent her from using the Portago name. Much to Andrea's chagrin, she even uses it incorrectly—the title is de Portago, but the name is just Portago.

Six years after the breakup of his first marriage, Anthony was ready to try again. This time he chose another regular at Studio 54, former model Antonia Lynch-Vernier, who sang onstage dressed as Marie Antoinette. They had known each other as children in Biarritz. They had frequented Biarritz's Hôtel du Palais, built by Napoléon III for his Empress Eugénie to summer, where Antonia recalled being taught to swim by the Duke of Windsor. Their families' Paris apartments were also close. "Both of us had spent some time doing social things, and we had had enough of that and were interested in holistic medicine and spirituality, especially Buddhism," Antonia said. Anthony vacillated between Catholicism and New Age spiritualism. He loved music and put on a free concert by Argentine nuevo tango master Astor Piazzolla in Central Park. "I studied some dancing. I also studied acting," he told Scavullo. "I went into a lot of arts at one point until I got fairly sick of trying to show myself through art. A lot of people are very much into self-expression, but I really believe that that's beside the point. The point is that we *are*. We are living and we are alive. It's irrelevant who we are: we just are."

Contrary to the blasé image he affected when speaking with Scavullo or showing a girlfriend the family album, Anthony adored his father's memory, according to Antonia. The tough talk was bravado. "Antonio put his father on a pedestal," recalled Antonia. "I heard so much about Fon that I felt I knew him. Antonio felt a pressure to be as dazzling as the late marquis. It wasn't very good for him, and he was ambivalent about that."

Anthony even drove in a few automobile races to emulate his father. But he found that racing wasn't for him. He also found, once again, that marriage wasn't for him. The second marriage lasted less than a year, though he and Antonia remained devoted to each other. "We were really true, true friends," she said, "but we were not meant to be married. We have given each other a rendezvous in the next life. We felt we'd known each other before and we will again."

Anthony was not the only Portago son living in New York in the early 1970s—Kim was also living on the Upper East Side, and the brothers became friends before Kim, most likely under the influence of drugs, committed suicide by jumping out a window sometime in the late 1970s. Kim had sent his girlfriend out to buy drugs and jumped while she was gone. "During the last few years of Kim's life, he and Antonio became very close," recalled Antonia. "Kim was tall, slim, dark; charm oozed out of every pore. He was quite desperate in a way. We were very good friends. Very shortly before he killed himself, he invited us to his apartment on Park Avenue and the walls had been painted gray and his bedroom was black. I told Antonio that I was quite worried about him." Kim is buried in a beautiful cemetery overlooking the sloping Basque country hills, next to his father and his grandmother.

Andrea was also living in New York and breeding dogs. In a "like mother, like daughter" scenario, she was, as her mother had been, a model. Andrea represented Farouche, a perfume from Nina Ricci. She also had the honor of being the first cover girl for her friend Andy Warhol's *Interview* magazine. She had a good time, showing up at a birthday party for Rolling Stone Mick Jagger sometime in the 1970s "half-naked" and "bald"—her hair was close-cropped and dyed red. David Geffen, the Hollywood mogul, teased Andrea about it when the two were present when Warhol and the writer Bob Colacello talked to Cher at the Pierre Hotel for *Interview* magazine.

Andrea seemed ready to follow in Carroll's footsteps in a second way: by making a Midas marriage. On January 16, 1978, Andy Warhol noted in his diary: "We found out that Andrea Portago is marrying Mick Flick this weekend in Switzerland. And then [socialite] Barbara Allen came by with [another socialite] Lacey Neuhaus. . . . When [Barbara] heard about Mick Flick and Andrea, she tried not to look shocked—she recovered in a second and said, 'I only had one date with him and he was so boring that

I left before the espresso.' " Flick is Friedrich Christian Flick, a Mercedes-Benz heir, one of the world's richest art collectors. Mick Flick and his brother, Muck Flick, as they are called, were known for their all-night parties and being, in the words of Taki, "famous skirt chasers." Though Andrea was a brunette, Mick preferred blondes—the ill-fated Christina Onassis was so smitten with Mick that she dyed her hair blond for him. Revolted, he fled, and for years she would pester his other female conquests for information about him. Because the Flick fortune was built on the endeavors of his grandfather, a Nazi war criminal who benefited from slave labor, art galleries were sometimes hesitant to show works from the Flick collections. Andrea and Mick were married only a few months, during which they lived in New York—on Fifth Avenue, across the street from the Frick Museum. Andrea was amused that the Flicks lived across the street from the Frick, but the brief marriage, which remains something of a mystery, left bitter feelings. "She had nothing nice to say about him," said an insider. Flick went on to marry and be divorced by Countess Maya von Schonburg.

After Jackie died, John Kennedy pursued a project about which his mother had doubts—founding a magazine. She had told her friends that she worried because John knew little about journalism and, having been the quarry of journalists, she didn't like the idea of her son entering the profession. John launched *George* in September 1995, genially quipping to the assembled newshounds that he hadn't seen so many of them in one place since he flunked his bar exam. John had good editorial instincts, according to a *George* staffer, but he probably would have been more fulfilled if he had been allowed to go into acting. He was struggling to put the floundering magazine on a firm financial footing at the time of his death and was contemplating a run for office.

People who knew Anthony Portago felt he was on the verge of getting his life together in the 1980s. He had moved to New Mexico and found the perfect job—a fund-raiser for the United World Colleges. It was a good fit. He loved the work and was good at it, and it was the sort of posh cause where the son of a marquis would be an asset. Prince Charles was president of the United World Colleges until Queen Noor succeeded him in 1995. There were ten campuses throughout the world. The Santa Fe campus where Anthony worked had originally been named for Armand Hammer, a longtime benefactor. Best of all for Anthony, it was a paying job—he insisted on that and a college official said it was "very important to him." Not because of the money but because of the self-respect. "The last time I saw him he was coming out of St. Vincent Ferrer Church [on Lexington Avenue in New York]," said Francesco Scavullo. "He said he was feeling very good and was very happy."

In May 1984 Anthony married for the third time, to Linda Spier, of Santa Fe, an attractive woman with deep family roots in New Mexico. He bought a ranch near Santa Fe and the couple soon had two daughters, Theodora, who is called Teddy, born the year they married, and Carolina, born two years later. He loved showing pictures of his daughters to everybody. "I look at the move to Santa Fe as an effort to center his life in some way," said somebody who knew him then. "He went to Santa Fe to distance himself from the social set into which he was born," said another. "He was a drifting, semi-tragic figure, and I think he knew it. He was struggling. He was a decent human being who was struggling. If he'd lived longer, he would have overcome what he tried to."

As with John Kennedy, Anthony's life was careening off course in the last years, but in a different way. John was finding that his storybook marriage was a facade. Perhaps John's life would have turned out better if he had become an actor, for which he had a real genius and was the one career in which his megacelebrity might have been nothing out of the ordinary, and if he'd married Daryl Hannah, who was probably more in love with John the man than John the image of perfection than was Carolyn Bessette. Whatever John was going through before he died, Anthony was living with darker demons. His marriage to Linda ended in divorce, and Anthony's friends were subsequently saddened to learn that he was suffering from HIV. A loyal friend insisted, "He did not have the kind of lifestyle of men who die of AIDS. He told me of one experience and said 'Can you imagine? It was that one time.'" While living in Spain, Portago took a turn for the worse. He first went to New Mexico and was then flown to New York, where he was operated on to no avail, and was so sick that he could not speak. Anthony died in New York on March 6, 1990. Like John Kennedy, who was thirty-eight when he died, Anthony was young and, despite his struggles, left behind a legacy of love from those who had watched him try to overcome his demons. He was thirty-five, seven years older than his father had been when he died.

Jackie had died first and been spared the agony of losing John, but

Carroll Petrie, now married to Milton Petrie, an elderly multimillionaire, had to endure Anthony's. She was not equal to the task. For one thing, she could not bring herself to admit that her son was dying of AIDS. Because of her refusal to acknowledge this, many New York socialites thought they saw glimmers of Carroll Petrie in Liz Altemus, a heartless society matron who refuses to give emotional support to her charming son who is dying of AIDS in Dominick Dunne's novel *People Like Us*. Andrea adored her brother and was "in shock" when he died. "Andrea has complained of Carroll's not being a good enough mother to Tony," said a family friend.

The funeral service was held in the private chapel of New York's John Cardinal O'Connor (who would later try to help John Kennedy and Carolyn Bessette Kennedy save their marriage). O'Connor preached on sin. Several of Anthony's friends felt it was an allusion to the cause of Anthony's death and were furious. This was not the only cause for tension. Making arrangements for the funeral had not brought out the best in Carroll. When somebody asked about inviting Andrea, Carroll said, "Oh, certainly not—we're not speaking." Andrea did attend her brother's funeral Mass, but she did not sit with her mother. Society gossips were intrigued by Carroll's choice of outfits for her son's funeral—she wore a vibrant purple, not a usual hue of mourning, ("It might shock a lot of people," Andrea said years later, "but my brother adored the way my mother would get dressed up. She may have done that as a thing between them.") After the Mass, the mourners adjourned to Carroll's apartment for a mournful lunch.

A few weeks after Anthony's death his friends gathered on what would have been his birthday—March 29—for a life celebration at the loyal Antonia's New York apartment. Carroll Petrie begged off, saying, "Oh, no, I couldn't. I have a very important dinner." But the friends went ahead. Twenty or so people, including Antonia, Lady Jean Campbell, and socialite Nicky Vreeland, met and, amid white candles and lilies, listened to Stevie Wonder, Bob Marley, and other musicians Anthony had loved. When Antonia and Lady Jean sang a song they'd composed in memory of Anthony, most of those present dissolved into tears.

Though Jackie Kennedy moved easily into being Grandma Jackie, Carroll didn't have smooth sailing as a grandmother. Shortly after Anthony's death, she said that she wanted the girls to come to New York to see her. Linda Spier, who did not trust Carroll, was frantic. According to a friend, she feared (perhaps wrongly) that Carroll wanted to do with her daughters what she felt that Olga, Carroll's mother-in-law, had done with Kim—take them away from their mother. Carroll and Linda ended up in a protracted legal wrangle, with the court setting the rules of visitation, down to how Carroll's dog, which scared the children, had to be handled during visits. "She dragged Linda to court because Linda said no, and nobody says no to Carroll Petrie," said a woman close to the situation. In addition to visiting schedules, there was also the matter of Anthony's ashes. Carroll had claimed them as hers, keeping the urn on a mantel in her bedroom. But Teddy Portago wanted her father's ashes. In a letter in the court documents, Teddy Portago begged for them. "I'm writing this letter not only because I want you and Mom to make up," ten-year-old Teddy told her grandmother, "but because I would like to have Daddy's ashes." In a warm but brief handwritten reply, Carroll said she was looking forward to seeing her grandchildren and promised to "have discussions about your father." But the bulk of the letter was devoted to the real focus of Carroll's life, Milton Petrie, who was gravely sick. "He doesn't speak anymore and he sleeps a lot but we also keep seating him upright so many hours each day," the anguished woman wrote, "and then I can hold his hand and he knows I'm there."

While Caroline Schlossberg and Andrea are the upholders of the family legacies, they perform their filial duties in different ways—Caroline appears at functions that honor the Kennedy memory; Andrea petitioned for and received the family title. She is now the Marquise de Portago. She lives in California and is a talented photographer who travels frequently to New Mexico, where she photographs Pueblo, Hopi, and Zuni. She is on better terms with her mother than in the past—for the most part—and though they still may go long intervals without speaking, they are friendly and agreeable when they do talk. "There's one big problem with my mother. I lived in Europe and my base is European. It's hard for my mother to realize that there is a cultural difference," she said. "Jockeying for position in society is irrelevant to the Portago family. But it might be my mother's story because she is a Southern woman. As different as we are, we get together and have the same things to say about a lot of people. But I really am probably more like my dad."

$\mathcal{E}pilogue$

FORTUNE HUNTING FOR FUN AND PROFIT (AND—QUITE OFTEN—LOVE):
It's Your Choice

Socialite Nan Kempner, who died in 2005, went out as she had lived—with style and a sense of humor. Of course, *The New York Times* observed, she would have considered the pre-noon hour of her memorial at Christie's, the posh auction house, "ghastly." The seventy-four-year-old socialite was never awake at ten in the morning. Nevertheless, so many pencil-thin A-listers did rise at what a socialite regards as daybreak to toast her memory with fine champagne that it looked as if "upper Park" had been "drained" for the occasion. Society bandleader Peter Duchin provided the music. Amid the festive tributes ("Nan's very sorry she couldn't be here, today," jewelry designer and Kempner confidante Kenneth Jay Lane was quoted, saying, "but as you all know, she would never want to see any of you, no matter how much she loved you, before lunch"), there was a genuine sense of loss. "She was my own Holly Golightly," a saddened Pat Buckley mused to *New York Times* journalist Joyce Wadler.

Buckley's allusion to Truman Capote's devil-may-care character from *Breakfast at Tiffany's* summed up Kempner's approach to life—or at least part of it. Nan Kempner had lived life to the fullest, even dragging her oxygen tank to fashion shows in New York and Paris as her emphysema worsened. Her fortitude and effervescence had won the day. But her life also embodied a key tenet of fortune hunting—you must not allow your-self to be buffeted by fate. You must learn to regard life as composed of the choices you make. Like many women who marry rich men, Nan Kempner's marital bliss had been marred by her husband's propensity for to seek love outside his marriage. In the mid-1990s Tom Kempner's affair with Iris Sawyer, a former actress, made it into the gossip sheets. For a short time, at the end of their eight-year affair, Kempner reportedly lived with Sawyer. A non–fortune hunter might have panicked, lost her nerve. She might have been devastated that her husband did not love her and her alone. Nan simply did what had to be done. "Nan Kempner threatened to take him to the cleaners, so Tom returned," gossip writer Roger Friedman wrote. Kempner had made her choice to remain in the marriage. Behind the frothy facade, there was determination. Friedman alleged that Sawyer was financially "ruined," attributing this to Nan's behind-the-scenes machinations. Not every muse of fashion is so capable of taking care of herself, but every fortune hunter must be if she is to continue the life to which she has become accustomed in the face of marital adversity. Nan was once quoted saying of the rumors, "It just washes off." Could you be-have in this fashion in order to be fashionable? A postscript: Barely a week after Nan's September memorial at Christie's, gossip doyenne Cindy Adams announced the impending nuptials of Nan's bereaved husband. He was planning to marry sawyer. SOCIALITE'S HUBBY WORKS FAST was Adams's headline. Tom and Nan Kempner had been married fifty years.

As I have said over and over again in this book, being a successful for-tune hunter is a matter more of talent and will than of looks. The job re-quires a certain degree of determination and dedication. In Kempner's case, it was not, of course, her Holly Golightly side that enabled her to preserve a marriage that a more sentimental woman might have fled. It was something harder and more calculating, something tough behind the fashionable exterior. Something, in short, alien to Miss Golightly. You might, after all, remember that the model Dorian Leigh—the woman who bore the Marquis de Portago's doomed illegitimate son—also likened her-self to Holly Golightly and may, in fact, have been Capote's real-life model for the character. Unlike Kempner, this free spirit never married the man. She had a career as a professional cook and now lives in Paris. A pure Holly Golightly will not make a successful fortune hunter. Having fun all the time must be secondary to having money all the time. Unlike most fortune hunters, Kempner had a sense of humor to carry her through life's tough patches. But when the chips were down, she was able to call upon her inner fortune hunter to defeat a rival. Better than having breakfast at Tiffany's, Nan could shop there.

But nothing, least of all shopping at Tiffany's, is free. If you are not a highly resourceful woman capable of single-mindedness, fortune hunting is not the right choice for you. Even Ivana Trump, who fell romantically in love with Donald Trump, could be hard-nosed in pursuit of a good settlement when her marriage failed. She hired private detectives to spy on her beloved. But Ivana didn't stop there. She wrote a novel, *For Love Alone,* which told the story of a wonderful, wonderful gal who marries a sleazy, sleazy tycoon. All of this was helpful in her ending up a very rich woman. Only those with this kind of grit and strength of mind should pursue wealth through fortune hunting.

But hardness swathed in couture is not the only trait you must have. You must, if you opt for this choice, resign yourself to doing what somebody else wants to do almost all the time. You must be willing and able to preserve your status by putting him first. Could you endure the tirades of an elderly man who was jealous of every man who came into your houses? Marylou Whitney could.

Most of the older fortune hunters in this book devoted themselves full-time to attending to their husbands. Even in an era when young socialites have chosen to work, the contemporary successful wife must make certain that her house is run perfectly in a way that ensures the uninterrupted comfort of Mr. Rich. If you lack this kind of stamina and self-discipline, why not plan to just live, live, live—and maybe not be rich, rich, rich?

Still, if you are up to the job, it can, as Nan Kempner demonstrated, be fun at the top. Paris a few times a year, gowns that cost what many pay in rent annually, and, at the end, a champagne send-off. Whether you are a natural beauty or a woman who has made herself beautiful, the choice, whether you are willing to sacrifice to be dazzlingly rich, is yours.

Notes

PREFACE

xv Pamela Harriman's stationery   Christopher Ogden, *The Life of the Party,* p. 394.

1
PROSPECTING FOR GOLD

2 "You'll never make it on your face"   "How to Be a Park Avenue Princess," *New York,* Aug. 23, 2004.

7 Charles Wrightsman's demands on Jayne   Francesca Stanfill, "Jayne's World," *Vanity Fair,* Jan. 2003.

8 the news of the Robert and Blaine Trump divorce was broken by Suzy,   *W,* Sept. 2005.

2
THE POWER OF BEAUTY AND THE PHILANDERING MARQUIS

11 Carroll's appearance as a girl   Interviews and *Nautilus,* the 1940 yearbook from Greenville, S.C., High School.

14 she bought a fur coat   Confidential interview and Leonard Lyons, "Lyons Den," *New York Post,* July 1954.

14 El Morocco description and nightlife of the era   Interviews and Jerome Zerbe's privately printed photo album of El Morocco (introduction by Lucius Beebe); Neal Gabler, *Winchell;* Ralph Blumenthal, *The Stork Club;* Gilbert Millstein, "The Twilight of a Zany Street," *New York Times Magazine,* Jan. 1950; "El Borracho, Café Society Likes Its Old Gage," *Life,* Feb. 17, 1947; Tryra Sampter Winslow, "To Eat Drink and Be Mentioned," *New York Times Magazine,* Feb. 24, 1946.

16 Dodero's friendship with Peróns   Alicia Dujovne Ortiz, *Eva Perón,* pp. 143–215; Joseph A. Page, *Perón: A Biography,* pp. 190–238; and Nicholas Fraser and Marysa Navarro, *Eva Perón,* p. 75.

16 international travel with Dodero   Confidential interview and "The New Queen of Hearts Collects Diamonds Too," *New York Mirror Daily,* Jan. 23, 1949.

16 Alfonso Portago   Brock Yates, "The Search for the Marquis Alfonso de

Portago, Myth Versus Reality: Gentleman Racer or Aristocratic Clown?" *Car and Driver,* May 1986; letter to editor in *The Times* (London) by C.K.W.S.; Ken W. Purdy, "Portago," *Car and Driver,* Aug. 1957; obituary in *The Times* (London), May 13, 1957; Alan Henry, *Fifty Years of Ferrari;* "A Driver to Remember," *Motor Trend,* May 1986; "The Search for the Marquis de Portago," *Car and Driver,* May 1986; Phillip Knightley, "Big Dance Hunter," *Mail on Sunday,* Nov. 26, 1995; Ivor Herbert, "I Won't Miss the Job of Calling the Race . . . or the Anxiety," *Mail on Sunday,* Mar. 29, 1998.

18   She took him to Greenville   Lutie McGee, "The Breakfast Hour," *Greenville* (S.C.) *News,* Dec. 23, 1950 (with picture).

19   the stunning Dorian Leigh   Confidential interviews and Michael Gross, *Model.*

21   "What? Are you seriously turning down a Marquis of Spain . . . ?"   Linda Christian's autobiography, *Linda: My Own Story,* is source of this anecdote and much of the affair with Portago.

21   Portago's death and funeral   "Linda's Racer Hits Crowd; He and 11 Die," *New York Daily News,* May 12, 1957; "A Kiss from Linda Before Dying," *New York Daily Mirror,* May 13, 1957; "Four Women Race to Dead Marquis; Linda Is First," *New York Daily News,* May 13, 1957; "14 Killed at Race in Italy, Marquis' Car Hits Crowd," *New York Times,* May 13, 1957; "Give Up Racing? Not for the Greatest Love Marquis Told Linda" "Marquis Felt Death Was Near," and "Mass Funeral for Crash Dead," INS, May 14, 1957; "Widow Calls Linda 'Just Another Girl,' " INS, May 15, 1957; "Car Race Victim Buried: Widow and Linda Christian Go Separate Ways to Grave," *New York Times,* May 15, 1957; "Bury Marquis; Linda Keeps Her Distance," UP, May 15, 1957; "Widow, Linda Attend Mass for Marquis," UP, May 16, 1957; James McGlincy, "Screen Career Is Almost a Minus: Linda's Loves," *New York Daily Mirror,* June 1957; Andrew English, "Memories of the Mille Miglia," Telegraph Group, Oct. 25, 1997.

22   documentary about Portago   *Alfonso Cabeza de Vaca, Marquis de Portago, un documentaire en deux parts de Philippe Alfonsi,* parts produced by Planette, Taxi Productions, Paris.

24   Carey-Hughes wedding   "Marquesa de Portago Married at the Carlyle," *New York Times,* Apr. 12, 1964; Doris Lilly, "In Town and Out" *New York Post,* Aug. 9, 1961.

25   "Carroll simply hadn't counted on Jane Engelhard"   *W,* Aug. 7–14, 1989, which refers to Carroll's "alleged interlude" with Charles Engelhard.

26   Richard Pistell and his business dealings   "Big Game Hunter Says Pup Is the Tiger in Marital Tank," *New York Daily News,* Feb. 20, 1969; "She Signs Big Names for Her Divorce," *New York News,* Mar. 19, 1969; "From Board to Bush," *Business Week,* Jan. 10, 1970; "Suzy Says," *New York Daily News,* Oct. 2, 1974, gives a one-sentence lead item announcing Carroll and Richard Pistell's divorce.

27   marriage to Pistell   "R. C. Pistell Weds Marquesa de Portago," *New York Times,* May 23, 1969.

27   life with Pistell   Interviews and Eugenia Sheppard, "Inside Fashion," *New York Post,* Apr. 7, 1970; A. L. "Ike" Eisenhauer, *The Flying Carpetbagger;* and a profile of Mrs. Richard C. Pistell, by Jerry Tallmer in the *New York Post,* Dec. 11, 1971.

27   Pistell's financial troubles   Stanley Penn, "Suit Charges Pistell Used Assets of IOS Totaling $3 Million for Own Enrichment," *Wall Street Journal,* June 12, 1974, and "Money from Gold and Wine Promoter," *Wall Street Journal.*

27   Milton and Carroll Petrie's life   Interviews and *New York Post,* May 30, 1986; David Remnick, "The Artful Codger," *Manhattan, Inc.,* June 1986; "Now That's a Party!" *New York Post,* Dec. 8, 1987; "Petrie Will Be Cited by Cops for Charity," *Daily News,* Mar. 11, 1988; Joanna Molloy, "Thanks a Million," *New York Daily News,* Nov. 11, 1994; "Milton Petrie's Stores Go Bust," *New York Post,* Oct. 13, 1995; "Retailer Assists Detective's Widow," *New York Times,* Aug. 1997.

28   "dug through the diamonds"   *W,* Aug. 7–14, 1989.

29   Petrie apartment on Fifth Avenue   Intelligencer, "Petrie's Dish," *New York,* Apr. 19, 1999.

3

IF AT FIRST YOU DON'T SUCCEED . . .

32   Nouvelle Society   Charlotte Curtis, "Society's New Order Takes Over," *New York Times,* Mar. 18, 1986; "Nouvelle Society," *W,* Jan. 5, 1987.

33   "It's so expensive to be rich"   John Taylor, "Hard to Be Rich: The Rise and Wobble of the Gutfreunds," *New York,* Jan. 11, 1988. This article is a source in part for descriptions of Susan's parties and of John as a "brutal" trader.

33   Gutfreund apartment   "Too Far, Too Fast," *New York Times Magazine,* Jan. 10, 1988.

33   "My wife has spent all my money"   "Hard to Be Rich," op. cit.

34   Jayne Wrightsman   Francesca Stanfill, "Jayne's World," *Vanity Fair,* Jan. 2003. (This article also documents the subsequent cooling of the relationship.)

34   "*Bonsoir, Madame*"   "Hard to Be Rich," op. cit.

34   Mrs. Gesternblatt   Michael Thomas, "Mrs. Fish's Ape, Society and Hospitality in New York, Vignettes and Reflections," *Vanity Fair,* 1983.

34   Gayfryd's epic parties   "Let 'Em Eat Cake," *W,* May 16–23, 1988; Liz Smith, "Saul Steinberg's Birthday Bash Is a Genuine Work of Party Art," *Orange County Register,* Aug. 9, 1989; Martha Sherrill, "Abuzz About a Million Dollar Bash: For Saul Steinberg's 50th, an Embarrassment of Riches," *Washington Post,* Aug. 19, 1989; Richard Cohen, "Wretched Excess, 1989," *Washington Post,* Aug. 20, 1989; "Plutocrats and Moralizers," editorial, *New York Times,* Aug. 22, 1989; John Kenneth Galbraith, "Nothing Succeeds Like Excess," *New York Times,* Aug. 28, 1989; Michael Kilian, "The Party Poop: People Outraged by Steinberg Shindig . . . Are Missing the Point," *Chicago Tribune,* Sept. 6, 1989.

37   "J.R.-ed" into Gayfryd's life   Tina Brown, "Gayfryd Takes Over," *Vanity Fair,* Nov. 1986.

37   Dominican divorce not valid in Louisiana   *Times-Picayune,* May 8, 1983.

38   Some harbored a grudging admiration   Ibid.

41   Johnson's tax debt   "N.O. Businessman May Owe Millions in Tax and Penalty," *Times-Picayune,* Oct. 19, 1982.

41   she stored nine valuable paintings   *Times-Picayune,* May 8, 1986.

41   Gayfryd quickly obtained an order   Susan Finch, "Tax Evader's Divorce Is a Federal Case," *Times-Picayune,* Oct. 5, 1983.

42   "not in keeping with the décor"   *Times-Piscayne,* May 8, 1986.

45   "Everyone was surprised she stayed around"   "Hard to Be Rich," op cit.

46   Tina Brown placed their meeting in November 1982   Tina Brown, "Gayfryd Takes Over," *Vanity Fair,* Nov. 1986.

47   In granting her divorce   Dawn Ruth, "Imprisoned Businessman Is Divorced," *Times-Picayune,* Dec. 23, 1983; Joan Treadway, "Wife Is Bigamist, Tax Evader Johnson Charges," *Times-Picayune,* Mar. 3, 1984.

48   "had it for ages"   "Hard to Be Rich," op. cit.

49   Saul Steinberg's downfall   Johanna Berkman, "After the Fall," *New York,* June 19, 2000; Suzanna Andrews, "Vanished Opulence," *Vanity Fair,* Jan. 2001; Geoffrey Colvin, "Beward the Buccaneer," *Fortune,* July 9, 2001.

50   John Gutfreund's fall   James Sterngold, "Too Far, Too Fast, Salomon Brothers' John Gutfreund," *New York Times,* Jan. 10, 1988.

50   "If I were her"   Kevin West, "School for Scandal," *W,* Dec. 2000.

4

THE GREAT COURTESANS

53   "hooked the biggest fish of all"   Locution of hooking her Bass seems to have originated in *W* magazine.

54   "Iranian firecracker"   *Vanity Fair.*

55   married in Geneva   "Miss Tavicola Marries Here," *New York Times,* Oct. 13, 1972.

55   "a hearty, vodka-drinking extrovert"   *Vanity Fair.*

56   "She has all the fashionable ladies"   S. M. L. Aronson, "The Bolters," *New York,* Oct. 20, 1986.

57   incident with the horse   Michael Schnayebon, *Vanity Fair,* August 1995.

58   "much too plebian"   "Charles Ventura Reports," H.I., Jan. 31, 1958.

59   how Marylou met Whitney   Jeffrey L. Rodengen, *The Legend of Cornelius Vanderbilt Whitney,* pp. 114–15; "Sonny Whitney," *New York Post,* Aug. 1, 1957; Sheilah Graham, "Socialite in Greasepaint," Feb. 1, 1958.

59   Graham's allegation removed from subsequent editions   Michael Schnayerson, *Vanity Fair,* Aug. 1995.

59   Sonny's divorce and remarriage   "Whitney Defies N.Y. Court; Takes Off with Wife No. 4," *New York Post,* Jan. 1956; "Mrs. Whitney Is Ready at Last to Free Sonny," Jan. 8, 1957; "Whitney Sheds and Weds in Defiance of N.Y. Court," *New York News,* Jan. 25, 1958; Earl Wilson, "Altar-Bound, His Fourth Wife," *New York Post,* Jan. 26, 1958.

62   food fight at Blenheim   *W*; "The Bolters," *New York,* Oct. 20, 1986; *Vanity Fair,* March 2002.

62   the Ice Princess   "Anne Bass, Empress of Fort Worth," *Texas Monthly,* Feb. 1987.

64   "Mercedes Bass sounds so much better than Mercedes Benz"   *Vanity Fair.*

67   "I thought of every day with Sonny as a performance,"   David Patrick Columbia, "Wild Life: Betrothed Anew: The Queen of Saratoga Hits Her Stride," *Quest,* July/Aug. 1997.

70   notoriously shy about publicity   "Driving Mercedes," *W,* Oct. 5, 1992.

5

BRINGING DOWN THE HOUSE

73   celebratory bonfires   Nigel Dempster and Peter Evans, *Behind Palace Doors,* p. 112.

73   "I was calm, deathly calm"   Andrew Morton, *Diana: Her True Story—In Her Own Words,* p. 83.

73   "exquisitely pretty, a perfect poppet"   *Behind Palace Doors,* p. 39.

74   "He has all the makings of a curmudgeon"   Ibid., p. 98.

75   "It was the most tragic thing I've ever seen" Sally Bedell Smith, *Diana, In Search of Herself,* p. 98.

75   "fallen in love with an idea" and "auditioning for a central role"   Jonathan Dimbleby, *The Prince of Wales,* p. 282, and *Diana, In Search of Herself,* p. 93.

77   "Yes, please"   *Behind Palace Doors,* p. 103.

77   Lady Fermoy felt it was a mistake   She "had her doubts." *Diana, In Search of Herself,* p. 89.

78   "last night of freedom" and "a sword through my heart"   *Behind Palace Doors,* p. 106.

79   "She went to Buckingham Palace, and then the tears started"   *Diana: Her True Story,* p. 119.

79   She asked Cornish if Charles was still in love with Camilla   *The Prince of Wales,* p. 346.

79   "Well, bad luck, Duch"   *Diana, Her True Story,* p. 39.

79   "My accident was on July 29, 1981"   Paul Burrell, *A Royal Duty,* p. 303.

80   "oozed class"   Michael Bergin, *The Other Man,* p. 18. Bergin's book is a primary source on Carolyn's affair with him and the timing of her courtship and marriage to Kennedy, and quotes in this book are drawn from there.

80   Eugene Carlin's description of Carolyn's sexuality   Christopher Andersen, *The Day John Died,* p. 218.

80   affair with Cullen and his roommate   Ibid., p. 219.

80   "Calvin just flew in on her broom"   Rebecca Mead, "Instant Princess," *New York,* Oct. 7, 1996.

83   Littell's meeting Carolyn   Ibid., pp. 155–56.

84   Carolyn was a "Rules Girl"   "Instant Princess," op. cit.

84   "I'm not waiting around for him"   Ibid.

85   "She's the best shot I've got"   *The Men We Became,* p. 177.

85　Ann Freeman's toast　Ibid., p. 184.

86　"Jackie must be smiling in heaven"　Christopher Andersen, *The Day John Died*, p. 229.

86　honeymoon and Prince Charles's letter　*Diana, In Search of Herself*, pp. 118–19, and *The Prince of Wales*, p. 134.

87　"My dad says give us a kiss"　*Behind Palace Doors*, p. 159.

87　"Duty is the rent"　Ibid., p. 83.

87　"sick as a parrot"　*Diana, In Search of Herself*, p. 125.

87　suicide attempt　She presented it as a suicide to Andrew Morton. *Diana, Her True Story*, pp. 129–30.

87　"haplessly trying to soothe her back to cheerfulness"　*Diana, In Search of Herself*, p. 136.

88　"The trouble is"　*The Prince of Wales*, p. 104.

88　"German parvenus"　*Diana, In Search of Herself*, p. 123.

88　"that fucking family"　P. D. Jephson, *Shadows of a Princess*, p. 138.

89　Bashir interview conducted on Guy Fawkes Day　*Diana, In Search of Herself*, pp. 283–84.

89　Gallup poll　Ibid., p. 286.

89　queen asks them to agree to a divorce　Ibid., p. 290.

90　"I have to do it, Patrick"　*Shadows of a Princess*, pp. 141–42.

91　she became convinced she had a healing power　*Shadows of a Princess*, pp. 141–42.

91　overheard editors on honeymoon　*The Day John Died*, p. 231.

91　"This is a big change"　*New York Daily News*, Oct. 7, 1996.

91　"I can't see"　*Newsweek*.

91　She refused to stop for a second　Laurence Leamer, *Sons of Camelot*, p. 428.

91　John spoke to a lawyer　Various published accounts.

92　first wedding anniversary　*The Men We Became*, p. 211.

92　scene with prostitutes　*A Royal Duty*, p. 276.

93　"In the event of an accident"　*Shadows of a Princess*, p. 135.

94　"Not bad—for a whore!"　Ibid., p. 388.

97　Cardinal O'Connor　Ed Klein, *The Kennedy Curse*, p. 214.

6
GOLD-PLATED GODMOTHER

100　wedding of Wallis's parents　Greg King, *The Duchess of Windsor*, pp. 3, 10. (King thinks there is evidence that Wallis was born prematurely.)

100　Mrs. Warfield wore widow's weeds　Ibid., p. 18.

100　a dignified house　Ibid., p. 5.

100　Uncle Sol's erratic financial contributions　Duchess of Windsor, *The Heart Has Its Reasons*, p. 14.

100　Uncle Sol's infatuation with Alice　Ibid., pp. 11–12, and King, *The Duchess of Windsor*, p. 19.

100　"the finest dining club in Baltimore history"　*The Heart Has Its Reasons*, pp. 15–16.

100 John Freeman Rasin   *The Heart Has Its Reasons; The Duchess of Windsor;* J. Bryan III and Charles J. V. Murphy, *The Windsor Story;* Charles Higham, *The Duchess of Windsor: The Secret Life;* and Frances Donaldson, *Edward VIII.*

101 "world's most fascinating aviator," Earl Winfield Spenser   *The Heart Has Its Reasons,* pp. 36–37.

101 "I can't ask Mrs. Townsend to invite my mistress!"   *The Secret Life,* p. 41.

102 introduced her to Ernest Simpson   King, *The Duchess of Windsor,* p. 68.

102 "I am very fond of him"   Michael Bloch, *Wallis and Edward, Letters, 1931–1937,* pp. 20–21.

102 first meeting with Prince Edward   *The Heart Has Its Reasons,* pp. 153–65, and Duke of Windsor, *A King's Story,* pp. 256–62.

103 Freda Dudley Ward   King, *The Duchess of Windsor;* Donaldson, *Edward VIII;* and Philip Ziegler, *King Edward VIII.*

103 "She did not have the chic she has since cultivated"   Gloria Vanderbilt and Thelma Furness, *Double Exposure,* p. 274, quoted by Donaldson in *Edward VIII,* pp. 171–72.

103 "something of a joke"   Michael Bloch's characterization in his commentary in *Letters,* p. 41.

104 "Uncle Arthur" and subsequent quotations   *The Heart Has Its Reasons.*

105 Wallis's replacing Thelma   *Double Exposure; The Heart Has Its Reasons;* Donaldson, *Edward VIII;* King, *The Duchess of Windsor;* and *Windsor Story.*

107 "I could have dominated him"   Nigell Blundel and Susan Blackhall, *The Fall of the House of Windsor.*

107 cigar incident   Donaldson, *Edward VIII,* pp. 174–75.

108 "a nice, quiet, well-bred mouse"   Sir Henry Channon, *Chips, The Diaries of Sir Henry Channon,* p. 22.

110 Wallis and Edward quotations   *Letters.*

111 mood of the voyage changed   Donaldson, *Edward VIII,* pp. 227–28.

111 "Becky Sharpishness"   Cooper, *The Light of Common Day,* pp. 174–90, quoted in Ziegler, *King Edward VIII,* pp. 285–86.

111 Wallis snubbed by Duchess of York   King, *The Duchess of Windsor,* pp. 170–72.

112 "Do you really think I would be crowned without Wallis at my side?" Quoted from Sir Walter Monckton's papers by Donaldson, *Edward VIII,* p. 221.

112 "May I have a whisky"   Baldwin's request for a drink and the meeting following the request are recorded (without direct quotation) in *A King's Story,* pp. 318–19.

112 "Sooner or later my Prime Minister"   *The Heart Has Its Reasons,* p. 225.

112 "Mrs. Simpson has stolen the Fairy Prince"   Quoted in *The Secret Life,* p. 114.

113 the matter as a public relations issue   *Windsor Story,* p. 269.

113 something similar to Roosevelt's "fireside chats"   King, *The Duchess of Windsor,* pp. 210–11, and Donaldson, *Edward VIII,* pp. 289–90.

113 "I feared for him"   *Windsor Story,* p. 255.

114 "Mrs. Simpson . . . preferred the morganatic proposal"   Donaldson, *Edward VIII,* p. 276.

115 "I can't support you"   *Letters,* pp. 262–63.

116 "glittering tip of an iceberg"   *The Heart Has Its Reasons,* p. 207.

117 "I drove up with no small degree of anticipation"   Quoted from Prince Charles's diary in Jonathan Dimbleby, *The Prince of Wales,* pp. 178–79.

118 the duchess's last years   Caroline Blackwood, *The Last of the Duchess.*

7
GOLD-PLATED GODMOTHERS

120 stalled-car incident   Sally Bedell Smith, *Reflected Glory,* pp. 24–25, and Christopher Ogden, *Life of the Party,* p. 27.

120 relationships of Digby children and parents   *Reflected Glory,* p. 30.

121 "When I am grown up"   Marie Brenner, "The Prime of Pamela Harriman," *Vanity Fair,* July 1977.

121 Janet, who embellished her family tree   Jan Pottker, *Janet and Jackie,* p. 30.

122 Black Jack's game at Miss Porter's   Sarah Bradford, *America's Queen,* p. 6.

122 all men were "rats"   Ibid., p. 30.

122 SOCIETY BROKER SUED FOR DIVORCE   The *Daily Mirror* went into detail about Bouvier's extracurricular activities, including tidbits supplied by Janet's lawyers. Ibid., p. 13.

123 she was a poor relation   Ibid., p. 67.

124 "red-headed tart"   *Life of the Party,* p. 74.

124 Pamela's wedding attire   *Reflected Glory,* p. 61.

124 Randolph read Gibbon in bed on honeymoon   Ibid., p. 63.

125 a Churchill inside her and another above her   Ibid., p. 171.

125 she had devoted her life totally to her husband   Ibid., p. 67.

125 "catalyst on a hot tin roof"   *Life of the Party,* p. 123.

126 always leaving something... where Janet would find it   Ibid., pp. 119–20.

126 she slapped Jackie   Edward Klein, *All Too Human,* p. 108.

126 Louis Auchincloss   Ibid., p. 113, and *Quest,* May 1997.

127 "If you're so much in love with Jack Kennedy"   *Janet and Jackie,* p. 126.

127 encounter with Joe Kennedy   *All Too Human,* pp. 126–37.

129 "just like *Tobacco Road*"   *Reflected Glory,* p. 145, and *Life of the Party,* p. 195.

129 he was awed by the Churchill connection   *Life of the Party,* p. 123.

129 very much in love with Agnelli   Ibid., p. 232.

129 using cocaine   Ibid., p. 223.

129 covered his eyes   Ibid., p. 224.

130 "Love, fascination with, and a focus on a single man"   Ibid., p. 232.

131 "too much status and not enough quo"   *Janet and Jackie,* p. 55.

132 Black Jack helped Jack procure women   *America's Queen,* p. 100.

132 "She has no children and no estate!"   *Janet and Jackie,* p. 157.

132 "I'll always remember the sweet smile on his face"   *America's Queen,* p. 114.

133 "Jackie wanted to do Versailles in America"   Sally Bedell Smith, *Grace and Power,* p. xxi.

133 "and I think he does now"   Ibid., p. 352.

134 little John wanted to go to airport   *Grace and Power,* p. 436.

134 "My God, what are they doing?"   Quoted in William Manchester's account.

135 the PBO (polite brush-off)   *Grace and Power,* p. 252.

135 they ended up in bed that first night   *Life of the Party,* p. 267

136 "no marriage is perfect"   Ibid.

136 Elie and Gianni showed up   Ibid., p. 269.

136 for half a million dollars   *Reflected Glory,* p. 211.

136 Pamela cooked chicken hash   *Reflected Glory,* p. 227; *CBS Morning News* interview with Diane Sawyer, Mar. 2, 1983.

137 Pamela verbally attacked Bill   *Reflected Glory,* p. 237.

138 Onassis slept on a sofa   *Grace and Power,* p. 452.

139 second cruise on the *Christina*   Nicholas Grace, *Greek Fire,* pp. 264–66.

140 "a monthly presentation of bills"   Ibid., p. 350.

140 she asked Fiona Thyssen   *America's Queen.*

142 Teddy Kennedy at Ari's funeral   *Greek Fire,* p. 362.

143 Pamela called the Duchins   *Reflected Glory,* p. 261.

143 Courtship with Harriman   Ibid., pp. 261–64.

144 reinvented herself as a policy wonk   Ibid., p. 342.

144 Pamela would talk about Sir Winston   Ibid., p. 298.

144 Dr. Sherrell Aston   Ibid. pp. 326–27.

8

TRUMPING EACH OTHER

146 Trump spotted her in Maxwell's Plum   Harry Hurt III, *Lost Tycoon,* pp. 95–96.

147 family background in Zlín   Ibid., pp. 96–100.

147 Ivana's relationships with George Syrovátka and Jiří Štaidl   Bob Colacello, "Ivana Be a Star," *Vanity Fair,* May 1992, and *Lost Tycoon,* pp. 97–102.

149 in a letter to "Sweetie Pie"   *Lost Tycoon,* p. 102.

150 prenuptial negotiations   Ibid., pp. 106–8, 143.

151 Ivana was already pregnant   ibid., p. 109.

151 "Ivana was great"   Gwenda Blair, *The Trumps: Three Generations That Built an Empire.*

152 "What do they prefer—"   *Lost Tycoon,* p. 128.

152 "Donald started referring to himself in the third person"   Ibid., p. 174.

153 "The first time we met"   Quoted in *The Trumps,* p. 358.

153 "wife-twin"   Term attributed to Ivana in *Lost Tycoon.*

153 Ivana's competitiveness with Donald   Ibid., *The Trumps,* and Donald Trump, *Art of the Deal.*

154 Dr. Steven Hoefflin   *Lost Tycoon,* pp. 52–54.

156 "Killer Blondes"   Art Harris, "The Hometown of the Killer Blondes," *Washington Post,* Feb. 27, 1990.

156 Reddi-wip quote   Mauren Orth, *Vanity Fair,* Nov. 1990.

156 "I held her gently in my arms"   Jeff Sandlin in *National Enquirer,* Apr. 17, 1990.

158 confrontation in Aspen   Liz Smith columns and Michael Gross, "Ivana's New Life," *New York,* Oct. 15, 1991.

159 Valentine's Day lunch Jeannette Walls, *Dish,* pp. 220–21.

163 "Riccardo always walked about eight steps behind Ivana" *People Weekly,* July 21, 1997.

164 "My prenup says what's mine is mine" Ibid.

9
UNIVERSALLY ACKNOWLEDGING

167 Melania's reluctance to go to Kit Kat Club Edit Molnár and Paolo Zampolli quoted in Marianne Garvey, *New York Post,* June 16, 2005.

167 Tory's childhood and relationship with Chris Burch Roxanne Patel, "Paging Lilly Pulitzer!" *Philadelphia,* Feb. 2004.

168 married William Macklowe Engagements, *New York Times,* Jan. 31, 1993.

169 "Donald did all the work" *New York Post,* June 16, 2005.

173 "For Melania, it's never, Ask . . ." Tina Brown, "Donald Trump Settling Down," *Washington Post,* Jan. 27, 2005.

174 planning the Trump wedding "Donald Trump's New Bride, the Ring, the Dress, the Wedding, the Jet, the Party," *Vogue,* Feb. 2005.

10
AFTERWARD . . . UNSTOPPABLE REDHEADS

The story of Georgette's life is constructed from her own autobiographical books, *Feminine Force* and *It Takes Money, Honey.* Unless otherwise stated, all quotes are from these books.

178 "I don't remember ever wanting anything" Jesse Kornbluth, "The Rise and Fall of Arianna Stassinopoulos," *New York,* July 25, 1983.

180 John-Roger baptism Maureen Orth, *Vanity Fair,* Nov. 1994.

185 How did Arianna support her fabulous life Ibid.

185 "I've met the man you're going to marry" William Hamilton, "Her Brains, His Money," *Washington Post,* June 5, 1994.

187 "The funny thing is" Orth, *Vanity Fair,* op. cit.

11
SACRIFICIAL LAMBS?

203 "My children never knew their father" Quoted in Edward Klein, *The Kennedy Curse.*

203 "My grandmother had a lot of pictures of him" Francesco Scavullo, *Scavullo on Men,* pp. 153–54.

207 "I was deeply in love" Ibid.

212 Teddy Portago's letter Documents from First Judicial District Court, Santa Fe County, New Mexico.

EPILOGUE

213 "Nan's very sorry she couldn't be here," *New York Times,* Sept. 24, 2005.

Bibliography

Abramson, Rudy. *Spanning the Century*. New York: William Morrow, 1992.

Andersen, Christopher. *The Day Diana Died*. New York: Morrow, 1998.

————. *The Day John Died*. New York: HarperCollins, 2002.

Atholl, Desmond. *Your Service, Memoirs of a Majordomo*. New York: St. Martin's Press, 1992.

Auchincloss, Louis. *The Vanderbilt Era: Profiles of a Gilded Age*. New York: Scribner, 1989.

Barry, Joseph. *Passions and Politics*. Garden City, N.Y.: Doubleday, 1972.

Bagehot, Walter. *English Constitution*. Cambridge: Cambridge Univiersity Press, 2001.

Blundell, Nigel, and Susan Blackhall. *Fall of the House of Windsor*. Chicago: Contemporary Books, 1992.

Bergin, Michael. *The Other Man*. New York: Regan Books, 2004.

Blackwood, Caroline. *The Last of the Duchess*. New York: Pantheon, 1995.

Blair, Gwenda. *The Trumps: Three Generations That Built an Empire*. New York: Simon & Schuster, 2000.

Bloch, Michael, ed. *Wallis and Edward: The Intimate Correspondence of the Duke and Duchess of Windsor, Letters 1931–1937*. New York: Summit Books, 1986.

Blow, Richard. *American Son*. New York: Henry Holt, 2002.

Blumenthal, Ralph. *The Stork Club: America's Most Famous Nightspot and the Lost World of Café Society*. Boston: Little, Brown, 2000.

Bradford, Sarah. *America's Queen: The Life of Jacqueline Kennedy Onassis*. New York: Viking, 2000.

Bryan, J. III, and Charles J. V. Murphy. *The Windsor Story*. New York: Morrow, 1979.

Burrell, Paul. *A Royal Duty*. New York: Signet, 2004.

Buskin, Richard. *Princess Diana: Her Life Story, 1961–1997*. Lincolnwood, Ill.: Publications International, 1997.

Channon, Sir Henry, ed. by Robert Rhodes James. *Chips, The Diaries of Sir Henry Channon*. London: Weidenfeld & Nicolson, 1967.

Christian, Linda. *Linda: My Own Story*. New York: Crown, 1962.

Dempster, Nigel, and Peter Evans. *Behind Palace Doors: Marriage and Divorce in the House of Windsor*. New York: G. P. Putnam's Sons, 1993.

Dimbleby, Jonathan. *The Prince of Wales: A Biography*. New York: Morrow, 1994.

Donaldson, Frances. *Edward VIII*. Philadelphia: Lippincott, 1975.

Eisenhauer, A. L. "Ike" (with Robin Moore and Robert J. Flood). *The Flying Carpet-bagger*. New York: Pinnacle, 1976.

Fraser, Nicholas, and Marysa Navarro. *Eva Perón*. New York: W. W. Norton, 1980.

Gabler, Neal. *Winchell: Gossip, Power, and the Culture of Celebrity*. New York: Vintage Books, 1995.

Gage, Nicholas. *Greek Fire: The Story of Maria Callas and Aristotle Onassis*. New York: Alfred A. Knopf, 2000.

Graham, Sheilah. *How to Marry Super Rich: or Love, Money, and the Morning After*. New York: Grosset & Dunlap, 1974.

Gross, Michael. *Model: The Ugly Business of Beautiful Women*. New York: Morrow, 1995.

Haden-Guest, Anthony. *The Last Party: Studio 54, Disco, and the Culture of the Night*. Reprint edition. New York: Harper Perennial, 1998.

Hatch, Alden. *The Mountbattens: The Last Royal Success Story*. New York: Random House, 1965.

Hayward, Brooke. *Haywire*. New York: Knopf, 1977.

Henry, Alan. *Fifty Years of Ferrari*. Motorbooks International, 1997.

Hewitt, James. *Love and War*. London: Blake, 1999.

Higham, Charles. *The Duchess of Windsor: The Secret Life*. New York: McGraw-Hill, 1988.

Hosford, Mary. *The Missouri Traveler Cookbook*. New York: Farrar, Straus and Cudahy, 1958.

Huffington, Arianna. *The Female Woman*. New York: Random House, 1974.

———. *Fourth Instinct: The Call of the Soul*. New York: Simon & Schuster, 2003.

———. *How to Overthrow the Government*. New York: Regan Books, 2001.

———. *Picasso: Creator and Destroyer*. New York: Simon & Schuster, 1988.

Hutchison, Robert A. *Vesco*. New York: Praeger, 1974.

Hurt, Harry III. *Lost Tycoon: The Many Lives of Donald J. Trump*. New York: W. W. Norton, 1993.

Jephson, P. D. *Shadows of a Princess*. New York: HarperCollins, 2000.

Junor, Penny. *Charles: Victim or Villain?* London: HarperCollins, 1998.

———. *Diana Princess of Wales: A Biography*. London: Sidgwick & Jackson, 1982.

Kendall, Paul Murray. *Richard the Third*. New York: W. W. Norton, 1956.

Kelley, Kitty. *The Royals*. New York: Warner, 1997.

King, Greg. *The Duchess of Windsor: The Uncommon Life of Wallis Simpson*. New York: Citadel Press, 1999.

Klein, Edward. *All Too Human: The Love Story of Jack and Jackie Kennedy*. New York: Pocket Books, 1996.

———. *The Kennedy Curse: Why America's First Family Has Been Haunted by Tragedy for 150 Years*. New York: St. Martin's Press, 2003.

Leamer, Laurence. *Sons of Camelot: The Fate of an American Dynasty*. New York: Morrow, 2004.

Leigh, Dorian (with Laura Hobe). *The Girl Who Had Everything*. New York: Bantam, 1981.

Leigh, Wendy. *Prince Charming: The John F. Kennedy Jr. Story*. New York: Dutton, 1993.

Leslie, Anita. *Cousin Randolph*. London: Trafalgar Square, 1987.

Lever, Evelyne. *Madame de Pompadour, A Life*. New York: St. Martin's Press, 2003.

Lewis, Michael. *Liar's Poker: Rising Through the Wreckage on Wall Street*. New York: Penguin, 1990.

Lilly, Doris. *How to Meet a Millionaire*. New York: G. P. Putnam's Sons, 1951.

Littell, Robert T. *The Men We Became: My Friendship with John F. Kennedy Jr.* New York: St. Martin's Press, 2004.

Manchester, William, *The Death of a President: November 20–November 25*. New York: Harper and Row, 1961.

Martin, Ralph G. *Charles and Diana*. New York: Putnam, 1985.

———. *A Hero for Our Time*. New York: Faucett Books, 1984.

———. *The Woman He Loved*. New York: Simon and Schuster, 1974.

Mitford, Nancy (with an introduction by Amanda Foreman). *Madame de Pompadour*. New York: *New York Review of Books,* 2001.

Morton, Andrew. *Diana: Her New Life*. London: O'Mara, 1995.

———. *Diana: Her True Story—In Her Own Words*. New York: Simon & Schuster, 1997.

Mosbacher, Georgette. *Feminine Force*. New York: Simon & Schuster, 1994.

———. *It Takes Money, Honey*. New York: Regan Books, 1999.

Mulvaney, Jay. *Diana & Jackie: Maidens, Mothers, Myths*. New York: St. Martin's Press, 2002.

Ogden, Christopher. *Life of the Party: The Biography of Pamela Digby Churchill Hayward Harriman*. Boston: Little, Brown, 1994.

Ortiz, Alicia Dujovne. *Eva Perón*. New York: St. Martin's Press, 1995.

Page, Joseph. *Peron: A Biography*. New York: Random House, 1983.

Pasternak, Anna. *Princess in Love*. New York: Dutton, 1994.

Pottker, Jan. *Janet and Jackie: The Story of a Mother and Her Daughter, Jacqueline Kennedy Onassis*. New York: St. Martin's Press, 2001.

Rautbord, Sugar. *Chameleon*. New York: Warner Books, 1999.

Rollins, Ed. *Bare Knuckles and Back Rooms: My Life in American Politics*. New York: Broadway, 1997.

Rodengen, Jeffrey L. *The Legend of Cornelius Vanderbilt Whitney*. Fort Lauderdale, Fla.: Write Stuff Enterprises, 2000.

Scavullo, Francesco. *Scavullo on Men*. New York: Random House, 1977.

Sheehy, Sandy. *Texas Big Rich*. New York: St. Martin's Press, 1992.

Smith, Sally Bedell. *Diana in Search of Herself*. New York: Times Books, 1999.

———. *Grace and Power, The Private World of the Kennedy White House*. New York: Random House, 2004.

———. *Reflected Glory: The Life of Pamela Churchill Harriman*. New York: Simon & Schuster, 1996.

Spoto, Donald. *The Decline and Fall of the House of Windsor*. New York: Pocket Books, 1996.

Tanner, Lawrence E. *The History of the Coronation*. London: Pitkin, 1952.

Taylor, John. *Circus of Ambition: The Culture of Wealth and Power in the Eighties*. New York: Warner Books, 1989.

Trump, Donald J. (with Tony Schwartz). *Trump: The Art of the Deal*. New York: Ballantine, 2004.

Vanderbilt, Gloria, and Thelma Lady Furness. *Double Exposure: A Twin Autobiography.* London: Frederick Muller, 1959.

Vickers, Hugo. *Alice: Princess Andrew of Greece.* London: Hamish Hamilton, 2000.

Walls, Jeannette. *Dish: The Inside Story on the World of Gossip.* New York: Avon, 2000.

Warhol, Andy, edited by Pat Hackett. *The Andy Warhol Diaries.* New York: Warner Books, 1991.

Williams, H. Noel. *Madame de Pompadour, A Portrait.* New York: Scribner, 1902.

Wilson, A. N. *The Rise and Fall of the House of Windsor.* London: Sinclair-Stevenson, 1993.

Wilson, Christopher. *Dancing with the Devil: The Windsors and Jimmy Donohue.* New York: St. Martin's Press, 2001.

Windsor, Wallis Waffield, Duchess of. *The Heart Has Its Reasons.* New York: David McKay, 1956.

Windsor, Edward, Duke of. *A King's Story.* New York: G.P. Putnam's Sons, 1951.

Ziegler, Philip. *King. Edward VIII.* New York: Knopf, 1991.

Zerbe, Jerome. *John Perona's El Morocco Family Album.* New York: privately printed, 1937.

Index

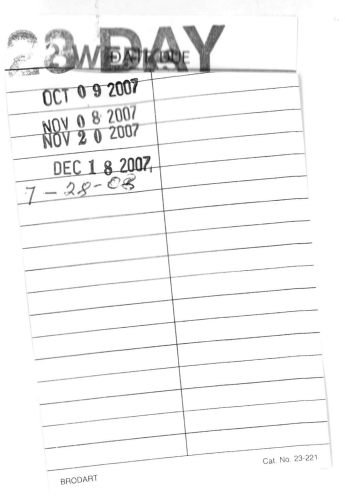